REAGAN AT REYKJAVIK

REAGAN
AT REYKJAVIK

Forty-Eight Hours That Ended the Cold War

KEN ADELMAN

BROADSIDE BOOKS
An Imprint of HarperCollins*Publishers*
www.broadsidebooks.net

HarperCollins books may be purchased for educational, business, or sales promotional use. For information, please e-mail the Special Markets Department at SPsales@harpercollins .com.

Broadside Books™ and the Broadside logo are trademarks of HarperCollins Publishers.

Grateful acknowledgment is made to reproduce illustrations on the following pages:
Page 24: Carlson © Milwaukee Journal Sentinel. Reprinted with permission of Universal Uclick. All rights reserved.
Page 35: Mike Keefe/Denver Post. Reprinted with permission from Mike Keefe.
Page 53: Jack Ohman/Portland Oregonian. Reprinted with permission from the Permissions Group. All rights reserved.
Page 76: Used with permission from the Conrad Estate/The Huntington Library, San Marino, CA.
Page 83: Mike Peters/Dayton Daily News. Reprinted with permission from Mike and Marian Peters.
Page 111: MacNelly/Chicago Tribune. Reprinted with permission from Sue MacNelly.
Page 143: Auth © The Philadelphia Inquirer. Reprinted with permission of Universal Uclick. All rights reserved.
Page 176: Draper Hill, courtesy of The Detroit News Archives.
Page 209: A 1986 Herblock Cartoon, © The Herb Block Foundation.
Pages 299–300: Courtesy of the Ronald Reagan Library.

Designed by Renato Stanisic

FIRST EDITION

Library of Congress Cataloging-in-Publication Data has been applied for.

ISBN 978-0-06-231019-4

14 15 16 17 18   OV/RRD   10 9 8 7 6 5 4 3 2 1

Dedicated to Carol and Will
I can't imagine life without them.

Contents

Introduction

The Reykjavik summit is something out of an Agatha Christie thriller. Two vivid characters meet over a weekend, on a desolate and windswept island, in a reputedly haunted house with rain lashing against its windowpanes, where they experience the most amazing things. The summit between Ronald Reagan and Mikhail Gorbachev on October 11 and 12, 1986, was like nothing before or after—with its cliffhanging plot, powerful personalities, and competing interpretations over the past quarter century.

A decade later, Gorbachev felt the drama was something out of the Bard, William Shakespeare, rather than the Dame, Agatha Christie:

> Truly Shakespearean passions ran under the thin veneer of polite and diplomatically restrained negotiations behind the windows of a cozy little house standing on the coast of a dark and somberly impetuous ocean. The accompaniment of grim nature is still lingering in my memory.

For those of us in the American delegation, Reykjavik was supposed to be an uneventful weekend, with the real action happening the following year at the real summit in Washington. Instead, in Iceland we rode an emotional roller coaster, full of twists and turns, ups and downs, all weekend long. NPR's Rod MacLeish deemed it among "the most amazing events in diplomatic history," while the ace *Washington Post* diplomatic correspondent turned Cold War historian Don Oberdorfer called it "one of the most controversial—and most bizarre—negotiations by powerful heads of state in modern times." To Gorbachev, it was exhausting with its "wearying and grueling arguments."

Unlike other summits and dramas, Reykjavik's plot unfolded off script. The session itself came as a surprise and ended up delivering surprise after surprise. We didn't know what to expect next or how it all would end—not just over that weekend, but over the months and years that followed.

Besides Reykjavik's gripping plot were its oversize personalities. Reagan and Gorbachev stand among the most intriguing and important characters of the twentieth century. For some ten and a half hours at Reykjavik, they dealt directly with one another—void of staff advice, detailed talking points, or guiding memos—acting more like themselves than at any time in office.

Thanks to the now-declassified American and Soviet notes of their private discussions, we can peep through the keyhole of their small meeting room to see them, hear their back-and-forth repartee, and come to understand their core beliefs, patterns of thought, and fundamental characters in a way that history rarely offers.

Reykjavik changed each man, changed their relationship and thus that of the superpowers. The day after returning from Iceland, Gorbachev said on nationwide Soviet television that, after Reykjavik, "no one can continue to act as he acted before." Neither man did, and neither country did.

Beside these two leading characters were two others in key supporting roles. Most constructive and then tragic was the chief of staff of the Soviet military, the five-starred Sergei Akhromeyev. Having been shrouded and operating behind the scenes for decades, he emerged at Reykjavik for a few shining hours to help change the course of history.

He could never have imagined that his contribution would end up helping to destroy the country he loved and the life he led.

The other key character in this drama was Hofdi House, the cozy and stunning structure said to be haunted by a people inclined to believe such things. At the time of the summit, more than half of Icelanders believed in elves and leprechauns, including the country's prime minister. Hofdi House provided a weird yet hospitable site for the world's two most powerful men to meet.

As if its twisting plot, outsize characters, and unique setting weren't enough, the Reykjavik summit has been hotly debated and differently interpreted over the years. Immediately afterward, it was universally deemed an abject failure since the two leaders left without a joint statement, clinking of champagne glasses, or promises of future meetings. They left each other glowering and, in Reagan's case, steaming mad. The White House chief of staff, Donald Regan, asserted that the two would never meet again. The session was nearly universally condemned, even by those as astute in foreign policy as Richard Nixon, who declared, "No summit since Yalta has threatened Western interests so much as the two days at Reykjavik."

The following year, 1987, Reykjavik received some acclaim when agreements reached over that weekend were signed in the White House as part of a sweeping arms control treaty.

Since then—despite the earth-shattering events of the fall of the Berlin Wall, the demise of Communism in Eastern Europe, the collapse of the Soviet Union, and end of the Cold War—Reykjavik has mostly been relegated to a footnote in history, something akin to the Glassboro summit of 1967 between U.S. president Lyndon Johnson and Soviet premier Aleksey Kosygin. Specialists have debated the summit's significance, particularly at four conferences held on its anniversaries, but their debates have largely remained there—among specialists at conferences.

And most of those specialists believe that the momentous events of that era sprang from internal weaknesses in the Soviet economy rather than from any outside events, such as Reykjavik, or outside pressure, such as Reagan's rhetoric or plans for strategic defense. Indeed, this view has become the conventional wisdom of how and why the Cold War ended.

With the gifts of historical perspective and declassified documents—both of the Reykjavik discussions and of Soviet meetings, before and after the summit—a different interpretation has become possible, and possibly more accurate. I, for one, have come to believe that Reykjavik marked a historical turning point, by leading to:

1. a steady stream of unprecedented arms control agreements;
2. a remarkable decline in the number and danger of U.S./Soviet-Russian nuclear arsenals;
3. an unexpected flowering of the anti-nuclear movement worldwide;
4. and even—the mother of all historical consequences—the end of the Cold War itself.

The case for this interpretation will be laid out in the final chapter, bolstered by such standard methods of substantiation as expert witnesses, evidence, and logic.

One such witness, Mikhail Gorbachev, has been clear over the years. U.S. Secretary of State George Shultz, at Reagan's side during Reykjavik, had a conversation with the last general secretary of the Soviet Communist Party some years after the summit, and described the scene:

> We were sitting around with the interpreter, and I said, "When you entered office and when I entered office, the Cold War was about as cold as it could get, and by the time we left it was all over. What do you think was the turning point?"

He didn't hesitate a second. He said, "Reykjavik."

And I said, "Why?"

"Because," Gorbachev said, "for the first time the two leaders talked directly, over an extended period in a real conversation, about key issues."

This is the story of what happened during that weekend, and what I believe to be its significance—why it deserves to be called the forty-eight hours that ended the Cold War.

CHAPTER 1

Departures

Thursday, October 9, 1986
Washington, DC

Ronald Reagan was beaming as he stood outside the White House on a beautiful Indian summer morning. He embraced his wife Nancy and then turned to acknowledge the greetings of the assorted members of Congress and his cabinet, who had come to wish him well and farewell. Attending a South Lawn departure ceremony was one of the perks of White House employment and the small crowd of staff, interns, supporters, and friends applauded enthusiastically.

The president, on that unseasonably warm October morning, was riding high. His reelection in 1984 had almost been by acclamation: he won forty-nine of the fifty states, most of them by hefty margins. The economy, so dismal when he took office in 1981, had gone through a painful readjustment and emerged stronger, just as he said it would. Reaganomics, as he quipped, was no longer a dirty word. Now, two years into his second term, he was near the height of his impressive popularity and power.

Having started to fix things at home, he was ready to take on the world.

That morning he was headed to Iceland, of all places, to negotiate about nuclear weapons with Mikhail Gorbachev. Negotiating was something Reagan loved to do, something he felt he was good at doing, something he most wanted to do with a Soviet leader.

Before boarding Marine One, the president had a few remarks to offer about the trip. There was a slight disconnect since his delivery was characteristically upbeat while his message was designed to lower expectations.

The upcoming meeting would be a quiet and intimate session, all business and no protocol. Reagan called it "essentially a private meeting between the two of us. We will not have large staffs with us," nor will they "dash off a few quick agreements, and then give speeches about the spirit of Reykjavik." That just wasn't in the cards.

Although it was to be a meeting of the superpower leaders, Reykjavik shouldn't even be called a summit. After all, summits were staged, theatrical events culminating in the clinking of champagne glasses to celebrate, well, usually little of lasting significance. A real summit fulfilled what Franklin Roosevelt once told Charles de Gaulle, who needed no guidance on such matters: "In human affairs, the public must be offered a drama."

But Reykjavik wasn't going to offer a drama. Rather, the president went on, this meeting would be a mere base camp leading to that "full-scale summit" he was "looking toward" in Washington, DC, the following year.

Just by chance, the president noted, he was leaving for Iceland on Leif Erickson Day—the day named for the mighty Viking explorer who had discovered America nearly a thousand years before. Reagan's linking that man with that land was a subtle diplomatic reach out to mollify some irritation in Iceland over Erickson's exact nationality. Days earlier, Iceland's foreign minister Matthias Mathiesen got cranky and blurted out: "In the U.S., they call him Norse—whatever that means. But he was born and bred in Iceland!"

As the president was speaking, a low-flying plane drowned out his remarks. When this had happened to Lyndon Johnson during some South Lawn ceremony years before, LBJ whispered in an aide's ear to call the head of the Federal Aviation Agency and have him stop all (expletive deleted) flights from taking off or landing at National Airport—NOW!— and keep them away—FAR AWAY!—until his ceremony ended.

That was Johnson's way. Reagan handled it his way. He paused dramatically, glanced up smiling, waved his hand gently and said, "Get out of the way!" and then joined the gales of laughter.

The president's peroration ended on an upbeat. He quoted "a great American who knew the extremes of hope and despair" and who said such immortal words as: "History teaches us to hope." Reagan then extolled the "nation's unified support," and said, "Today we're making history, and we're turning the tide of history to peace and freedom and hope." The man who found hope in history was none other than Robert E. Lee, who was not necessarily "a great American" who shared our "nation's unified support."

As another plane approached, Reagan raced through the rest of his prepared remarks. He then wrapped an arm around Nancy's waist as they strolled across the lawn to the white-topped presidential helicopter. In an elegantly choreographed move, he hugged his wife with one arm, waved to the crowd with the other, bent down to bestow a farewell kiss, and completed the pivot with a crisp salute to the marine saluting him at the helicopter's steps. Just before he boarded the khaki green chopper, the president turned and waved to his wife. She waved back and he ducked into the cabin.

As the chopper began its slow rise, the president was framed in one of the windows. He waved again to his wife and blew her one last kiss. They would be apart two full days.

THE REYKJAVIK MEETING HAD come suddenly and the first lady had chosen to stay behind. She had several events long scheduled to advance her "Just Say No" anti-drug campaign. Neither she nor

Reagan's staff knew that the Soviet first lady would be accompanying her husband to Reykjavik. Mrs. Reagan would not be pleased when later seeing Raisa Gorbachev careen around Reykjavik with the world press in tow reporting everything she wore and everywhere she went.

Not that the ladies would miss being with each other. The two had not gotten along in Geneva the year before. Mrs. Gorbachev was political, even ideological to the core—more of a committed Communist, it was said, than her husband. Mrs. Reagan had scant interest in politics and none whatsoever in ideology. She was interested in one thing, "Ronnie."

After the seventeen-minute hop to Andrews Air Force Base, Marine One set the president down on the tarmac, just steps away from the Air Force One ramp. The big jet's engines began revving as soon as the door closed behind him. It was wheels up three minutes later.

After being welcomed aboard by the captain, Reagan went into his private cabin and settled in for the long flight. His cabin, directly off the long corridor, had sitting and working areas, a bedroom with the presidential seal sewn into the covers and linens, and a bathroom with toilet and shower.

As was his wont at the outset of any foreign trip, the president reset his watch to local time at his destination. As he twisted the set wheel, 10:30 a.m. became 2:30 p.m. When the plane reached its cruising altitude, an Air Force steward announced lunch would then be served. Reagan was delighted to hear that meatloaf was on the menu. It was his favorite meal aloft, yet one which was served only when Mrs. Reagan was not aboard.

The early meal service was another of his travel preferences. Just as his watch should move to Iceland time, so should his stomach. Now on that time, he was already late for lunch. He paired his meatloaf with water and decaffeinated coffee since he seldom drank alcohol on the plane, except for an occasional glass of wine if Nancy was having one.

. . . .

AFTER THE MEAL, THE president picked up a black three-ring binder. The title—*The Meetings of President Reagan and General Secretary Gorbachev, Reykjavik*—was embossed in gold above a presidential seal.

The binder's eight tabs began with "General Information," which contained a map with the flight path between Washington and Reykjavik presented in curved red lines drawn between the two cities. Beneath it was the "Statute Miles"—2,880 in either direction—and "Flight Time"—5 hours and 20 minutes outbound riding the headwinds, and 6 hours and 5 minutes back home bucking them. The next tab was "Notes on Gifts and Customs." Further tabs had papers about the country, converting money, and the names of professionals at the U.S. Embassy—all nine of them. The final tabs on "Soviet Union" and "Security and Arms Control" included his administration's public positions.

The material was mostly pap. But that was just as well, because Reagan, at best, only skimmed his briefing books. This happened famously in May 1983 when he was hosting a critical session of the economic summit with all eight Western leaders. The picturesque backdrop of Colonial Williamsburg was pure Reagan, as was his performance there.

On the summit's opening morning, then White House chief of staff James Baker asked the president if he had questions about the material in the briefing book handed him the night before. The president said that, no, he really didn't. Well, he hadn't actually opened the briefing book since *The Sound of Music* had been on TV and he simply couldn't resist watching it again.

The story created rounds of guffaws in Washington. It reinforced the notion of Reagan as—in the memorable sobriquet of the capital's most esteemed wise man, Clark Clifford—"an amiable dunce." He wouldn't even read his briefing book for a top meeting that he was hosting!

Lost among the snickers, however, was how Reagan ended up running the economic summit differently, and better, than had previous hosts. He insisted that the eight leaders of the industrial democracies hold real discussions rather than just regurgitating their staffs' talking points. Reagan deftly steered the leaders onto topics that went beyond the E-8's province, yet ones that he considered more critical than those on the official agenda, including NATO unity while the United States deployed intermediate missiles in Europe later that year. Even Reagan's most scornful colleague, the oft-snickering Canadian prime minister, Pierre Trudeau, publicly called Reagan's economic summit "an unprecedented success."

A FOLDER ON THE desk in the president's cabin provided more sensitive Reykjavik material than the black briefing book. Several classified memos focused on the next forty-eight hours.

A memo from Secretary of State George Shultz, dated October 2, was stamped SECRET/SENSITIVE. Lest there be any doubt, someone had written in longhand "Super Sensitive" on it. In the memo, the secretary urged the president to take "a positive, self-confident, and commanding approach to this meeting"—as if Reagan could take any other—and then advised: "We should not try to separate form from content or appearance from substance. As far as Reykjavik goes, they will be intertwined." Shultz left it up to Reagan to fathom what this might mean.

While the president should "stress the potential for substantive progress," he must still be careful not to go "permitting the impression that Reykjavik itself was a Summit." Shultz ended on an ingratiating note: "The policies you set in motion six years ago have put us in the strong position we are in today." That solid foundation opened an opportunity to achieve "real reductions in nuclear forces—a historic achievement in itself, and a major step towards your vision of a safer world for the future."

Reading such supersensitively secret solicitous secretarial boiler-plate, Reagan may have considered watching *The Sound of Music* yet again a better use of his time.

As Air Force One continued eastward toward Iceland, the president munched contentedly on fruit and a few jelly beans which the blue-attired Air Force stewards kept in steady supply on his side table.

To break up the trip, he popped into the staff conference area, right behind his cabin, to chat with those gathered there and tell a tale or two. He told about recently reading Tom Clancy's novel *Red Storm Rising*, with its vivid scenes of Iceland, and about an astronaut who said that the moon had a more hospitable landscape than where he had trained, outside of Reykjavik.

Many of Reagan's stories harked back to his Hollywood days, but his favorites were about growing up in Dixon, Illinois. He would regale his time as a lifeguard at Lowell Park Beach, where he cut a notch on a log for every life he saved. According to his story, the log ended up having a truly incredible seventy-seven notches.

Throughout the rest of his life, Reagan sought to add to those seventy-seven notches. He envisioned himself as a lifeguard, though on a far grander scale than at Lowell Park Beach.

RETURNING TO HIS CABIN, he read a second memo in his red folder, one also classified as SECRET/SENSITIVE. Another clear case of classification creep, this memo, from a Soviet expert in the White House, Stephen Sestanovich, was at least clear: "We go into Reykjavik next week with very little knowledge of how Gorbachev intends to use the meeting." He had recently displayed "coyness" and "may be genuinely undecided, even skeptical which is why you [the president] will have to smoke him out."

Rather than concentrating on policy, Reagan had mostly prepared for Reykjavik by focusing on psychology. According to Jack Matlock, the top Soviet expert in the White House and the American notetaker the first morning at Reykjavik, the president had concentrated "on the psychology of Soviet leaders—an attempt to understand their mode of thinking and to find actions and arguments that would induce them to change their behavior."

There had been top-level meetings in the White House and Foggy Bottom to prepare for Reykjavik. Shultz had hosted a few in his wood-paneled, private office on the seventh floor of the State Department. Yet no one had proposed preparing, and then sharing with the Soviets, such basic elements of a professional meeting as an agreed agenda, session times, and attendees on each side.

With midterm elections just three weeks away, the president had been campaigning hard for Republican candidates across the country. In order to refocus his attention on international affairs, he had convened his own meeting on Reykjavik, in the Roosevelt Room, just across the hall from the Oval Office.

The key question at all pre-Reykjavik meetings was the same: "What should we expect from Gorbachev there?" And the experts' key response was the same: "Not much."

Connecting scattered intelligence dots outlined the picture of Gorbachev proposing Reykjavik to boost his domestic standing. Facing mounting resistance at home, he needed to show global leadership. This was deftly done by summoning the president of the United States to a windswept island in the middle of nowhere. This assessment was shared by the U.S. and Soviet ambassadors—Arthur Hartman in Moscow and Yuri Dubinin in Washington—during separate meetings in Shultz's inner office.

Secure in our assessment, we had no problem with the grip-and-grin session we came to expect, if that would indeed help Gorbachev. After all, nobody was better at gripping and grinning than Ronald Reagan.

. . . .

The Air Force One carrying Reagan to Iceland—Sam 27000—
had joined the presidential fleet in 1972. Although it was small compared with the 747 that would replace it, it had a history and a scale
that Reagan loved. It was good that he did, since he would log more
miles on it (630,000) than any of his predecessors. Fittingly, that plane
now resides in the Ronald Reagan Presidential Library, seeming
almost airborne on display in its own pavilion.

Behind the presidential quarters were the staff conference area and
a handful of seats for top presidential aides and secretaries. Other sec-
tions were designated for lower staff members, a few for the press, and,
at the very back, Secret Service agents.

Donald Regan settled into the seat reserved for the White House
chief of staff—the first seat in the first section. The son of an Irish
Catholic Boston cop, Regan worked his way through Harvard College but dropped out of his freshman year at Harvard Law School
to join the U.S. Marines when World War II broke out. He fought
in five South Pacific battles, including the vicious ones of Guadalca-
nal and Okinawa. Anyone who called him "a former marine" would
be dressed down and quickly corrected. "I am a marine," he would
counter. And he stayed a marine.

A brisk, focused man, Regan had joined Merrill Lynch as a trainee
and ended up as the CEO. He had a temper and colorful vocabulary
and was used to being obeyed and getting stuff done.

Regan did a fine job as Reagan's first secretary of the treasury, managing through Congress the most far-reaching tax reform bill of the
preceding quarter century and promoting Reaganomics. He shared
the president's desire to cut taxes and government spending, although
both goals were more touted than achieved.

By the end of Reagan's first term, Regan was becoming restless at

Treasury. He had mastered the brief, had performed well, and was thus eager for a new challenge. Luckily, White House chief of staff James Baker was feeling the same way. Baker's patrician background of hunting parties and private rail cars differed from Regan's scrappy youth on Boston's mean streets. Still, they liked one another. Both believed in firm management. Both produced impressive results.

While chatting one time, they realized their respective restlessness and concocted the novel solution of switching jobs. Baker could move to the Treasury and Regan to the White House. They walked right into the Oval Office to propose this unconventional idea. The president readily agreed, seeming indifferent as to who occupied either position.

Thus did Regan become the White House chief of staff at the outset of Reagan's second term. He fancied himself more as a prime minister than a staff aide, keeping the administration on track and controlling the information flow to and from the Oval Office. As an offshoot of Harry Truman's sign on his desk "The buck stops here," Regan had a sign made up saying "The buck doesn't even pause here." He was all for efficiency. When issues were posed, decisions were made, fast.

While this new job did challenge him, it did not really suit him. Always assertive, he now became overbearing, if not officious. His salty language did not sit well with members of Congress or cabinet officers. He assembled a cadre of eager-beaver aides—quickly dubbed "the mice"—who seemed more loyal to him than to the president. He assigned himself round-the-clock Secret Service protection—something not even H. R. Haldeman had done at the height of Nixon's imperial presidency. And Regan entered large ballrooms with a flourish of his own, coming in just before the president but noticeably after the band began playing "Hail to the Chief."

In a town where status is an obsession and gossip a cottage industry, Regan's actions and pretentions were well noted. But nothing reached a critical mass until it came to the first lady's attention, and displeasure.

Before the first Reagan-Gorbachev summit—in Geneva in November 1985—Regan cracked that women cared little about arms control since they didn't, or couldn't, understand throw weight. That did not go over well.

During the summit, the official White House photographer snapped a shot of President Reagan and General Secretary Gorbachev seated side by side on a red couch craning their necks to look up at Regan, who was standing behind them and seeming to lord over them. When the photo appeared above the fold in the *New York Times* and on front pages around the world, Regan landed on the first lady's watch list.

Despite such faults, Don Regan served Ronald Reagan well at Reykjavik. For starters, he knew his man. The president of the United States was now seventy-five years old and had taken a bullet half an inch from his heart a few years earlier. Knowing that the president adjusted poorly to time changes, Regan built in two days' respite in Iceland. And knowing that he didn't exactly pore over official material, Regan kept the briefing books to a minimum.

Also seated in the Air Force One's front section was Regan's pal and fellow marine, Secretary of State George Shultz. He and his counterpart, Soviet foreign minister Eduard Shevardnadze, were the world's two top diplomats, though neither had done much in diplomacy before. They would be learning their craft together, especially during their thirty-plus meetings with one another. Instead, Shultz's experience lay in Regan's realm of economics and business, but more from the academic side.

On the back of each chair around the conference table in the White House Cabinet Room is a small brass plaque, with the name and title of its occupant. The plaque on Shultz's chair, to the right of the president's, bore four brass plates—"Secretary of Labor, 1969–70," a second "Budget Director, 1970–72," a third "Secretary of the Treasury,

1972–74," and the most recent one "Secretary of State, 1982–." It would be filled in with "89," giving Shultz the longest tenure—six and a half years—of any secretary of state since Dean Rusk.

His first three cabinet posts, all in the Nixon administration, won him acclaim for thoughtfulness, integrity, and tranquility. Even Henry Kissinger—unaccustomed to swooning over others in government posts, especially if they had been *his* posts—succumbed to Shultz. "I met no one in public life for whom I developed greater respect and affection," Kissinger wrote in his memoirs. "Highly analytical, calm and unselfish, Shultz made up in integrity and judgment for his lack of flamboyance. . . . He never sought personal advancement. . . . If I could choose one American to whom I would entrust the nation's fate in a crisis, it would be George Shultz."

It was less Shultz's intellect and experience than his temperament that most appealed to Reagan. After two years of endless Sturm und Drang with Al Haig as secretary of state, Reagan canned Haig in June 1982 and installed the Buddha-like Shultz at Foggy Bottom. "As I watched, the President just visibly relaxed with Shultz," longtime Reagan aide Mike Deaver recalled. "He has a marvelous staff style that appeals to Reagan, [who] was very comfortable with Shultz." The men got acquainted in California in the 1970s, when Reagan was governor and Shultz was CEO of the San Francisco–based multinational engineering firm Bechtel. In 1980 president-elect Reagan appointed him head of his economic transition team.

As secretary of state, Shultz was careful and workmanlike, with two real gifts. One was a knack for figuring out what his boss wanted and working hard to get it done. For six-plus years, Shultz kept one thought uppermost: What does Reagan want me to do? It is an admirable trait, one rare among Washington officials, who usually think uppermost on how to get the president to do what *they* want.

Second, Shultz practiced what he often preached, that "politics is the art of inclusion." Beginning in January 1985, at his crucial Geneva meeting with Soviet Foreign Minister Andrei Gromyko to reopen the arms talks, Shultz included representatives of the joint chiefs, the CIA, the U.S. Arms Control Agency, and even the Pentagon to join him. He drew on their varied knowledge and advice and got the oft-warring agencies to work together in a productive manner.

That's why a number of arms control experts were on their way to Reykjavik. Since the president thought little staff would be needed there, Regan kept scratching names off the manifest. Nonetheless, Shultz managed to wedge in a few arms officials, even though their expertise would probably not be needed.

I WAS DELIGHTED TO be among those on the backup plane, behind Air Force One, and felt lucky to be along. But then again, I had felt lucky about my whole experience in government.

After getting a master's in foreign service studies from Georgetown University, I had worked on legislation for a fabulous mentor, Hank Lieberman, in the Commerce Department. Then, by happenstance, in 1968 my father ran into fellow lawyer Don Lowitz on LaSalle Street in Chicago, which ended up with my landing a job in the "war on poverty" agency headed by a dashing young ex-congressman from the Thirteenth District of Illinois, Don Rumsfeld, with his even younger assistant from Wyoming, twenty-eight-year-old Dick Cheney.

Two years later, my wife—a career foreign service officer with the foreign aid agency—took me along to Zaire as her "dependent husband." There she worked while I conducted research for a Georgetown doctorate in political theory, collected African art, and translated for Muhammad Ali during his "Rumble in the Jungle" heavyweight bout.

The year after Ali's eighth-round knockout of George Foreman, I felt fortunate to be back in the United States with Rumsfeld—this time as assistant to the U.S. secretary of defense. That constituted my deep dive into strategic affairs, armaments, and arms control. It was a golden time, ended by the will of the American people, who tossed out the Ford administration and brought in that of Jimmy Carter in 1977.

Needing something to shove in his pocket in 1978 to read on a long plane ride to Tokyo, Reagan adviser Dick Allen grabbed the latest issue of the tall and narrow journal *Foreign Policy*. On the flight, he was startled to read a conservative piece in that liberal publication—by me. I had by then been publishing articles, some in the *New York Times* and fairly regularly in the *Wall Street Journal*.

Upon his return, Allen invited me to join his newly formed Foreign Policy Advisory Group for candidate Reagan. There, by fate, I got reacquainted with my favorite Georgetown professor, Jeane Kirkpatrick, who asked me to become her deputy at the United Nations after Reagan appointed her to be U.S. ambassador.

For all her hard-line ideology and image, Jeane had a pacifistic streak in her. She chose not to attend National Security Council (NSC) meetings on arms or arms control even though, as a full NSC member, she had a regular seat at the table. Luckily, Jeane asked me to fill that seat, which I did frequently.

Something I said—or, more probably, that I hadn't said much at all—made someone in the White House think of me when the president needed a new arms control chief in January 1983. I was in my third year as director of the U.S. Arms Control and Disarmament Agency when flying to Reykjavik.

It was an odd job. While my office was in the State Department, my views inclined closer to those in the Pentagon. Yet I reported to the secretary of state—but also to the president. Secretary Shultz didn't much like having a subordinate sit in White House meetings right beside him, usually disagreeing with him on issues before the president.

I can't say I blame him. It must have been especially exasperating since I could muster more information and better arguments than he or anyone else around that table—certainly not because I was any brighter, but simply because I had nothing else to do. Whereas Shultz and everyone else around the cabinet table had dozens of issues thrown at them every day, I focused on arms control all day and all night.

My long good luck streak in government extended to riding on the plane to Reykjavik. After many awkward moments with Shultz over the years, I felt especially grateful for his welcoming me aboard.

ON THE PLANE IN front of ours, on Air Force One, there was a seat in the front section reserved for John Poindexter, the fourth of Reagan's six national security advisers.

A true patriot who had graduated first in his class from Annapolis in 1958 and dedicated his life to service in the United States Navy, the admiral was sadly miscast in this post. While Poindexter mastered nuclear propulsion, he knew and cared little about how to work the Congress and press, or how to build consensus across warring bureaucracies.

For all their power, exalted titles, and real talents, the top trio of Regan, Shultz, and Poindexter—the White House chief of staff, the secretary of state, and the national security adviser—would end up contributing little in Reykjavik. Even Shultz played a small part in that big drama, providing more encouragement than expertise.

This trio of top advisers didn't give a lot of advice. But that was okay, since the president didn't want, or need, a lot of advice at Reykjavik. There, he was pretty much on his own, which suited Ronald Reagan just fine. And, although no one would have imagined it, each of the three would go through professional and personal traumas immediately after Reykjavik.

Friday, October 10, 1986
Vnukovo Airport, Moscow, USSR

A light snow dusted Moscow as the Gorbachev motorcade arrived. In the usual Soviet style, all traffic between the Kremlin and the airport had been cleared, so the armored Zil-115 limo and its surrounding motorcade could travel at breakneck speed down the middle of the highway.

At the airport, the closed-off official area was some distance removed from the commercial terminals. There, the Gorbachevs moved quickly through the geriatric men atop the Kremlin power structure, who had come to bid them farewell.

First was the recently minted chairman of the Presidium of the Supreme Soviet, Andrei Gromyko. As was the Soviet way, the more extensive the title, the less significant the position. It hadn't been easy for Gorbachev to dislodge the wily Gromyko, who had been Soviet foreign minister for a whole generation. The Soviet Union's face to the world had been a grim one; Gromyko's nickname was "Mr. Nyet." Yet replacing him had been a major milestone in the advent of Gorbachev's new-think on foreign policy.

Viktor Chebrikov stood at Gromyko's side to bid his supposed boss farewell. It was no secret that the chief of the secretive KGB harbored deep suspicions about all the drivel he had been hearing about sweeping reforms. More heartfelt farewells came from Yegor Ligachev, a Gorbachev appointee who had risen to number two on the Kremlin power meter. Behind these four stood lesser members and deputy members of the Communist Party Central Committee.

The Gorbachevs made their way down the line, shaking hands and exchanging the traditional Russian cheek-to-cheek-to-cheek triple kiss. The general secretary was typically dressed in a heavy gray wool coat and his favorite gray fedora. His wife, however, was providing a sneak preview of the fashion show that she had readied for Reykjavik.

The Associated Press noted that she was "elegantly attired" in a black coat and matching leather-trimmed hat.

The Gorbachevs' departure, though carefully scripted, was not carefully timed. In fact, it went against their hosts' explicit request. Iceland's ambassador had made strong and repeated pleas for Gorbachev to arrive at any time except between noon and 4:00 p.m. on Friday, October 10. During those four hours—and only those four hours, over the whole year—Iceland's top officials had to attend the annual opening of Iceland's thousand-year-old parliament, the sixty-member Althing.

But despite Gorbachev's burgeoning stab at modernization, the Soviet system was too rigid to bend. The Soviet government informed the Icelandic government that Gorbachev would arrive right during that window, since Politburo invitations to his airport sendoff ceremony had already gone out.

Apprised of this startling news, Iceland's prime minister went public with what, in the delicate nuances of diplospeak, constituted a slap across the face: "It is unfortunate," he said frowning.

As the Gorbachevs climbed the steps to the blue-and-white Aeroflot Ilyushin II-62M aircraft, the rest of his traveling party was already settled aboard.

Despite the American president's assertion that their big staffs would be left home, the general secretary's entourage numbered more than three hundred. A hundred carried diplomatic passports. The others consisted of KGB officers, sundry security officials, staff aides, and journalists.

And in the Soviet system—despite their various ranks, functions, and passports—they all worked for the government. Their journalists were thus both hacks and flacks.

In the middle of the aircraft, astride the Gorbachevs' cabin, sat the

key Soviet officials. Foremost was Shevardnadze, whom Gorbachev liked and trusted enough to appoint foreign minister, displacing Gromyko from his three-decade perch.

The fifty-eight-year-old Shevardnadze was an intriguing figure. His background had not been promising, as he had been chief of the secret police in his native Georgia. He rose to Communist Party chief there, occupying that post for some thirteen years.

Despite his pedigree as a local party hack, Shevardnadze had become increasingly convinced that reform was urgently needed and came to consider Gorbachev the man to lead it forth. The two found that they had much in common. Both hailed from peasant stock and had worked the land in their youth. Both were comrades in the Komsomol party youth organizations and then became party chiefs—Shevardnadze in Tbilisi and Gorbachev in nearby Stavropol.

Quietly at first, they increasingly spoke of the need for reform in the 1970s. They took long walks together through the Pitsunda

Woods on the Black Sea coast, during which, as Shevardnadze said in his memoirs, "We spoke of the many absurdities of our life, and came to the conclusion that we just couldn't go on like this." By 1984, their Pitsunda talks had grown more urgent. "Everything's rotten. It has to be changed," they agreed.

Shevardnadze had been seared by his upbringing in Stalin's native Georgia, and by his wife's father having been slaughtered during one of Stalin's serial purges. In 1956 the brutal Soviet putdown of the Hungarian Revolution overshadowed the Soviet police massacre of two dozen peaceful protestors on the streets of Georgia's capital, Tbilisi. "My generation and I acquired a '1956 complex' for the rest of our lives," Shevardnadze wrote, "rejecting force as both a method and a principle of politics."

Four months after Gorbachev became general secretary, he invited Shevardnadze to Moscow to become his foreign minister. The fact that the Georgian party chief lacked any diplomatic experience—he had scarcely ever been out of the country—seemed less important than to have an able and loyal ally in that critical post.

At Reykjavik, and for years after, their relationship remained airtight. Yet it was not always to stay tight. Nor was Shevardnadze always to perform nobly in public life. There would be as many gyrations in his performance over the decades as there would be in the negotiations over the days in Reykjavik.

A corpulent occupant of another prime seat on the flight was Anatoly Dobrynin, the previous Soviet ambassador to the United States. He squeezed in because even these seats on the Ilyushin Il-62Ms were no bigger than economy seats in a Western commercial aircraft.

Ambassador Dobrynin—after so many years, the title became affixed to his name—had served under six Soviet leaders and personally dealt with six American presidents. Trained as an engineer at the Moscow Aviation Institute, he began work in an aircraft plant. Stalin's solution to the postwar dearth of diplomats—caused primarily by his prewar purges of their ranks—was to recruit engineers instead of intellectuals. Although they were less capable in such a different field, Stalin deemed them more politically reliable, which counted far more.

Dobrynin was among the first so selected. He later recalled that his crash course in diplomacy consisted of language immersion and lessons in etiquette. Because trainees were not allowed to read "bourgeois" newspapers, he picked up English by reading the English-language Communist propaganda rag, *Daily Worker.*

It turned out that "Tolya" Dobrynin was a natural-born diplomat. He arrived in Washington when Harry Truman occupied the White House, became the Soviet embassy's number two man while Dwight Eisenhower was president, and was given the post of ambassador during the John F. Kennedy presidency. He more than filled that tricky post for another two dozen years, through the first five years of the Reagan administration, becoming dean of the Washington diplomatic corps along the way. During that long run in the spotlight, he traveled throughout the United States, deep-sea fishing regularly in Florida, attending the annual running of the Kentucky Derby, and hobnobbing wherever the rich and powerful capitalists and imperialists of America assembled.

It was during the dicey days of the Cuban missile crisis that Dobrynin's skills proved most valuable. He negotiated directly with President Kennedy and his brother, Attorney General Robert Kennedy. It was Dobrynin who first suggested that the United States remove its outdated missiles from Turkey after the Soviets removed their new missiles from Cuba. This provided a face-saving way out of a fix for his boss, Nikita Khrushchev.

Later Dobrynin became the back-channel contact between his superiors in the Kremlin and Henry Kissinger and President Richard Nixon in the White House. During the Nixon years, Dobrynin had a direct telephone line to the National Security Council, prompting staffers to become jealous over his having more access to their bosses than they had.

When Gorbachev called Dobrynin home in 1986 to be the powerful head of the international department of the Communist Party Central Committee, Reagan asked, "Is he *really* a Communist?" The answer was decisively yes, even though he did seem too nice and cosmopolitan. As urbane as he was, as much as he enjoyed the cultural and intellectual riches of Western life, he remained a dedicated Communist to the end. He later deemed the dissolution of the Soviet Union an avoidable tragedy caused by the misguided ambitions of incompetent leaders, presumably those along with him on that flight to Reykjavik.

Dobrynin was heading there as an adviser to Gorbachev, much as an NSC staff member would advise the U.S. president. His real contribution would stem from his intimate understanding of America and virtually all the Americans who counted in government.

Shortly before flying out, he had hosted a lunch for Richard Nixon, who happened to be visiting Moscow then. A dozen years after his 1974 resignation, Nixon had managed to plot, crawl, and will himself into yet another political resurrection. A 1984 cover of *Newsweek* magazine had confirmed—or, as some deemed it, warned—"He's Back." In Dobrynin's Moscow apartment over a long lunch, at least, Nixon was back in the middle of U.S.-Soviet relations.

Also on the way to Reykjavik, along with Shevardnadze and Dobrynin, were three other senior Soviet officials—Sergei Akhromeyev, Alexander Yakovlev, and Anatoly Chernyaev.

Akhromeyev was the least familiar to Americans, even though he was chief of the general staff of the Soviet armed forces and the country's sole living marshal. Among the combat ribbons bedecking his chest was one certifying him to be a Hero of the Soviet Union.

Even in a country with a bad case of medal inflation, Akhromeyev's take was impressive—nine Jubilee medals, four Orders of Lenin, a Lenin Prize, the Order of the October Revolution, Order of the

Patriotic War, Order of the Red Banner, Order for Service to the Homeland in the Armed Forces of the USSR, plus that Soviet Hero designation, the highest the state could bestow.

Slight tensions had arisen between Akhromeyev and Gorbachev over all the talk of military reform, which invariably meant scrapping costly defense programs. Hence it was not foolish for the *Washington Post*'s lead story that Friday morning of October 10 to place Marshal Akhromeyev "in the second echelon of advisors . . . who apparently will not play a direct role in the talks." Little did any of us know what lay ahead for that secretive and quiet man.

Yakovlev bore the most inflammatory title, as director of the propaganda department of the Central Committee of the Communist Party of the Soviet Union. In life, however, Yakovlev was a credible, noninflammatory man.

He had been chosen early on by Gorbachev in order to strengthen the party's reform wing. Yakovlev had grasped just how backward his country had become when serving as Soviet ambassador to Canada from 1973 to 1983. During that decade he learned a good deal about America.

"You have to understand what we inherited in 1986," Yakovlev said at the Ronald Reagan Presidential Library during a conference celebrating Reykjavik's tenth anniversary. "An economy that was heading towards catastrophe, the Cold War, stagnation in the country's development. We knew it was necessary to implement major change."

Yakovlev, the author of several scholarly books, came across as more of an intellectual than a propagandist. He was destined to become a critical player in the Kremlin, as Gorbachev began rolling out his reforms and in the troubled years to follow.

Everyone knew that Chernyaev was Gorbachev's senior aide, although no one knew exactly how he aided him. That would only become clear years later, when the Soviet documents of the summit were opened. Then it became clear that Chernyaev took notes during Politburo meetings and then made assignments to its members. In essence, he was Gorbachev's all-purpose notetaker and task-tracker.

IN OCTOBER 1986 MIKHAIL Gorbachev was, like Ronald Reagan, at the height of his power.

But unlike Reagan, who had been dubbed "the Teflon President" and who appeared worry-free, Gorbachev had worries galore. The younger man—Gorbachev was fifty-five at Reykjavik and relatively new in his office—faced far more serious problems than the old man, comfortably ensconced in his. All his options were bad; some were just less bad than others.

The years before Reykjavik had been a bad patch for Soviet leaders. Some hope sprang, after nearly twenty years of stagnation under Leonid Brezhnev, in the spring of 1983 when Yuri Andropov came to power. The former KGB head was seen as the man who could modernize the U.S.S.R. at home and abroad. Kremlinologists proclaimed his elevation a good thing, because Andropov would be both ready and able to change things.

Ready because only the KGB had access to the information that was available abroad, showing just how far behind the U.S.S.R. had slipped—compared not only with other industrialized nations, but also with its satellite minions in Eastern Europe. Perhaps unique in the annals of imperialism, the center of the sprawling Soviet empire, Russia, was poorer than the countries it ruled over.

Able because only the former head of the KGB could muster the power needed to push real change. The KGB chief, with a taste for single malts and an extensive collection of jazz LPs, which he played on a Bang & Olufsen turntable in his Danish modern–furnished Kremlin flat, was thought to be just such a new kind of Soviet leader.

The hope was that Andropov could effect reform at home while dealing with Reagan abroad, especially on arms control, which was thought to have real benefits for the Soviet economy. This hope may have been well-founded. But, after a lingering illness, Andropov died only fourteen months after becoming general secretary.

His successor, Konstantin Chernenko, was younger than Reagan, though he sure did not act it. Chernenko, a Novosibirsk-born Communist bureaucrat, had risen through the ranks in Siberia before being summoned to Moscow in the mid-1950s. Having served as Leonid Brezhnev's chief of staff, it was perhaps inevitable that he absorbed the Brezhnevian torpor. When, at seventy-three, his health began to fail, he went from lethargic to practically comatose.

Chernenko thus became the virtual embodiment of the late Soviet empire—sclerotic and pathetic, with nothing working well. At times, he was unable to enter a room without aides holding him up by the armpits. He mixed up pages when reading major addresses and wheezed so badly from asthma as to be unintelligible. These two traits drove to distraction the CIA analysts trying to decipher what he might have been saying and then what it possibly could have meant. Their, and the Kremlin's, agony was short-lived, as Chernenko became the Pope John Paul I of Moscow, dying right after becoming numero uno.

Two Soviet leaders in under two years was no recipe for stability. When I ran into the Italian ambassador in Washington, then set to fly back to Moscow for yet another state funeral, he told me, smiling, "You see, Ken, I bought tickets to the entire series."

Everyone knew the sprawling Soviet state needed revitalization. Maintaining superpower status on a third world economy with a totalitarian government was unsustainable in a world prospering and democratizing at the dawn of the information age.

Everyone knew what had to be done, namely modernization, but no one knew how to do it. Going too fast could be dangerous, while going too slow could be disastrous. And there was no experience to go by. Any new Soviet ruler had to lead his 280 million countrymen into uncharted territory. The twentieth century offered two dozen or so examples of countries going from capitalist to Communist, but not a single one going in the opposite direction. That was, in fact, enshrined in the Brezhnev doctrine, which asserted that no country becoming Communist could ever turn back. Once a red state, always a red state.

Moreover, real reforms could come only after a clean sweep of the antiquated Communist leadership. Wily and wary, moribund and entrenched, it was firmly anchored in the past, and determined to resist any change that undermined its power. Clearing away these brambles would take so much time, and consume so much political capital, that too little would remain for the reforms themselves, presuming any could be identified and agreed upon.

It was less than two months after Reagan's second inauguration that Gorbachev's moment came.

Western observers considered Gorbachev a surprise victor, since he was strikingly different from all recent general secretaries: he was young, in perfect health, highly personable, and a relative newcomer to Moscow, having moved there only in 1978.

Specialists pointed to three key factors in Gorbachev's rise. First and probably foremost, he excelled at ingratiating himself with powerful party elders, turning them into patrons. The country's chief propagandist, Mikhail Suslov, favored him as the local boy made good. Longtime number two in the Kremlin, Suslov took a personal interest ever since Gorbachev succeeded him as Stavropol party chief. Andropov elevated Gorbachev to be in charge of agriculture and planning for reforms. And Gromyko, the most crotchety of the old guard, personally nominated him for the top job.

Second, Gorbachev showed well. His grand audition came on a visit to London in December 1984, while still a party functionary.

The Soviet specialist Serge Schmemann, of the *New York Times*, described how a group of "heavyset men in dark coats and heavy fur hats marched across the frozen tarmac" in Moscow to send off the solemn Gorbachev, who paused "for the stiff wave required by the ceremony" while his wife slipped unnoticed into the rear of the aircraft. However, upon arriving in London, as Schmemann put it,

> the front door opened and the two popped out together, jubilantly waving to the welcoming officials. . . . It was a classic magician's trick: Put a Kremlin heavy into one end, quietly slip an attractive woman into the other, wave through the air and—Presto!—out comes the New Soviet Leader, smiling, charming, gregarious and complete with elegant, educated, and cultured wife. Few in Britain were disappointed.

The habitually cynical London press became starstruck by the Soviet couple. Typical was the gossip columnist Peter Tory of the London *Daily Mirror*, who gushed: "What a chic lady is Mrs. Gorbachev!"

Third, Gorbachev had a pulse. After a decade of defibrillated Brezhnev, a year-plus of a kidney-failing Andropov and another of comatose Chernenko, the Soviets needed a leader who was fit. Gorbachev, as James Gallagher of the *Chicago Tribune* put it, was "a refreshing change from the sick, old men who had occupied the office for the previous decade."

Regardless of the reasons, the Communist Party was cocked and ready to go when Chernenko went. State radio announced the rise of the new leader a mere four hours after announcing the death of the old.

Gromyko nominated Gorbachev as a man with "a nice smile and iron teeth." And then, after "a minute of mournful silence" for the fallen leader, a vote on the new leader was taken. It went unanimously for Gorbachev, who happened to be chairing the meeting. Skeptics doubted whether all 319 committee members—hailing from across a country eleven time zones wide—could have reached Moscow quickly enough in the frozen month of March to take such a unanimous vote.

Regardless, Gorbachev was in. He became the youngest Soviet leader since Stalin, the first—and, as it turned out, the only—Soviet leader born after the Revolution and the only one not to have served in the military.

The announcement was greeted with enthusiasm both within the Soviet Union and abroad. Gorbachev's nice smile was widely noted and welcomed. The iron teeth went unnoticed, at least initially.

Here, at last, was a leader who knew drastic change was needed and confident that he could bring it about. Others were less sanguine, given that the main cause of home fires in the U.S.S.R. then was exploding television sets. A now-declassified CIA report of the time explained that "Gorbachev still faces an economy that cannot simultaneously maintain rapid growth in defense spending, satisfy demand for greater quantity and variety of consumer goods and services, invest the amounts required for economic modernization and expansion, and continue to support client-state economies." Something had to give.

Thursday, October 9, 1986
Andrews Air Force Base, Camp Springs, Maryland

The third assault on Iceland came from journalists. The last time the world press had paid the least attention to the remote island was in 1972, when the world chess championship between the erratic American Bobby Fischer and the lively Russian Boris Spassky was held there. Dubbed the Match of the Century, the six-week contest brought an unexpected American victory and ended Soviet chess domination, which had begun at the dawn of the Cold War in 1948.

While making diplomatic rounds at the United Nations a week before the summit, Shevardnadze told reporters that Gorbachev had suggested meeting in Reykjavik since he sought "a working session in a working atmosphere, without unnecessary fuss, without advertising." He added, "The number of reporters will be small."

Not quite. Shortly before the summit opened, Marcus Eliason of the Associated Press estimated that there would be twenty-five hundred journalists—reporters, editors, producers, photographers, and cameramen—journeying to Iceland. Even that low-balled the media migration. By the time the summit opened, 3,117 foreign journalists were accredited to cover it.

American reporters and film crews had begun pouring into Reykjavik several days before the heavy hitters arrived on two official U.S. press planes. A small group of reporters chosen by their colleagues was aboard the presidential aircraft to file pool reports describing anything of note happening en route. Most such reports ended up revealing whether POTUS—the president of the United States—wore a cardigan or leather flight jacket and which movies the in-flight entertainment offered.

One of the two press planes had left Andrews earlier Thursday morning, before the president's appearance on the South Lawn, to enable reporters and crews to set up in time to cover the president's arrival ceremony at Keflavik Airport.

News organizations paid the U.S. Air Force full first-class fares for press-plane seats. Nonetheless, taxpayers provided a hefty subsidy. Reagan's press secretary, Larry Speakes, and his aides flew on the main press plane. Officials from the NSC or the State Department might also be onboard, to offer quotable insights from "a high administration source."

The atmosphere aboard press planes is, to put it mildly, freewheeling. Reporters and columnists are generally gregarious, with ego never in short supply. The bar stays open the whole flight, with stewards topping off drinks without being asked. Practical jokes are played, talking and laughing are loud. And rules are usually ignored, including the captain's routine request to fasten seat belts and bring their trays into a full upright and locked position.

THE ICELANDIC GOVERNMENT MADE a heroic attempt to accommodate the throngs suddenly arriving on its barren shores. Not accustomed to much change in their tradition-bound lives, the Icelanders faced a veritable media tsunami. Even providing basic services was, as AP's Eliason put it, "a remarkable achievement for a tiny nation of 240,000 accustomed to the obscurity of island life on the Arctic Circle, and plunged with little advance notice into the center of international attention."

When the summit was announced for Reykjavik, the whole nation had only 215 overseas phone lines. There were only 150,000 phones in operation. The Post and Telecom Administration quickly imported nine ground stations to facilitate overseas calls, and AT&T boosted that capacity by flying in its latest technology. ITT set up extra fax lines so that the script of Japanese reporters "would not need translation to a different alphabet for transmission." IDB Communications from Los Angeles installed a portable earth station to beam radio transmissions to the satellite. The main American television broadcasters spent $150,000 to charter cargo planes to bring in satellite dishes.

Expectations

Back then, three broadcast networks ruled the American airwaves and dominated the news. Each dispatched its anchor—CBS's Dan Rather, NBC's Tom Brokaw, and ABC's Peter Jennings—to read their nightly reports "live from Reykjavik."

ABC News alone sent a team of fifty to support the nightly broadcast. The ABC A-team included, in addition to Jennings, the network's three top White House and diplomatic correspondents, led by the irrepressible Sam Donaldson.

CNN, new on the scene and eager to wedge in as a real player, sent thirty people to Reykjavik. Ignoring Reagan's message that this would be a low-key event and Shevardnadze's remark that few journalists would come, and despite the summit having a news blackout announced ahead of time, CNN brazenly publicized that it would run twenty-four hours of live broadcasts from Reykjavik over the weekend.

Intelsat scrambled to set up seven satellites to receive signals from the ten or eleven dishes the European networks had already installed. The Western countries contracted for dish signal with the American-organized Intelsat, as did the Soviet Union, despite having its own satellite communications firm. Kremlin officials had more confidence in the competitor's service.

Finding lodging was proving a nightmare. Nearly half the city's hotel rooms had been reserved and a third of all its rental cars had been snapped up by the U.S. Secret Service and State Department before the summit was even announced. On any day, there were only a thousand hotel rooms in Reykjavik, which ran the gamut from four stars to minus stars. The government boldly announced that it had assumed "emergency powers" to force guests out of prebooked rooms in the better hostelries in order to accommodate the official diplomatic parties, assorted VIPs, and top-drawer journalists. It also commandeered private homes and public schools to furnish accommodations.

The few hotels with rooms still available quadrupled their rates, or more. Entrepreneurial locals offered their homes at up to $15,000 for the weekend. A Norwegian company ferried in a big ship with two hundred double cabins.

Tourists, homeowners, and schoolchildren weren't the only ones dispossessed by the onslaught. The Secret Service requisitioned the U.S. ambassador's residence for the president's use. The whole house would be needed, so the ambassador and his wife needed to move out for the duration.

By the time Ambassador Nick Ruwe was so informed, there was no suitable room in any inn. A proud and wealthy man, Ruwe wasn't used to being treated so cavalierly. So he and his wife, after greeting the president and welcoming him into their home, abandoned their embassy and left for points unknown. Thus the U.S. ambassador to Iceland was nowhere around at the most critical time of U.S.-Icelandic relations in history.

Despite the privations, most journalists were delighted to be covering the world's biggest story. Only a handful were reluctant to go, due to Yom Kippur, the holiest day of the Jewish year, which was to begin at sundown on Sunday, October 12. The summit was set to end at noon Sunday, enabling the press planes to be back hours before sundown. Nonetheless, reporters Daniel Schorr of National Public Radio, Barry Schweid of Associated Press, and several others decided not to chance it. That proved to be wise, since at Reykjavik nothing would go according to plans—not even for a holy day.

On the eve of the summit, while all the press was wondering "What will happen?" the locals were wondering "How is this happening?"

IT WAS HAPPENING BECAUSE of Gorbachev. He conceived the idea of a flash summit shortly after receiving a mundane letter from the president in July reiterating U.S. arms proposals and hoping that more progress could be made on them in Geneva.

Gorbachev's letter in response, dated September 15, was a strange one, auguring the strange events that would unfold from it. The letter began with him flashing those iron teeth. Gorbachev wrote that he took offense at Reagan's deliberate campaign to delegitimize the Soviet system, the "massive hostile campaign [that] has been launched against our country, which has been taken up at the higher levels of the United States Administration."

Gorbachev then reviewed the latest U.S.-Soviet crisis, which had begun on September 2, 1986, when the KGB had arrested on espionage charges an American journalist for *U.S. News & World Report*, Nicholas Daniloff. Making a big deal of this, Gorbachev claimed that the United States "deliberately sought to aggravate Soviet-American relations and to increase tension." Moreover, Reagan's stance on the Strategic Defense Initiative (SDI) seemed "a bypass route to securing nuclear superiority."

So maybe this wasn't the man about whom British Prime Minister Margaret Thatcher had said, "We can do business together" two years earlier. By then, Thatcher was already known as the Iron Lady, a sobriquet she relished even though it originally came from the Soviet Army newspaper, *Krasnaya Zvezda (Red Star)*.

The first part of the letter indicated that Gorbachev was more a fresh face on an old body, a new red star in world media but still an apparatchik spouting standard Moscow agitprop in private correspondence with the American president.

Then, at the very end of the six-page letter, in the final paragraph actually, came the first in a succession of surprises. The tone and message suddenly broke out of the old Soviet mold with the unexpected sound of a friendly voice.

"An idea has come to my mind to suggest to you, Mr. President," Gorbachev wrote. Maybe they could set "aside all other matters"—presumably those he ranted about in the first five pages—to "have a quick one-on-one meeting, let us say in Iceland or London, maybe just for one day" to deal with arms control.

The letter went from nasty to nice, from ideological to practical. Gorbachev further suggested that they "engage in strictly confidential, private, and frank discussion (possibly with only our foreign ministers present)." A simple, friendly meeting between the two of them—to be held in a matter of a few weeks.

Thinking back on how we had spent some six months preparing for the Reagan-Gorbachev meeting the year before, I must have looked worried when reading this correspondence. As I began to raise doubts in Poindexter's corner office, after he had shut the door and handed the letter to me to read there and then, he raised his hand indicating I should stop. The president wanted this meeting, he told me, so much so that he had already written Gorbachev back agreeing to it.

Reagan preferred Iceland since in Britain he would have obligations with the queen and Thatcher. In Reykjavik, they could keep it simple—with just the two of them talking quietly by themselves, or maybe with just one or two others along. In London, there would be considerable fuss. In Reykjavik, no fuss at all.

The exact dates were swiftly set—Gorbachev being as eager as Reagan—and the government of Iceland then duly informed.

Prime Minister Steingrímur Hermannsson was first told, not by his NATO ally but by the envoy of his alleged foe, the Russian ambassador, Yevgeny Kosarev. The prime minister said he was skeptical that such a big event could be staged in only twelve days, and that he would check this out with the American ambassador.

Hermannsson later related what happened next: "His Excellency"—meaning Ambassador Ruwe—"was, shall we say, not pleased." He distinctly recalled the ambassador saying, "Those bastards!"

The prime minister innocently asked, "The Russians?"

" 'No,' Ruwe replied indignantly. 'The State Department!' He had not been informed."

Soon, the entire world was informed. Hermannsson broke the news to Icelanders the next day, specifying that the Hotel Saga in downtown Reykjavik would be the chosen summit site.

The next Reagan-Gorbachev summit—which had been announced at Geneva the year before—would not be at the end of the year in Washington, DC. It would instead be in twelve days' time in Reykjavik, Iceland. It would not be at the Hotel Saga, but at Hofdi House. And it certainly would not be a vapid, all-for-show session.

CHAPTER 2

Arrivals

Thursday, October 9, 1986
Keflavik International Airport, Iceland, 7:00 p.m.

In the chilly twilight of an autumn evening, Air Force One touched down at Keflavik International Airport, on the coast some thirty miles west of Reykjavik. Keflavik did double duty as Iceland's main commercial airport and as an American-run NATO air base where three thousand airmen and women serviced jets flying north to track Soviet planes coming over the Arctic Circle. Before going there, Eduard Shevardnadze quipped that Iceland had been selected partly because its NATO base assured Russian leaders of their safety.

A few years back, a large demonstration was held to protest American military aircraft operating from there. While protests elsewhere were staged by peace demonstrators, those in Iceland were protesting the Phantom flights endangering "the wee folk," the local elves. A University of Iceland poll found that 55 percent of the population believed in elves and spirits of sundry sorts. In his UPI filing on October 4, Rolf Soderlind described Iceland as "one of the strangest places on Earth—a windblown volcanic moonscape populated by sheep, ponies, elves, pagan gods and 241,000 bookish descendants of the Vikings."

Rain pelted President Ronald Reagan as he emerged from Air

Force One. With his light tan raincoat buttoned to the neck, he shook hands quickly with those awaiting him on the tarmac. For a long-time politician, Reagan was remarkably bad at recalling or pronouncing names. So he did not even attempt to greet by name Vigdís Finnboga-dóttir, Iceland's president. She was the only elected female president in the world then, having been trained in theater and schooled in French literature. Nor did he make a stab at pronouncing Steingrímur Her-mannsson, the name of the prime minister standing beside her. As a wag put it, consonants were one of Iceland's main products.

Reagan wasn't the first American president to come there. Richard Nixon had made the journey in 1973, with disappointing results. A local photograph snapped Nixon's arrival at Bessastadir, the official home of Iceland's president, with the ever-awkward U.S. president being knocked over by a sudden gust of wind. After that awful moment was immortalized on film, Nixon dismissed Iceland as "that God-forsaken place" and claimed that the stench of fish is only relieved by its incessant winds.

Icelanders were able to watch Reagan's arrival live on nationwide television. This was a distinct honor, since Icelandic television, only one channel then, went black on Thursdays, as the nanny-state's way of fostering a more wholesome life for its citizens. When people feared that having a Thursday broadcast would spark an outbreak of per-missiveness, the station manager pledged that the weekly blackout would never again be violated. The Wednesday ban on all alcohol sales across the land, likewise imposed for public wholesomeness, continued uninterrupted.

Because the summit would be brief, the need for transportation around Reykjavik scant, the population tiny, and the nearby U.S. military huge, the Secret Service decided not to fly in one of its nuclear-holocaust-survivable presidential limos. Hence, twelve minutes after stepping onto the tarmac, Reagan ducked into a locally rented armor-plated limousine.

His motorcade then sped into town. The thirty-mile route had been closed to all traffic, reminiscent of Gorbachev's unimpeded progress through Moscow. Part welcome gesture, part peace protest, hundreds of citizens stood along the route holding candles.

It was dark by then, but the president wasn't missing any picturesque countryside. The airport road cut through monochrome stretches of wind-battered black carbuncled lava, unrelieved by trees or vegetation. It was more moonscape than landscape, evident from NASA choosing that area for astronaut rehearsals of their own version of a moon walk.

A half hour later, the president's limo pulled up at the American embassy on Laufasvegur Street. A small crowd, corralled behind yellow barriers, watched as Reagan emerged from his car, waved, and entered the blockish three-story, stucco-fronted building. He entered into the basement, as the house sits on a slope with its main entry one floor up. All homes in that affluent neighborhood had been searched the day before, and each neighbor given a special identity card for the duration of the president's visit.

The ambassador's residence was attached to the embassy. On the first floor—as we were to see the next morning—was a richly furnished living room, a den with a fireplace, a dining room, and a covered patio. Ambassador Nick Ruwe was a serious hunter, and striking amidst the residence's classical European décor was his overwhelming assortment of antlers on the walls. On the second floor, which we were not to see, the president slept in the master bedroom with an adjoining dressing area, its own bathroom, and a small study. The three other bedrooms and two baths were taken by the security and communications staffs and the president's physician.

While the president settled into Laufasvegur Street, the rest of the cars continued the few blocks along to the Holt Hotel, where the senior staff would be housed in clean, tidy, tiny rooms. A U.S. embassy information sheet admitted that the Holt's rooms "are not furnished to the standards of the grand European hotels" and instead called them "well-appointed." Rooms in the rear of the hotel, like Secretary Shultz's, looked out over the National Cathedral. Those in the front, like mine, had a fine view of the miniature downtown. The hotel lobby contained what was billed to be among Reykjavik's finest restaurants, which served horsemeat and whale chops along with other delicacies.

A block from the Holt was a grammar school which the government had seized under its emergency powers to provide the U.S. delegation with office space. Above the schoolhouse doorway someone pasted a sign "IEOB—Iceland Executive Office Building." The real executive office building in Washington, "the EOB," being the ornate structure adjacent to the White House that houses presidential staff.

As the summit progressed, no one actually worked in the cubicles assigned us in the IEOB. The mail cubbies were constantly replenished with State Department cables that might be skimmed and then tossed in the classified waste bin. Anything important happening in the world that weekend was happening right there.

On Friday morning, a number of us met in the living room at the ambassador's residence to brief the president. We sat under Ruwe's impressive antlers in massive, ornately carved furniture most befitting a first-class salon of a nineteenth-century luxury liner. Reagan was so groggy from jet lag that it quickly became painful to watch him endure us.

His relief was palpable when our session was cut short, so he could head off to Bessastadir. That was just as well, since we had little to brief him about.

One of the earliest Viking sites, Bessastadir was settled before the year 1000. Once the home of its conquering rulers—first Norwegians, then Danes—it had become the home of Iceland's elected leaders. It is a beautiful compound south of Reykjavik, with a ceremonial manor house where Reagan was received, an ancient church, and several old farm buildings. It is surrounded by pastures with Icelandic horses running free and, at that time of year, loads of geese and swans fluttering about.

Reagan wore a full-cut, fur-collared Ulster-like coat popular in the 1930s—which I never saw him wear before or afterward—as he strolled around the grounds with Vigdís Finnbogadóttir, who had run the City Theater before becoming the country's fourth president. As they walked, she observed that since there was no school to teach anyone how to be a president, "the best place you could learn that was at the theater, where you were defining life and society all the time." Reagan liked that notion, and her, so much that he called her "my old colleague" afterward.

After the stroll, President Reagan met with the prime minister and foreign minister. He wasn't any better with them than he had been with us. They tried to discuss nuclear weaponry with him, but it didn't take. Prime Minister Hermannsson later wrote that Reagan was "a very likable person but somehow distanced" since he "was not paying attention" to what the two Icelandic officials said.

Evidently, the president of the United States didn't much care about Iceland's views on nuclear disarmament.

Instead, Reagan told a series of jokes. As described later in a biography of Hermannsson, the prime minister again tried to "discuss nuclear disarmament [and] Reagan took a little note from his pocket and replied, 'Prime Minister, I announce to you that Icelandair will get a landing license for Boston." While welcome, that was surprising news to Hermannsson, who had "not known the airline had applied for that."

After twenty more minutes of agony, the meeting ended awkwardly. Per his biography, to Hermannsson "something felt not right" and he later wondered whether "Reagan's health problem [Alzheimer's disease] was perhaps affecting him already in 1986."

It was not an auspicious start to a critical weekend.

Friday, October 10, 1986
Keflavik International Airport, Iceland, 1:18 p.m.

When Mikhail Gorbachev stepped off his plane, a sudden gust of wind on that raw, blustery day made him grab his gray fedora and falter a bit, almost Nixon-like, as he descended the ramp. At the bottom, he became the first Soviet leader to ever visit Iceland and the first to ever step onto a NATO base.

The Icelandic police formed an honor guard along a red carpet but, as the Soviets had been sternly warned, Iceland's top leaders were elsewhere, leaving only a mid-level official of the Foreign Ministry to welcome the superpower leader. As if to compensate, the weather favored his arrival, albeit briefly. During Gorbachev's perfunctory remarks at the quick arrival ceremony—"The time has come for serious, decisive action . . ."—a burst of sunshine broke through the cloud covering.

At Gorbachev's side was a striking woman whom he referred to, Russian style, as Raisa Maksimovna but who was known everywhere outside the U.S.S.R. as Raisa Gorbachev. Wearing a black coat with a leather-trimmed hat, she was ushered over to meet her weekend host. Being more adept with names than Reagan, she greeted Edda Gudmundsdottir, the prime minister's wife, by name.

Mrs. Gorbachev, fifty-four, had become a sensation after the Gorbachevs' international debut in London. She was good looking and dressed fashionably, especially for a Soviet leader's wife—admittedly, a modest standard. As with her husband, the contrast with her predecessors was sharp. As one wag then put it, Raisa was the only wife of a Soviet leader who weighed less than her husband. Plus, she was intellectually as sharp as she looked. She had received a doctorate and lectured on philosophy, albeit of the Marxist-Leninist variety, at Moscow State University.

Unlike the Americans, the Soviets had flown in a bulletproof Zil limo for the Gorbachevs' use. As the motorcade pulled out of the airport, it passed a billboard with "Welcome" written boldly across it in Russian. This kindly gesture was marred only by the fact that the brief greeting was misspelled.

The bulk of the massive Soviet delegation stayed at the Hotel Saga—the KGB's pre-announcement booking made this possible—with its hundred rooms, close to the university. A large billboard facing the hotel had advertised the current hit film *Top Gun*, which glorified the prowess of American fighter pilots against threatening enemies. But that billboard had been removed by the time the Russians arrived there.

The Gorbachevs chose to stay aboard the *Georg Ots* in Reykjavik's large harbor. The five-hundred-foot Polish-built vessel was named for an Estonian singer nicknamed the "Soviet Sinatra," whose signature song was fittingly "The Impossible Dream" from *Man of La Mancha*. When asked why they had decided to stay aboard the ship, Mrs. Gorbachev said because it was "wonderful, very romantic."

Docked alongside the *Georg Ots* was the *Baltika*, a forty-six-year-old ocean liner that had carried Nikita Khrushchev to the United States in 1959. Those Soviets not at the Hotel Saga would stay aboard the *Baltika*.

Now full of Soviets, Reykjavik's harbor was thus full of security. Phalanxes of KGB officers—almost caricatures of themselves—wore long gray coats and black hats and carried boxlike walkie-talkies. A local resident was quoted in one of the mini town's four daily newspapers as saying, "They don't have to be afraid. There's no such thing as an Icelandic terrorist."

The KGB turned away the *Sirius*, a Dutch ship that Greenpeace had recently acquired to hassle Iceland's whalers. Some local officials objected when the Soviets kept the colorfully refitted *Sirius*, its hull decorated with a rainbow and the dove of peace, out of the harbor.

But the locals objected more to the KGB and U.S. Secret Service packing high-caliber heat in their weaponless land. The island nation had no armed forces, its police carried no weapons, there was no hunting, and virtually no armed robbery (one alleged incident had been recorded the previous decade). The prime minister's response to such objections—"These men are so accurate that they can shoot a man between his eyes in every single position imagined"—offered little comfort.

After getting settled in, the Gorbachevs headed out, with their big Zil surrounded by police cars and motorcycles. Dark-windowed KGB vans were trailed by reporters and cameramen and emergency medical vehicles, with an ambulance at the end, caboose-like. Reykjavik had never seen anything like it, a huge motorcade speeding through its closed-down, closed-off narrow downtown streets.

Their destination was Bessastadir, where President Reagan had made his call earlier. Finnbogadóttir returned from the Althing's opening to meet Gorbachev, who would greet but not eat at Bessastadir. The week before, Gorbachev had told his staff to arrange "courtesy visits to the Icelandic authorities . . . but decline lunch politely" (according to Chernyaev's notes). He instructed staff to tell the Icelandic officials "that Raisa Maksimovna will be coming" and would like "a cultural program for her—everything that they offer." She would end up doing more than everything they offered.

Later that night, Ted Koppel devoted his *Nightline* broadcast to Reykjavik. At its close, the anchor mordantly observed that "Rarely does the payoff match the pomp." At that point, even the pomp had been anemic.

As the U.S. and Soviet delegations were settling in, members of the Fourth Estate were still streaming in.

The Icelandic government was trying its best. It had hired Gray & Co., then Washington's top-drawer PR firm, to show the country off to advantage. It printed up a handout explaining that Iceland meant "island" and not "ice-land," and that Reykjavik meant "smoky bay" because the steam rising from its underground springs was mistaken by the town's Viking founder, Ingolfur Arnason, for smoke. The handout boasted that Iceland had more geysers than anywhere on earth, its hot springs supplying the hot water for all those above, that its capital lies midway between Moscow and Washington and contains half of the nation's 240,000 population.

The Gray & Co. spinmeisters also presented material on the culture, especially Iceland's sagas. Written between AD 1200 and 1300, the sagas are all but bred in the bones of every Icelander. They chronicle epic battles of gods, elves, and leprechauns through the centuries and across the land. *Time*'s essayist Roger Rosenblatt wrote that "the Icelandic sagas [were] populated by heroes with unpronounceable names who made elegant speeches and went at each other with axes." He summarized one:

In Njal's Saga, known to every schoolchild, the hero is burned to death, and it falls to his son-in-law Kari to avenge the family. Coldly, he knocks off fifteen of his enemies, but then suddenly the killing stops. He feels he has overdone it.

Horses are revered along with legends, there being sixteen Icelandic words for the proud beast, frequently seen in odd positions—they sleep on their sides, looking dead—and in odd places. "Along the steepest mountainsides, small horses stick like burrs, grazing where no American horse could maintain its balance," Meghan O'Rourke wrote in the *New York Times*. "The Icelandic horse, too, is unique with its quick, short-steeped gait, so smooth a rider wouldn't spill a drink." For centuries horses were the main mode of transport, since the country never had a railroad and cars were not introduced until the 1920s.

Iceland's government-run tourist bureau established a clearinghouse to find housing for journalists, but it was quickly overwhelmed. The government did better with its international press center, which opened Thursday morning with celebrity speeches and a noisy brass band. A lottery was held with such prizes as smoked salmon and woolen sweaters for lucky winners. The center offered journalists local delicacies, including cod liver oil. "We encourage you to take it," the spokesman said. "You will feel better, stronger, and live longer."

Outside the center there were six tan Icelandic ponies carrying U.S., Soviet, and Icelandic flags. And for all four days, reporters could meet and interview the newly crowned Miss World, Iceland's own Hólmfríður Karlsdóttir, who had been summoned back from an Asian goodwill tour for the summit festivities. She wore a white T-shirt with sketches of Reagan and Gorbachev during her press availability. When not reigning globally, the blue-eyed, blonde Karlsdóttir taught nursery school. Also in the international press center was Miss Young Iceland, who was available for interviews each day after her high school classes ended.

The onslaught of voracious journalists and probing photographers had descended on a people unaccustomed to change and resigned to their fate. "In Iceland the geology is primary, humans are secondary," O'Rourke observed. "In Iceland, you are aware at every turn of your smallness, the irrational, slow forces at work."

As in most cultures, language captures essence. Icelandic is antique Danish flash-frozen for the past thousand years. Hence, an eleventh-century Viking suddenly returned to Reykjavik could understand what his startled hosts were saying about the startling happenings in his ancestral land.

Because of its lack of much happening and long dark winters, Icelanders can be fond of drink. Visiting in 1872, the linguist and explorer par excellence Richard Burton found "more cases of open, shameless drunkenness . . . during a day in Reykjavik than a month in England." The Reykjavik city administrator blamed this on the inhabitant's heritage: "We are the descendants of the most boring people in Europe, the Norwegians," Bjorn Fridfinnsson told foreign reporters, "and the drinkingest, the Irish."

. . . .

"AND NOW, THE REYKJAVIK summit," intoned ABC's Peter Jennings at the top of his evening broadcast on Friday, October 10. "President Reagan doesn't begin to meet with Mr. Gorbachev until Saturday, but already on this island there is a very heightened sense of anticipation. . . . There was some indication . . . how [Reagan] felt about the prospects. ABC's Sam Donaldson traveled with him." The broadcast then cut to the intrepid Donaldson, who tried to eke some significance out of Reagan's anodyne arrival remarks.

For television viewers around the world, Hofdi House became the signature site, practically the logo, of Reykjavik. Yet, it was not the government's first choice to host the summit sessions.

When, shortly after midnight on September 29, the prime minister received the call that Iceland had won the summit sweepstakes, the exact meeting place was undecided. He had announced and personally preferred the new Hotel Saga, or an old mansion downtown that had just been remodeled to host conferences. As third choice was the rickety old Hofdi House.

The government hastily formed a Summit Preparatory Committee to decide on arrangements. The committee, like the summit itself, soon got bloated, with more than fifty members from U.S., Soviet, Icelandic, and Reykjavik government agencies. Its first agenda item was the site where the superpower leaders would actually meet. Iceland's recommendation was opposed by both superpowers. They preferred Hofdi House solely because its physical isolation offered greater security.

Nonetheless, it was an inspired choice. A stunning art nouveau wooden structure in a land void of trees, Hofdi House was built with large wooden planks running horizontally on all sides. There are symmetrical windows on every side of the boxlike structure and a mansard roof with dark shingles. It is fairly small, each floor some twenty-two hundred square feet. There are six small rooms, a kitchen pantry, and a bathroom on the main floor. Upstairs are an additional six rooms as well as one bathroom with a tub, ordinarily an unremarkable feature but one which would play its own supporting role in the weekend's drama.

Given more time, Hofdi's history may have discouraged the committee, as the striking white structure has a distinctly dark side. Its construction was linked with death, its history marked by spirits.

At the turn of the twentieth century, French fishing crews began working the cod-rich northern seas. The unpredictable weather and turbulent waters soon claimed some four hundred French ships and four thousand sailors. The French government established a hospital in Reykjavik to treat survivors and appointed a French consul to oversee the operation.

The first consul, J.-P. Brillouin, asked to build his residence adjoining the new hospital, but his request was turned down. He was offered land a mile away, on a forlorn hayfield on the bleak Felagstun Bay. Reluctantly, he accepted. Brillouin hired a French architect who admired Norwegian wood.

Above Hofdi House's living room entrance is an inscription: "Anno 1909, J.-P. Brillouin, Consul Erat." But Brillouin spent only a few years in his striking new house. When World War I began in 1914, the fishing lanes were closed, and he returned home to join the army.

The house was then occupied by Iceland's foremost poet, Einar Benediktsson, who christened it Hofdi House after his childhood home. In the late 1930s, it was rented to and then bought by the British government for its ambassador's residence. Winston Churchill spent a night there in August 1941, after meeting President Franklin Roosevelt on the battleship *Prince of Wales*, where they sang hymns together and wrote the Atlantic Charter.

According to the Iceland government, when "the war between the British empire and Hitler's Third Reich was at its peak, Hofdi became the nerve center of British operations in Iceland," such as they were. Marlene Dietrich also spent the night there.

After the war, the British ambassador, John Greenway, came to believe he had company in Hofdi House since dishes fell off his shelves at night; framed pictures got twisted or tumbled down; walls cracked; and the whole house creaked. He felt the spirit of a young girl who had drowned, or committed suicide, or both, when living on that land. Another legend had the spirits being Viking warriors, whose fort on that site had burned down a thousand years before.

No matter where the spirits came from, they were there, according to the ambassador. He felt that the "bumps in the night" he heard were because of spirits and not because of Hofdi House's being wooden and situated on lava soil which expands and contracts with temperature changes in the springs below. Wooden structures, unlike those built of brick or stones (like nearly all other buildings in Iceland), react to such fluctuations by moving a bit.

The city of Reykjavik took the house off the jittery ambassador's hands in 1958 and refurbished it for use on ceremonial occasions, the zenith of which was about to take place. Neighborhood kids still refer to it as "the ghost house." On the summit's eve, NBC anchor Tom Brokaw interviewed the prime minister during his daily dip in the thermal springs. Standing poolside in his skimpy bathing suit, Hermannsson said that all his family believed in ghosts, so if any resided in Hofdi House, they were most welcome there.

When the Foreign Ministry spokesperson was asked about that legend, in that land filled with glorious legends, he replied: "We do not confirm or deny that the Hofdi has a ghost."

CHAPTER 3

Minds and Moods Going into Hofdi House

Ronald Reagan was seventeen when Secretary of State Frank Kellogg and French Foreign Minister Aristide Briand signed the Pact of Paris, which outlawed war forevermore. The 1928 Kellogg-Briand Pact soon attracted sixty-two more signatories, who proudly called themselves "the established nations of the world."

They were established, but not all were peaceful. Three years later, a pact signatory, Japan, invaded China. A few years after, signatory Italy invaded Ethiopia, and then signatories Germany and the Soviet Union tore apart Poland. A decade and a year after the pact outlawing war forevermore, the world was engulfed in war bigger than any before.

Nonetheless, fifty-eight years later, the idealism of the pact still moved Reagan. He mentioned it often, aware that it had failed but inspired by its nobility. His view was, as Samuel Johnson once said of second marriages, a triumph of hope over experience.

Like most people living in that era, Reagan fretted about the unimaginable devastation from a nuclear exchange. "Nuclear war can never be won, and must never be fought" was a favorite adage of his.

Even Communists, Reagan believed, would be rational enough to avoid triggering a nuclear exchange that could destroy their own country and much of humanity.

In 1946, with nuclear weapons still an American monopoly, President Harry Truman's adviser Bernard Baruch proposed turning over America's atomic bombs to the United Nations, if other nations abjured developing their own. Had Truman pushed the Baruch Plan, it would have met a firestorm of congressional and popular opposition as an infringement on American sovereignty. However, the Soviets turned the proposition down flat, as they wanted a bomb of their own. And thanks in part to the network of spies—both American and Russian—it was running, it would soon have one.

In the early 1960s President John F. Kennedy asked John McCloy, the wisest of the Establishment's wise men, to help create a new agency named the Arms Control and Disarmament Agency, or ACDA. By a series of improbable happenings, that was the agency I was to head up two decades later.

In 1963 Kennedy concluded the Limited Test Ban Treaty with the Soviet Union, which he heralded as a key step in "man's effort to escape from the darkening prospects of total destruction." His appealing rhetoric equated arms control with peace and goodwill, a mind-set that prevailed at the time of Reykjavik.

Yet Kennedy's treaty constituted more of an environmental than a disarmament measure. Banning nuclear testing in the atmosphere precluded mushroom clouds from frightening the public. Consequently, both America and Russia could, with impunity, step up their nuclear testing and development programs. And both did.

Kennedy's rhetoric soared when he spoke of the nuclear threat. "Every man, woman and child lives under a nuclear sword of Damocles," he told the UN General Assembly in September 1961, "hanging by the slenderest of threads, capable of being cut at any moment by accident or miscalculation or by madness."

Kennedy's secretary of defense, Robert McNamara, shortened the president's "madness" to MAD as he adopted an approach which *assured* that every man, woman, and child would live under Damocles's nuclear sword forevermore. MAD was short for "mutually assured destruction," an idea that had been around for years before McNamara embraced it.

The idea, though appalling, was appealingly simple: if both sides had enough nuclear arms to wipe out the other, then the prospect of mutually assured destruction would render their use irrational and hence preclude such use.

As became unmistakable at Reykjavik, the MAD doctrine offended Reagan's moral sense. It was what George Orwell might have included as a scheme so stupid that only an intellectual could have created it. Reagan's opposition to MAD propelled him toward the Strategic Defense Initiative, which was disparagingly dubbed Star Wars. The showdown in Reykjavik would be waged in this intellectual arena of MAD, SDI, and the Anti-Ballistic Missile (ABM) Treaty.

Many serious people subscribed to MAD, and for good reason. By the early 1960s the United States and the Soviet Union had developed intercontinental ballistic missiles, which could be launched from land or sea to demolish the other country within a half hour. Before long, each ballistic missile became capable of carrying many warheads—three on American Minuteman missiles and up to ten on Soviet SS-18s. This heightened the danger, since it made each new missile as devastating as three, or ten, had been before.

Moreover, these weapons, once launched, could be neither brought back nor shot down. Unlike strategic planes carrying bombs—which could be shot down by air defenses or recalled by their commanders—nothing could be done once a ballistic missile was on its way. While theoretically possible to being shot down in mid-flight, doing so required successfully aiming at and hitting an object traveling at bullet speed far off in space—all within twenty minutes. That was too tough to do in the 1970s and '80s, and remains tough to do still.

Thus there was some logic to MAD, but there was no comfort in MAD. Nuclear theologians touted the beauty of their strategic theory and defense experts implemented it, but Americans were scared to death by it. From such fear sprang the "ban the bomb" movement across America and around the world. Parents fretted over strontium 90 in their children's milk. Families, encouraged by the Kennedy administration, built fallout shelters. Schools across America braced for Armageddon.

On the South Side of Chicago, at 10:30 each Tuesday morning in the late 1950s, an alarm would wail through Bryn Mawr Grammar School, prompting us to walk, calmly, down the hallway and kneel down and shove our heads into our hall lockers. Ours was not a unique experience at that time.

During an eminently forgettable summit in Glassboro, New Jersey, in June 1967, President Lyndon Johnson informed Soviet premier Aleksei Kosygin of this new MAD approach and then unleashed the brainy, assertive McNamara to explain it all. In the post-Reykjavik edition of *Time* magazine, McNamara recalled what happened: "Kosygin was furious. The blood rushed to his face, he pounded on the table and said, 'Defense is moral. Offense is immoral.' That was essentially the end of the discussion."

It wasn't. Nearly twenty years later, at Reykjavik, the roles became reversed while the arguments and emotions remained the same. There, the Soviet leader reasoned as calmly and as cogently pro-MAD as had the U.S. secretary of defense, while the U.S. president reacted against MAD as passionately as had the Soviet premier in 1967.

A year after Glassboro, in 1968, Johnson concluded the Non-Proliferation Treaty. Based on the criterion of Parkinson's second law—namely, that the success of a policy is best measured by the catastrophes which do *not* ensue—this treaty was the most successful arms accord ever, at least until Reykjavik. In 1963 President Kennedy had warned of twenty countries acquiring nuclear weapons by 1975. Yet in 1975 there were only six states with nuclear weapons, not twenty. Over the next thirty-eight years, only three more would be added—Pakistan, Israel, and North Korea—three too many but far fewer than Kennedy anticipated in 1963. This becomes more impressive when realizing that forty-plus countries have the technical know-how to build a bomb, but have chosen not to.

It was Richard Nixon who developed the nuclear terminology and approach that Reagan and Gorbachev would bring into Hofdi House.

Nixon concluded arms accords with the Soviets on both offensive and defensive systems. Offensive systems were constrained in their growth, yet not reduced in their numbers, by the Strategic Arms Limitations Talks (or SALT I), signed in Moscow in the spring of 1972. It wasn't much in itself, but for Nixon and his negotiator Henry Kissinger, it was the beginning of a bright new era of arms controls.

Just as critical was the arms accord on defensive systems, the ABM Treaty. A few years after Kosygin's outburst at Glassboro, the Soviets bought into MAD. The ABM Treaty prohibited either superpower from building defensive systems, except for one system around its capital. The Soviets built a system around Moscow (as Reagan would mention many times at Reykjavik), but the Americans found it politically impossible to build one around Washington, which would have protected the politicians but left "real Americans" beyond the Beltway vulnerable.

The ABM Treaty marked a big change—not so much in theory as in mind-set. The *descriptive* fact that each side was vulnerable— that Kennedy's nuclear sword of Damocles was dangling overhead— became a *prescriptive* tenet, that each side *should be* vulnerable, that Damocles's sword should remain dangling there. This was what Reagan abhorred, as he would tell Gorbachev in no uncertain terms at Reykjavik.

. . . .

IT WAS DURING THE Jimmy Carter years that Reagan solidified his main beliefs on foreign policy and arms control. Beginning in 1979 he called Carter's SALT II agreement "fatally flawed" and urged the Senate to reject it. But the Senate never got the chance to do so, as Carter withdrew the treaty after 120,000 Soviet troops stormed into Afghanistan on Christmas Day 1979.

After trouncing Carter in the 1980 election, Reagan crafted his new administration's approach to foreign policy. Unlike all presidents since Nixon, he was not content to limit the growth of nuclear arms but sought to cut them, massively if not entirely. Reagan thus changed the *L* in SALT, for Strategic Arms *Limitations* Talks, to an *R* in START, for Strategic Arms *Reductions* Talks.

Washington's arms experts denigrated his change. It was clear—to most everyone, except the new president—that the Soviet leadership could never navigate and the Russian military leadership would never tolerate massive nuclear cuts. This, after all, was the Kremlin's ticket to superpower status. Reducing weapons would reduce Soviet power and status in the world. Hence, it would never happen. Hadn't Soviet Premier Nikita Khrushchev quipped to President Dwight Eisenhower, "You have your Senators, and I have my generals"?

Since experts knew this approach was a nonstarter, Reagan's adopting it meant either that he was duplicitous or—more likely, since he wasn't that shrewd—woefully ignorant. In either case, he was, in the prevailing cliché of its day, "not serious about arms control."

The second element of Reagan's new foreign policy was a massive military buildup. Proclaimed under his banner of "peace through strength," it was promoted as needed to close the window of vulnerability opened by the relentless twenty-year Soviet arms expansion. Harold Brown, President Carter's secretary of defense, summed up the situation nicely by saying, "When we build, they build. When we stop building, they build." The U.S. buildup was also needed to prod the Soviets to bargain seriously—in Reagan's view, for the first time ever.

For these reasons, Reagan rallied Congress to put its money where his mouth was. And it did. Defense procurement—the purchase of planes, tanks, ships, and other matériel—more than doubled from when Reagan took office to the time of Reykjavik, rising from $71.2 billion to $147.3 billion yearly. Overall defense spending also hit a peak the year of Reykjavik, upward of $450 billion, compared with less than $340 billion when Reagan assumed office.

One part of the Reagan military buildup was the missile buildup in Europe. When the Soviet intermediate missile was deployed in 1976, it was a real game changer. Soviet nukes were now pointed at the heart of Europe. Consequently, NATO nations asked for U.S. intermediate missiles and cruise missiles to be deployed on European soil to counter this new, grave Soviet threat.

The Soviets desperately tried to split NATO, and the West European peace movement demonstrated massively against the U.S. deployment of missiles to defend their homes, even though they had not demonstrated against the Soviet deployment of missiles to target their homes.

Reagan, supported by Margaret Thatcher and others, insisted that the NATO Alliance stay the course. The U.S. missiles *would* be deployed unless an arms agreement with the Soviets precluded it. But everyone knew that the likelihood of that ever happening ranged from dubious to preposterous—everyone, that is, until Reykjavik.

Reagan's third radical innovation was the Strategic Defense Initiative (SDI). He startled everyone when announcing it on March 23, 1983, including his own secretary of defense. Caspar Weinberger and his assistant secretary, Richard Perle, were attending a NATO meeting in Portugal when informed that SDI would be announced hours later. They tried to stop it, but the announcement came anyway, at the end of an otherwise unexceptional TV address to garner support for his defense buildup. Coming to the close, the president said:

Tonight, consistent with our obligations of the ABM Treaty and recognizing the need for closer consultations with our Allies . . . I am directing a comprehensive and intensive effort to define a long-term research and development program to begin to achieve our ultimate goal of eliminating the threat posed by strategic nuclear missiles.

Reagan said that to launch "an effort which holds the promise of changing the course of human history," he was asking the scientific community "who gave us nuclear weapons" to turn their talents toward peace and find a way "to rendering these nuclear weapons impotent and obsolete."

REAGAN'S WORDS CAME AS a bolt out of the blue, but the notion of strategic defense had been marinating in his brain for years.

His aha moment had come in July 1979. Having completed two terms as California governor, with his eyes on the White House, Reagan began boning up on security issues. So he headed to the headquarters of NORAD, the North American Air Defense Command, outside of Colorado Springs. He was given the usual VIP dog and pony show and heard what thousands before him had heard. Yet he saw things differently.

Visitors to NORAD walked through gigantic steel doors, some five feet thick, to access the granite core of Cheyenne Mountain. After touring the facility, Reagan was led into something out of *Dr. Strangelove*, a room with massive screens on the walls to track Soviet ballistic missiles that might have been launched.

The NORAD brass was accustomed to visitors then leaving wowed. Yet Reagan began leaving perplexed. So he stopped and asked the commanding general, James Hill, just what would happen if those big panels ever did light up. The general pointed to a row of colored phones along the side table. Pick that one up, he said, and the White House Situation Room instantly answers. That phone there connects us to all U.S. commanders across the country. And on the one over there, we can talk to U.S. base commanders all around the world.

Reagan got more frustrated. Well, what happens then?

They call their subordinates, Governor, and on down the chain of command. The president may order a retaliatory strike or take other measures. No one can be sure, but NORAD is, and must be, prepared.

That was the moment of revelation for Reagan. After those gigantic NORAD panels lit up like a Christmas tree, indicating a nuclear attack against America, everyone would scramble to phone everyone else—up and down the chain of command—each with a variant of the same message: "Holy shit!"

Well, Reagan mused, shouldn't someone be able *to do* something? Something more than calling everyone else to convey the *really* bad news? Something more moral than wiping out the other guy's country? Shouldn't the president be able to do something to protect America? Maybe by shooting down those incoming missiles before they get here?

"We have spent all that money, and have all that equipment," he mused afterward to an aide, "and there is *nothing* we can do to prevent a nuclear missile from hitting us?" He was sure that there was *something* out there, something better for the future than that, and kept pondering the problem.

Two years later, he was in a place where he could do something about it. He was in the Oval Office.

BEFORE SDI WAS ANNOUNCED, Reagan worked the issue with the Joint Chiefs of Staff. In a letter to a friend, the president said that he reminded the top brass that every offensive weapon had inspired a defensive one "all the way back to the spear and shield. Then I asked them if, in their thinking, it was possible to devise a weapon that could destroy missiles as they came out of the silos. They were *unanimous* in their belief that such a defense system could be developed. I gave the go-ahead that very day." That, it turned out, was the easy part. Garnering support for the program and then devising such a weapon—those would prove the tough parts.

When Reagan launched SDI, all hell broke loose. Senator Edward Kennedy, with the family's gift for PR, dubbed the program Star Wars, after George Lucas's 1977 fantastic intergalactic movie epic. Like "Deep Throat" in an earlier administration, it was catchy and understandable. So it stuck.

SDI launched a thousand irate articles and editorials. The Union of Concerned Scientists, 100,000 members strong, was fierce in its opposition. The Arms Control Association declared that SDI would end arms control, while some Soviets felt SDI would end the world. Domestic critics became furious and the Kremlin went ballistic.

THE FOURTH ELEMENT OF Reagan's new foreign policy—along with deep cuts in nuclear arms, a military buildup à la "peace through strength," and SDI—was a campaign to delegitimize the Soviet system. Along with SDI, this was both his most innovative and effective element.

All Reagan's predecessors had dealt gingerly with the world's other superpower. Since the U.S.S.R. was here to stay, powerful and fearsome, a president had to be respectful. Harsh rhetoric would only be counterproductive.

Reagan opposed the two pillars of postwar policy, containment and détente. "Containment is not enough," he said, preferring to go on the offensive. Détente was, to his mind, accommodation at best and sellout most probably.

He desperately wanted the Cold War to end. On the flight to Detroit to accept the 1980 Republican nomination, Reagan was asked by longtime political adviser Stuart Spencer, "Why are you doing this,

Ron? Why do you want to be president?" Without a minute's hesitation, he blurted out, "To end the Cold War." And beginning in the 1970s if not earlier, Reagan envisioned how that would happen: "We win, they lose."

As president, he lost no time in trying to make that happen. At his very first White House press conference, he asserted that "détente's been a one-way street that the Soviet Union has used to pursue its own aims," foremost "the promotion of world revolution and a one-world Socialist or Communist state." That explains why "the only morality they recognize is . . . [to] reserve unto themselves the right to commit any crime, to lie, to cheat, in order to attain that" world domination.

As if that wasn't tough enough, Reagan told members of the British Parliament the next year that Communism would end up on "the ash heap of history." The following year, he famously called the U.S.S.R. an "evil empire." Speaking to evangelists in Florida, he urged true believers

> to beware the temptation of pride, the temptation of blithely declaring yourselves above it all and label both sides equally at fault, to ignore the facts of history and the aggressive impulses of an evil empire, to simply call the arms race a giant misunderstanding and thereby remove yourself from the struggle between right and wrong and good and evil.

WHERE THESE FOUR MAJOR foreign policy innovations came from is, even now, tough to say. Ronald Reagan was neither inwardly reflective nor outwardly revealing. He certainly was no grand strategic theorist. But somehow his four elements fit together to form a coherent strategic approach. And somehow that approach fit his overarching goal of ending the Cold War, with our winning and their losing.

Though Reagan may not have been widely read, he was widely

written. From the time he entered politics, he wrote, and rewrote in longhand, his speeches, columns, and radio broadcasts. He realized that ideas have consequences, and thus grappled with the right choice of words to convey the right ideas.

Though just weeks shy of turning seventy when entering the White House, Reagan was still a policy entrepreneur, still brimming with ideas, most of them new, which he wanted implemented during his limited time in office. While boosting the military was standard conservative fare then, his other three innovations—deep nuclear cuts, SDI, and the war of ideas to delegitimize the U.S.S.R.—were all Reagan, and only Reagan.

While still unable to determine where Reagan's ideas came from, we can now determine where his ideas led to. They led to outcomes that ended the Cold War.

But Reagan's innovations didn't do that, or much of anything for that matter, during his first term as president. Hence in 1984, his critics were right to claim that the new Reagan foreign policy, though full of sound and fury, had signified nothing. All there was to show from the harsh talk was heightened world tensions. Indeed, had Reagan been a one-term president—like both his predecessor and his successor—he would have been judged an abject failure in foreign policy.

How much of a failure can be appreciated by glancing back at two prestigious publications of the 1980s—*Time* magazine and the *New York Times*. Both describe the dangerous landscape of Reagan's years. Both attribute it largely to Reagan's dangerous leadership.

Time's premier edition each year is its "Man of the Year" issue. For 1983 it was a "Men of the Year" issue with a dramatic cover portrait of Ronald Reagan and Yuri Andropov back to back, as if in a duel. They stand ready to take ten paces, turn, and fire at one another—not with pistols drawn, but with missiles launched.

The *Time* cover story relied heavily upon its key diplomatic correspondent, Strobe Talbott, who went on to write best-selling books deriding Reagan's arms control policies. Its punch line was: "The deterioration of U.S.-Soviet relations to that frozen impasse overshadowed all other events of 1983." *Time* lamented how "the superpowers for the first time in 14 years [had] no arms-control talks of any kind in progress."

The main problem was, in a word, Reagan. "At times," the cover story revealed, "Reagan has talked of the Soviet Union as a phenomenon that a resolute West could cause to disappear." Something worse was identified next: "Moreover, Reagan's closest aides say he consistently speaks exactly this way in private." In short, here was a president who said in public what he believed in private. Here was one who believed something as radical as that "a resolute West" might just cause the Soviet Union "to disappear."

While such a view sounded alarming to a *Time* diplomatic correspondent here, it sounded even worse to diplomats elsewhere: "To Soviet ears, the President seems not only to be denying the U.S.S.R.'s coveted claim to equal status with the U.S. as a superpower, but even challenging its right to exist as a legitimate state."

Though unflattering, *Time*'s reporting was accurate. Reagan was not only *seeming* to delegitimize the U.S.S.R.; he was *intending* to do so.

Months after the most prestigious newsweekly's assessment came the most prestigious newspaper's verdict on Reagan's presidency. On October 28, 1984, in its most important quadrennial editorial, the *New York Times* endorsed Reagan's opponent, Walter Mondale, for president. It cited as its "most important" factor "Mr. Reagan's diplomacy" which had taken "the nuclear arms race . . . to new heights." Reagan's "lifelong opposition to arms control" made him "unlike every other President of the nuclear era." His rhetoric was deplorable, though its motivation was clear: He "tickles the religious right by reviling the Soviet Union as an Evil Empire." The editorial quoted esteemed historian Henry Steele

Commager as calling Reagan's evil empire speech "the worst Presidential speech in American history, and I've read them all." One can question whether even an esteemed historian could read every presidential speech delivered since George Washington and find Reagan's the very worst. But no matter; Commager represented the conventional view of the time.

WHILE THE EVENTS FOLLOWING Reykjavik later disproved these points, Reagan's behavior before Reykjavik disproved that he opposed and cared little for arms control.

He cared a lot. This was evident in his choice of topics for his radio broadcasts in the 1970s. Of his thousand or so broadcasts, more than 20 percent were devoted exclusively to arms control and another 20 percent to Soviet policy—hence, nearly half, some four hundred broadcasts, to this overall topic. A surprisingly few were on the hot-button items politicians commonly use to garner support—abortion and what nowadays we'd call issues relating to guns, gays, and God.

Upon becoming president, Reagan kept up his keen interest in arms control. From April 1983—the month I became arms control director— until the end of that year, the president presided over fourteen White House meetings *exclusively* on arms control—eight NSC meetings in the Cabinet Room and six small sessions in the Oval Office. Moreover, twenty-five arms control meetings were held in the White House without him but with his top staff. All told, I attended forty White House meetings on arms control in forty weeks, which is more than nearly any cabinet officer would attend over a four-year period. Most amazing was how all this top-level attention in Washington came at a time of little movement in Geneva at the formal arms talks.

During his first term, Reagan was roundly condemned for not having met with any Soviet leader. He sloughed it off by quipping, "How am I supposed to get any place with the Russians, if they keep dying on me?"

Nonetheless, the criticism got to him. He was failing at the one thing he most wanted to succeed at, and failing at what he likely considered God's mission for him. For a man who seldom failed in life, this was tough to take.

WE DON'T KNOW JUST what Reagan had in mind before Reykjavik but we do know his mood. He was awfully excited.

Part of it was his fondness for big events. And Reykjavik was, despite his attempts to dampen it down, shaping up to be a very big event.

He also liked negotiating, and considered himself quite a master of it. During White House meetings, Reagan would regale us with bygone triumphs when negotiating as president of the Screen Actors Guild. He particularly relished the instance—or maybe it was several instances—when he triumphed through urinal diplomacy. The talks were deadlocked; tension was rising; much was at stake; and Reagan called a bathroom break. As he and his counterpart stood side by side at the urinals, Reagan whispered how he would propose this, suggest the other fellow counter with that, and then he would offer something they could both support. Back from the bathroom, hands washed, it happened just that way! A broad presidential smile would accompany the story's happy ending, each and every time.

AT LAST, LATE IN 1985 came the opportunity for Reagan to meet a live Soviet leader and to use his finely honed negotiating skills at a summit of the superpowers.

This would be historic, as the first summit in six and a half years, the first for either Reagan or Gorbachev. After some haggling with the Russians, both sides settled on the dates—November 19 and 20—and the location—the lakeside chateau of His Highness the Aga Khan, a neutral venue in a neutral city (Geneva) of a neutral country (Switzerland). No session would have a host. Everything would be equal, the playing field absolutely level.

The summit's most memorable moments were its opening ones. The president, looking fresh and chirpy, was chatting with some of us in the Aga Khan's ornate hallway, seeming without a care in the world, when a Secret Service agent whispered that the general secretary's limo was coming up the circular driveway.

This being late November in Central Europe, it was cold. Yet Reagan bounded out of the hallway, not stopping to don a coat or hat, and sprang down the steps, just as the boxy black Russian limo pulled to a stop. Reagan gracefully walked over to greet Gorbachev, who was making a rather clumsy exit from the big Zil, wrapped up in a heavy coat, a black fedora, and a thick gray scarf.

They stood for a minute seeming to chat but actually posing for the world's photographers, Reagan looming six or eight inches taller, looking sprightly and healthy in his finely cut suit. Gorbachev was shorter and swaddled from head to foot in dark wool. Coming out of the massive boxy vehicle, he looked like a gangster from some 1940s noir movie.

Before a sea of cameras, the two leaders continued their performance, full of smiles and handshakes and gestures, uttering greetings unintelligible to each other. After this *pièce de théâtre*, the president extended his arm expansively toward the grand entrance of the Maison de Saussure. It was the gesture of a gracious host welcoming an important guest, turning the maison from a neutral location into Reagan's private abode. Gorbachev nodded, appreciating his host's hospitality, and the two of them turned and headed up the grand stairway.

Then came the most remarkable stagecraft. While climbing up, the president, who was nearly a generation older, eased his hand under Gorbachev's arm and elbow—not aggressively, but helpfully—in case his guest needed some assistance mounting the stone steps.

Reagan may have planned this opening gambit or, more probably, it came from instinct. Regardless of its origins, its effects were clear. Gorbachev's public affairs chief, Sergey Tarasenko, surprisingly admitted what had just happened: "I felt that we lost the game during these first movements. You can compare this to a chess game. We started with the wrong move."

THEREAFTER, THE SUMMIT PROCEEDED according to script. For two days and nights, the leaders and their attractive wives shared fancy meals and receptions. The men seemed to like double dating.

Though the Cold War had turned chillier since Reagan entered office, the mood in Geneva was warm. The summit's most enduring image, besides its opening, was of the two men sitting chummily before a blazing fire, which bestowed the tagline of "The Fireside Summit."

Reagan and Gorbachev would have four more summits together, Reykjavik being far and away the most substantive and momentous. During them, the two would undergo the usual ups and downs of any human relationship. Some staff claimed they became friends, but that would be an overstatement. Their contrary values and interests precluded any real friendship. Besides, they had each chosen the all-consuming life of politics, which left little time or space for friends.

Luckily, each found a partner to fill that space. Raisa Gorbachev had the smarts and political canniness to help guide her husband during her perilous journey. On a staff memo sketching his schedule at Reykjavik, Gorbachev scribbled on its margins: "You have reserved no time for me to consult my wife," clearly wanting her advice during such a critical event. As an extrovert with a genuine interest in foreign cultures, Raisa was the personification of the transformation of Soviet life that was Gorbachev's cause and trademark. Moreover, she cared deeply for him, as he did for her.

Reagan's needs were different, less political and more emotional, and thus his choice of a mate and subsequent relationship with Nancy were different. As the son of an alcoholic, he remained an emotional loner in the crowded worlds of Hollywood, Sacramento, and Washington, DC. Unwilling, perhaps even unable, to establish close relationships, even with his brother and children, Reagan needed someone totally devoted to him, as he would be to her. It was as if all of Reagan's emotional capital went to Nancy, with none left over for others.

She had the added advantage of serving him as head of personnel. She was a keen judge of people and could fire those who proved incompetent or unreliable, a skill which eluded him. While that served Reagan well, it was more a side benefit than a central feature of their unique relationship.

NANCY AND RAISA MAY have been all their husbands needed in their personal lives. But they did not need one another in their personal lives. While their husbands got along fine, they got along less than fine.

Such gossip mattered little in the larger scheme of war and peace. Yet, like most gossip, it was more intriguing and easier to understand than issues of war and peace. Journalists spotted a juicy story, which they needed to soften their submissions otherwise filled with mind-bending arms control lingo.

Thus the Superwife Summit would play out within the Superpower Summit. *Le Figaro* called Raisa "Nancy Reagan's great rival" before the two had ever met. Boning up for the competition, Mrs. Reagan watched videotapes of Mrs. Gorbachev before heading to Geneva.

While the men were debating Star Wars, the women were engaging in Style Wars. Nancy was declared first-round loser after landing in Geneva wearing an oilcloth raincoat, which got "everyone wondering if she had left her sense of style at home," as the UPI article had it.

But she recovered in subsequent rounds. Her attire at the Geneva dinners and receptions showed the advantage of shopping on Rodeo Drive near Hollywood rather than at the GUM department store near

Red Square. "On the fashion front," the *Washington Post* concluded, "there was no contest. Rather than continents apart, the two women were worlds apart." The UPI put it punchier: "Mrs. Reagan . . . easily outglittered Mrs. Gorbachev."

The first ladies made it through the summit by confining their mutual disdain to chilly glances. Each was careful not to utter an unkind word about the other. But no such discipline was shown by Mrs. Reagan's hairstylist, Julius Bengtsson of Los Angeles. Asked about Raisa's hairdo, "Mr. Julius," as he called himself, told reporters, "I'm not crazy about her hair. It looks like it has a freeway or a grand canal coming down the middle . . . It's not natural," he opined, as if it *was* natural for a hairdresser to criticize the first lady of the Soviet Union during a superpower summit.

The sole substantive accomplishment out of Geneva came on its final morning, when Gorbachev agreed to another summit the next year in Washington, DC, and Reagan to one the year after in Moscow.

Neither of these summits would happen as they had agreed. Those carefully scripted plans at the close of a carefully scripted summit went awry as contentious issues arose in 1986.

THOUGH A CONSERVATIVE, REAGAN approached Soviet affairs and arms control with radical innovations. Though a Marxist, Gorbachev approached American affairs and arms control with conservative instincts. He sought no massive military buildup, no radical cuts, no SDI, and no delegitimization of his adversary. He merely wanted the standard-fare Nixon-Ford-Carter arms control to move along faster. That's why he proposed a no-frills meeting on arms control, to push it along.

Unlike Reagan, who remains mysterious, Gorbachev has become transparent since the release of Anatoly Chernyaev's notes of top-secret pre-Reykjavik Kremlin meetings. On September 22, 1986, Gorbachev directed his staff "to turn on some propaganda" and "create a leak about Reykjavik" that the U.S.S.R. wanted real breakthroughs on arms control there. "Don't we have some brains?" he asked out loud.

Besides a PR push, Gorbachev sought real results. "We cannot make offers to the Americans which we know beforehand they would not accept. This is not a policy," he told a top aide reframing their same old policies.

Five days before taking off, Gorbachev told the "Reykjavik Preparation Group" he had established that "most likely nothing can really be done with [the Reagan] Administration." Nonetheless, he hoped for something with "breakthrough potential," something "significant and bold." He recognized that "in order to move Reagan, we have to give him something."

Gorbachev said his prime focus would be on strategic arms, as they "concern everybody [above] all other issues." Given their importance, "we should not link" strategic arms deals to SDI. His second priority was to knock "the U.S. intermediate missiles out of Europe. It is a gun pressed to our temple." Four days later, he called these U.S. missiles "a serious threat to us."

In fact, they were nothing of the sort. While our new missiles were reliable and accurate—with high-precision guidance and flying at Mach 8, more than 6,000 miles per hour—their prime attribute was their mobility. And, in fact, they could move mobilely around U.S. Army bases in America, accompanied by the army-mandated caravan of thirty specialized support vehicles. But they were not being deployed on bases in America, but in West Germany, where army plans called for the missiles and their thirty accompanying vehicles to go cruising down the autobahn during a crisis. In reality, no German government would ever allow that, *especially* during a crisis. Even if it did, the peace movement would block the convoy before it ever reached the ramp onto the highway.

Hence those of us briefed on the army procedures concluded that our missile, despite its mighty reputation, was a lemon. Luckily,

Gorbachev received no such briefing. And thus he came to no such conclusion.

Gorbachev sensed how keen Reagan was for him to visit America, telling his Kremlin colleagues that "if there is no agreement" at Reykjavik "there will be no Gorbachev visit to the States. This is a hook on which we can hold Reagan."

THE MOST STUNNING REVELATION of Chernyaev's notes is how much Gorbachev feared failure at Reykjavik.

At an October 4 meeting, he said that should Reykjavik fail, "we will be pulled into an arms race beyond our power, and we will lose this race" because "we are presently at the limit of our capabilities."

Here, remarkably, was Gorbachev saying what Reagan had long been saying. In contrast, the foreign policy experts "knew" that—as large as the Soviet defense effort was—it could grow much larger.

This, they taught, was why arms control benefited us far more than them. For without arms agreements in place, the Soviets would be unconstrained and grow even mightier, while the United States would still be constrained—by Congress with higher budget priorities and by peace groups with higher callings.

Yet here was the general secretary of the Soviet Communist Party telling his Politburo what Reagan had been telling anyone who would listen—that the U.S.S.R. was at the end of its rope, with a military budget that simply couldn't be boosted. Without an accord coming out of Reykjavik, Russia would be up the proverbial creek.

Lest his colleagues miss the point, Gorbachev reiterated it many times during the lead-up to Reykjavik. "If the new round [of the arms race] begins, the pressure on our economy will be inconceivable," he said at one point. At another: "The arms race overburdens our economy. That is why we need a breakthrough." Soviet military efforts "first and foremost lead to a wearing-out of our economy. This is impermissible." And finally: "If they impose a second round of arms race upon us, we will lose!"

What Gorbachev was saying was at odds from what other powerful Russians were saying then. Indeed, the Communist Party Central Committee issued a secret report claiming that "the meeting at Reykjavik will be conducted in an atmosphere where people from all over the world are turning towards the policies of the Soviet Union." Given this global wave of support for the red team, Reagan was on the ropes: "It will be difficult for him to leave the meeting without positive results."

Gorbachev never bought that line. To drive his point home, he reminded the Politburo on October 4 of what had happened the day before, when a missile onboard a Soviet nuclear submarine accidentally exploded during a routine patrol off Bermuda. That caused it to plummet to the bottom of the sea along with its sixteen nuclear-tipped missiles. "Because of the submarine which just sank," Gorbachev explained mournfully to colleagues, "everybody knows, everybody saw, the shape we are in."

"IN THE INTEREST OF MISSILE REDUCTION AND DISARMAMENT, WE SANK
ONE OF OUR NUCLEAR SUBMARINES... NOW ITS YOUR TURN."

The Soviets were stretched beyond anything the CIA imagined. At the time of Reykjavik, they were estimated to be devoting 12 to 14 percent of their gross national product (GNP) to defense. Soviet archives opened later revealed that the real figure was more *twice* that, or around 30 percent of GNP—some four times America's level of effort for our military (slightly over 7 percent of GNP).

During Gorbachev's final preparatory meeting, held on October 8 in the Kremlin, he revealed how much he resented Reagan's delegitimizing campaign, "speaking of a crusade and threatening to send Socialism to the scrap heap of history."

THANKS TO THE CHERNYAEV notes, we get insight into Gorbachev on the eve of Reykjavik. Keenly sensitive to attacks on his country, he was nonetheless a man in charge and a man charging.

No other Politburo member makes any decisions. No other, not even those with far more experience, raises any resistance or offers any ideas. Andrei Gromyko, past foreign minister for more than thirty years, and Eduard Shevardnadze, present foreign minister for more than a year, contribute nothing of substance. Everything is generated by Gorbachev.

Beyond the macroeconomic impetus for an arms accord—his country was going broke and needed relief—there were security incentives. Gorbachev fretted over our missiles in Germany and our SDI in space. In both cases, he was wrong. Our intermediate missiles weren't mobile in reality and SDI was little more than pie in the colorful sky of Ronald Reagan's imagination. But Gorbachev didn't know what he didn't know and was determined to act on what he thought he did know.

GORBACHEV AND REAGAN HAD reasonable priorities to push at Reykjavik—Reagan to cut down nuclear weapons and raise up SDI,

Gorbachev to cut down U.S. intermediate missiles along with SDI and raise up his economy.

Beyond such rational factors were emotional ones. For Reagan, it was fulfilling the mission he felt he had been given after being saved from an assassin's bullet.

Most people would be resentful if they had been shot, but not Reagan. Instead, he was grateful to have been spared. Reagan felt the Lifeguard on High had saved the American lifeguard in chief for some grand life-saving mission.

Reagan was reluctant to talk about the shooting. He skirted all unpleasant topics and this was the mother of all unpleasantness. Nonetheless, he did in a later interview:

There are moments you never erase from your memory, ever. I didn't know I was shot. In fact, I was still asking, "What's that noise?" I thought it was firecrackers. And the next thing I knew, Jerry, the Secret Service agent, simply grabbed me and threw me in the car, and then he dived on top of me. It was only then that I felt a paralyzing pain, and I learned that the bullet hit me up here.

When I walked in, they were just concluding a meeting in the hospital of all the doctors. And when I saw all those doctors all around me, I said I hoped they were all Republicans.

One of the surgeons looking down at him—lying on the operating table, waiting to be cut open—said quietly, "We all are today, Mr. President."

Reagan, to conclude this interview, showed his sunny disposition and deep faith:

God must have been sitting on my shoulder. Whatever time I've got left [he then points up], it now belongs to someone else.

. . . .

GORBACHEV'S MOST COMPELLING EMOTIONAL factor was the fallout of Chernobyl. Like the spirits said to inhabit Hofdi House, Chernobyl was a ghostly presence at Reykjavik, invisible yet strongly felt.

Several months earlier, on April 26 during a series of routine overnight tests, a nuclear reactor in the massive power plant near Chernobyl, Ukraine, caught fire and exploded. It was, and remains, the worst nuclear accident in history.

Although Gorbachev was fully informed about the horrors it unleashed, he reacted with first denial and then misinformation. Even after alarming radiation levels reached neighboring nations and led to worldwide outrage, Gorbachev held off for two and a half weeks before informing his people just what had happened. And even then, he took a page from the old Soviet playbook and blamed the West for an "unrestrained anti-Soviet propaganda campaign" in response to the tragedy.

This inane explanation, on top of his absence from the scene and delay in reacting, added to delegitimizing his system. For the Soviet, and especially for the Ukrainian, people, all the hiding, cheating, lying, and uncaring nature of their government—even under the seemingly kinder, gentler Gorbachev—was infuriating. Only a rotten system would allow children to play in a hot nuclear zone or to stage a soccer match with a large audience near the melting nuclear reactor in a vain attempt to cover up, or at least minimize, the radioactive catastrophe.

BY THE TIME HE arrived at Reykjavik six months later, Gorbachev's reputation had mostly recovered. Over the summer, he pushed internal reforms at home and peace and disarmament abroad.

While he offered far-reaching arms accords notions, such was dismissed as standard Soviet fare. After all, Khrushchev regularly delivered rousing calls for "complete and total disarmament" while accelerating the Soviet military buildup, as did his successors. We in the Reagan administration remained skeptical, never for a minute imagining that *this* time *this* Russian leader might actually be serious about seeking fewer weapons.

Gorbachev and Reagan, reflecting these rational and emotional factors, knew their briefs going into Reykjavik. They had their priorities clear on strategic arms, to cut them where possible. On intermediate missile systems, Reagan wanted them zeroed out, while Gorbachev wanted ours removed from Europe. On SDI, Reagan wanted expanded research or at least research not further constrained by the ABM Treaty, while Gorbachev sought just such constraint, by tightening the ABM Treaty.

Each man sought a businesslike session, to see if they might agree on accords which could be signed at the "real summit" the following year, in Washington, DC.

However, each worried that the other would not be equally serious. Neither needed to have worried on that score.

CHAPTER 4

Saturday in Reykjavik

Saturday, October 11, 1986
The Morning Session

The president got there first. Perhaps with his gotcha moment at Geneva still in mind—where his coatless welcoming of the bundled-up Gorbachev sent a strong image of American vitality and Soviet vulnerability—Reagan again assumed the role of host at another hostless event.

The wind was brisk, the temperature low, and the sky overcast as Gorbachev's big Zil pulled into the circular drive, past the protective screens put up behind Hofdi House to provide yet another layer of security. The smiling president popped out to greet him, as if welcoming a guest to his northern White House. But this time Gorbachev was likewise without hat, coat, or scarf in weather that warranted all three.

As the two shook hands and made mutually unintelligible small talk, the sun suddenly broke through. Some said they spotted a faint rainbow over the sea, causing enterprising PR types to try to dub this "the rainbow summit." But because the weekend weather was generally harsh and the summit's ending harsher, the tagline didn't stick.

The two leaders entered Hofdi House together, where the mayor of Reykjavik, David Oddsson, directed them to chairs carefully positioned for an indoor, seated version of the outdoor, standup photo-op they had just completed.

The scene was nicely composed, with two low-backed, leather-upholstered chairs facing each other at a friendly angle in front of large picture windows filled with a high-horizoned ocean. The peaks of Esja, the volcanic mountain rising over Reykjavik, framed the president's head on either side of a tan curtain.

Strategically placed on a low table between them was a leafy plant with a small flag of Reykjavik stuck in it. Its blue background represented the ocean and its two white pillars represented Viking power. According to legend, Reykjavik was discovered after the Viking chief, Ingolfur Arnarson, tossed his pillars—what we'd call staffs—into the sea, asking the gods to guide them to fertile farmland.

In this case, the gods either lost their sense of direction or found their sense of humor, as Ingolfur's pillars landed on possibly the least fertile spot in the Northern Hemisphere. Yet Ingolfur—not one to question the ways of the gods—founded Reykjavik on the spot then, in AD 874.

Mayor Oddsson, recognizing the unique opportunity handed him, had not limited his boosterism to the symbol-rich flag. Artfully displayed in the three window panels behind the leaders were small bronzes crafted by the father of Icelandic sculpture, Asmundur Sveinsson. Homey representations of Iceland's daily life—*The Harp, Weather Teller,* and *The Laundress*—they were silhouetted against the sea.

However, more attention was paid to the men's heads than to Sveinsson's sculptures. Reporters had long doubted whether the natural hair of a seventy-five-year-old man like Reagan could remain that soft, that wavy, and that dark, without a streak of gray.

Consequently, some self-styled investigative reporters had scrambled into barber shops to scoop up strands of his hair left on the floor after a haircut. Chemical analyses never detected a trace of dye.

Gorbachev's head was more intriguing, with its distinctive wine-colored blotch on his right upper forehead. Although this birthmark had become Gorbachev's trademark in the West, the Soviet public had not seen it, since Soviet photographers were instructed to snap their leader only from the left. If they misaimed, they simply airbrushed the birthmark out of their published photos—just as Soviet textbooks airbrushed Leon Trotsky and other disgraced officials from photos of early Soviet leaders. History for Russians, as George Orwell once quipped, was created rather than learned. Similarly, contemporary photos of the Soviet leader were created rather than simply printed—at least, if snapped from the wrong angle.

Gorbachev's forehead marking, officially called hemangioma, is caused by high concentrations of blood vessels right below the skin. It is often accompanied by seizures, paralysis, or learning disabilities—none of which Gorbachev suffered. Such a birthmark can be removed by laser treatment, but he did not want to seem vain by having such a procedure performed abroad.

Finally, Reagan and Gorbachev stood, ready at last to begin the work that had brought them such a long way. But the hovering mayor had another task for them. In normal times, the mayor of a town with a population that of Topeka, Kansas, would consider himself lucky to be at a reception where he might glimpse one of these leaders. But here was the mayor of Reykjavik stage managing the leaders of the world's nuclear superpowers, now leading them over to sign his Hofdi House guestbook. With signatures from the full delegations added later, that guestbook sits there today under glass as a major tourist attraction.

The mayor's staging, at the outset of this no-staging "business meeting," had taken up more executive time than anyone but he wanted. At long last, the leaders were liberated from the clutches of Mayor Oddsson, walked the short distance to a small conference room, and sat down at a rectangular copper-inlaid table to do business together.

The president began by saying that he was "pleased that you had proposed the meeting, since it was important to make sure that your visit to the United States will be as productive as possible."

"I and the Soviet leadership," Gorbachev responded, "place real value on your agreeing to this meeting."

"I, too, am looking forward to this meeting, and suggest that we alternate one-on-one meetings, with meetings with our foreign ministers." Gorbachev readily agreed and added, "After lunch, we could discuss regional, humanitarian, and bilateral issues." To this, Reagan in turn readily agreed.

Reykjavik was off and running, with the two most powerful men on earth making their first two decisions. However, like nearly everything that weekend, neither happened as planned. The two men never again met one on one, nor did they discuss the broader "regional, humanitarian, and bilateral issues" after lunch that day.

Gorbachev explained that he had proposed Reykjavik since the Geneva arms talks had "a black eye or two and are virtually at an impasse." He sketched Soviet proposals on the numbers of strategic arms, to which Reagan replied that "these seem too high to us. It would still leave the world threatened by these highly destructive weapons."

"The Soviet leadership wants to solve the problem of the nuclear arms race," Gorbachev said, agreeing. That was why he had "formulated proposals which take into account the interests of both the Soviet Union and the United States. This is the only way the problem can be solved."

Reagan nodded and stressed verification by quoting an old Russian proverb—*Doveryai, no proveryai*, "trust but verify." Gorbachev smiled, perhaps because he knew the proverb well but probably because of Reagan's pronunciation.

"You and I must agree on effective verification," Reagan said. "That would be a great step, and the world would applaud."

"Both sides must be confident of compliance," Gorbachev said agreeing once again.

Having brushed on substance, the leaders turned to the meeting itself. Gorbachev had suggested Reykjavik since "it is almost exactly halfway between Moscow and Washington," and Reagan said that he had selected Reykjavik "over London because it seemed more suited to private, serious conversations."

The president then raised what was at the top of his priority list: "Do you have a date in mind for your trip to the United States?"

"I was just getting to that," Gorbachev responded, but said they first needed "concrete results . . . since it would be a scandal if we continued to meet and failed to reach agreements."

After more talk on how eager each was for progress, Gorbachev suggested "that our foreign ministers be invited in to join our meeting." Reagan nodded and word went out to fetch Shultz and Shevardnadze. They hadn't missed much.

WHILE THESE INITIAL EXCHANGES were being made inside the conference room, there was a haunting scene outside it. There in the corridor stood two military officers, one American and one Soviet, in their smartly pressed Class A uniforms, clutching their countries' "footballs," the briefcases containing the series of codes to authorize a nuclear attack. There they stood, a few feet apart, looking straight ahead, not acknowledging one another. It was a sight I couldn't help but watch, at times for minutes on end, over that tumultuous weekend. It was a sight which remains my most vivid image of the Reykjavik summit.

When Shultz and Shevardnadze got seated, Gorbachev started on his agenda with strategic arms, saying they "form the basis of the military strength of both sides." He proposed numbers for a strategic agreement which would "take the U.S. point of view into account" and realize Reagan's goal of a 50 percent cut.

Moving onto his second agenda item, that of intermediate missiles, Gorbachev said that he would "make the following major concession to you. The Soviets will drop the question of British or French nuclear forces. This is *a big step* on our part." After explaining why he could restrict such missiles only in Europe, and not in Asia as Reagan wished, Gorbachev reiterated how he had already made "a huge compromise on our part."

Reagan was encouraged by Gorbachev's apparent willingness to cut nuclear weapons but discouraged when he heard his views on the third agenda item.

"Both sides need to observe the ABM Treaty strictly and in full. What is important here," Gorbachev said, "is to get a mutual understanding which permits SDI research and testing in laboratories, *but not outside of laboratories.* This would not affect testing of systems allowed by the ABM Treaty." Once they agreed to restricting SDI to the laboratories, Shultz and Shevardnadze could "work out drafts of agreements to be signed during my visit to the United States."

"Everything I've heard is encouraging," Reagan said, even though "some points of difference remain," mostly over SDI. Gorbachev merely needed to understand the program better. So he explained it.

"The point is," Reagan said, "that SDI makes the elimination of nuclear weapons possible." He suggested a treaty that "supersedes" the ABM Treaty and requires each side to

> conduct testing in the presence of representatives of the other country. For example, if the U.S. were first, Soviet representatives would be invited to witness the testing. Then, if testing should reveal that a system is practical, we would be obligated to share it. The reason for this is that we can't guarantee in the future that someone—a madman like Hitler, for example—might not try to build nuclear weapons.

To Gorbachev, that would scrap the ABM Treaty: "You are proposing to renounce it. We want to preserve it. You want to destroy it. We just don't understand this."

Gorbachev was already frustrated. He had come to Reykjavik with high hopes for a breakthrough summit. But there, in its opening minutes, the American president had shown no flexibility and proposed nothing new. Gorbachev wondered if he had flown a thousand miles to hear the same old Reagan lines.

As GORBACHEV LOOKED ACROSS the table, his attention occasionally shifted to another set of eyes gazing right at him. For on the wall over Reagan's right shoulder was a large portrait of Iceland's former prime minister, Bjarni Benediktsson.

Reagan would have warmed to Benediktsson, who, like him, was stubborn once he latched onto a policy, a compelling speaker, and a great admirer of America. Gorbachev might have been less enthusiastic.

While studying law in Berlin in the 1930s, Benediktsson came to hate Hitler and Nazism. After the war, he came to hate Stalin and Communism. In 1949, as foreign minister, he pushed Iceland to become a founding member of NATO and, two years later, an American defense ally. As prime minister during the 1960s, with America mired in Vietnam, he defended the American alliance against mounting criticism around the country.

Benediktsson didn't get the chance to become Iceland's elder statesman, as he died tragically in 1970, along with his wife and grandson, in a fire at the government's summer house in Thingvellir National Park.

That was then, but there he was now, sixteen years later, larger than life, staring down at an incredible gathering in his hometown of the two most powerful men on earth discussing the most powerful weapons ever created.

After Reykjavik, three of the four key men sitting beneath Benediktsson would also experience tragedy, while a fifth there that weekend, Sergey Akhromeyev, would suffer a fate as tragic as Benediktsson's.

HAVING BEEN DASHED BY Reagan's unvarnished support of SDI, Gorbachev began to get antsy. Suddenly it was 12:30 p.m. and they had already gone half an hour over the time scheduled for their first morning session.

Gorbachev wished to end on a cordial note: "I hope that you will give careful thought to our new Soviet proposals," with his modifications on intermediate and strategic arms.

"I and the Soviet leadership would appreciate your reaction, point by point. It is important for us to know just what you can accept, and what you cannot accept—and why."

"I will look over your proposals," the president assured him, "but you are refusing to see something. If SDI research were successful, it would make possible the elimination of nuclear weapons." The accusations against SDI were unfounded. "We are being accused of wanting a first-strike capability. But we are proposing a treaty that would require the elimination of ballistic missiles before SDI was deployed. Therefore, a first strike would be impossible."

With that, Gorbachev began gathering his papers. But the president wasn't finished yet. He had another way to make his point, one that would *finally* persuade Gorbachev to come around to his view, to see the truth about SDI.

> The agreement which I have proposed would prohibit us from expanding a strategic defensive system until we reduced offensive arms. This system would be for our protection, and yours, in case of unforeseen situations—a sort of gas mask.
>
> After all, when the use of chemical weapons was prohibited after World War I, the world did not reject gas masks. They were the guarantee of our protection against such a weapon in case someone decided to use it.

Gorbachev listened, still unconvinced. Noticing that, Reagan made the analogy yet more explicit: "It is exactly the same with offensive strategic weapons. We need a gas mask here."

The general secretary didn't feel he needed a gas mask here, there, or anywhere. Not receiving the rousing welcome Reagan had expected—not receiving much of any reaction, except Gorbachev's greater impatience to leave—he said with quiet resignation, "Okay. We can discuss this in more detail at the next meeting."

"All right. We will continue the discussion," Gorbachev said hurriedly.

With that, the two leaders rose, quickly shook hands, gathered their papers—Reagan in his manila folder, Gorbachev in his tan briefcase—and parted. As they left, each was followed by the officer carrying a nuclear football.

. . . .

WHILE HER HUSBAND WAS lightly skirmishing at Hofdi House, Raisa Gorbachev was rapidly scurrying around town. In seven hours, she would visit eight tourist sites—all, and perhaps more, than the mini-metropolitan area had to offer.

Raisa, like the superpower leaders themselves, was then at the peak of prominence. With Nancy Reagan's staying back in Washington, she had the brightly lit Reykjavik stage all to herself. And with the news blackout slapped on all summit events, the opportunity to write about Raisa's day was a gift from the gods—of which Iceland had so many—for the hordes of journalists stranded with nothing better to cover. The KGB, tone deaf to the opportunities the situation offered, had initially restricted those accompanying Raisa to a dozen reporters, hand-picked from different countries. But such restrictions didn't last out the morning, as more and more reporters joined her cavalcade.

To play such a prominent role on the world stage, Raisa had to rely on her instincts. Except for the forays during the Geneva summit and several state visits, she had little experience to draw on. At home—where the role of first lady had not occurred to Lenin, much less to Marx—she was seldom noticed. The Soviet press never mentioned her as the wife of the general secretary. She was not even identified when appearing in photos or on TV along with her husband. Since 1917 the Soviet public had not become aware of a leader's wife until she was photographed at her husband's funeral.

But Raisa had tasted the international high life and found it to her liking. During a state visit to France, after the couple's 1984 debut in England, she had wowed the public. The impossible-to-please Parisian press did mildly chide her for wearing the same outfit two times in two days.

Whether she had taken this critique to heart or was just start-ing to flex her fashion wings, Raisa would make up for this faux pas by changing outfits four times as she careened around Reykjavik. A police motorcycle led the way, with press vans and security vehicles, an ambulance, and dozens of unsmiling KGB agents completing her touring convoy.

Shortly after her husband had left for Hofdi House, Raisa emerged on the deck of the *Georg Ots* wearing a turquoise blouse, a black pleated skirt, and suede boots with stiletto heels. So adorned, she turned the ship's gangplank into a veritable fashion runway as she sashayed her way down.

Within minutes, she arrived at the National Museum of Antiquities and admired the manuscripts of Iceland's revered sagas. One of them told the tale of some Nordic ruler who once traveled to Russia. Ah, she said smiling, "from these documents we can see deep roots in the relationship between Iceland and Russia. Our generation should promote these traditions."

At the National Museum, she held Viking helmets, spears, and shields and asked the curators a series of questions, as befitting her professorial background. She headed back to the *Georg Ots* for an outfit change, reemerging in a three-quarter-length silver fox jacket, appropriate to the onset of near-freezing temperatures with flurries of hail.

Next she took off for a huge outdoor thermal springs, where she clapped in delight at bathers paddling around amidst rising steam while the cameras rolled. Before dashing off, she extended a fox-clad arm to shake the hand of a startled young girl wearing a pink bikini.

For her visit to the City Museum, Raisa wore a fitted beige blouse and matching skirt. Her next stop was at a local school to meet with children who had written her husband a letter urging him to bring world peace. By the time she arrived for a luncheon at the prime minister's residence, she had changed into a black suit and white satin blouse. Her after-lunch ensemble involved a gray pinstriped skirt and large rhinestone earrings.

Since most Icelanders speak English, Raisa repeated two all-purpose

English phrases at every stop—"Good morning" and "It is beautiful." Accompanied by her broad smile, they applied equally well with everyone she met and everything she saw. One time, speaking in Russian, she told the adoring press that she relished two novels by Iceland's Nobel Prize winner, Halldor Laxness.

Along the way, Mrs. Gorbachev even managed to score a point in her smoldering relationship with Mrs. Reagan. While at the City Museum, she was asked why the first lady had not come to Reykjavik. "There must be a reason," she said, before helpfully suggesting, "Maybe she isn't well."

Within minutes, despite the total summit news blackout, White House Press Secretary Larry Speakes suddenly appeared at the international press center and rushed up to the podium. The world press, scrambling to attention, high with anticipation, heard Speakes emphatically declare: "Nancy is well!"

THE FIRST REAGAN-GORBACHEV SESSION yields some insights. Listening in nearly thirty years later, we hear an engaging conversation in which both men do a commendable job.

Each realized the high stakes involved and felt the tension, while still managing to express his goals, explain his positions, test the other, and remain personable. Each felt free to speak his own mind. As Shultz explained a quarter century later, by the time of the summit, both men felt that their own bureaucracies were blocking, not just their goals, but even a clear enunciation of their goals. "At Reykjavik," as Shultz put it, "there were no bureaucracies."

Most surprising to Reagan skeptics is the lack of any discernible difference between the men in the force of their presentations, quality of their arguments, or depth of their knowledge. Reagan was then widely seen as lacking in substance and smarts. Even someone as astute and pro-American as Margaret Thatcher's foreign secretary Lord

Peter Carrington years later would say that, while both Thatcher and Reagan considered the U.S.S.R. evil, "the difference between them was that while he had gut feelings, she had an intelligence that he did not have." In contrast to the prevailing view of Reagan as doddering and ill-informed was the image of Gorbachev—young and sharp, speaking in full paragraphs—who could run circles around the old man.

But that isn't what comes across in the record. Reagan knew enough about arms control to make his arguments adeptly. He made the case for SDI providing protection, not just against each other's nuclear arsenal but against another "madman like Hitler," who would seek nuclear weapons.

In short, there was no knowledge gap or information gap between the two leaders. The men who *should* have known more—Secretary of State Shultz and Foreign Minister Shevardnadze—contributed little of substance to this, or any other session. Their occasional interjections were organizational, and even these stabs at being helpful were unsuccessful.

The first session also made clear that—despite the American intelligence assessment that Reykjavik would be a glorified photo-op—Gorbachev had come loaded for bear. He arrived with a briefcase full of proposals and figuratively dumped them onto the Hofdi House conference table. He later said, "We believe the world wanted bold decisions."

Subsequent sessions, more than this opening one, showed that Gorbachev had deftly maneuvered his sclerotic Politburo into making bold decisions. But this wasn't yet apparent that morning. Gorbachev's dropping British and French systems for an intermediate missiles accord was, admittedly, dropping a long-held Soviet objection, but one without merit over the years it had been held. And his tweaking proposals on strategic weapons was indeed movement, yet still tweaking. Nonetheless, these two moves were two more than the Soviets had made since Reagan became president, more than five years earlier.

The first session also displayed the leaders' different personalities and temperaments. There was Gorbachev—always pushing, ever impatient, often chiding the president for often repeating himself, getting short and even snappy. And there was Reagan—tranquil, confident in his views, calmly pushing Gorbachev to see SDI and his arms proposals the way *he* saw them, the way he felt any reasonable person would have to see them. Reagan would become baffled that anyone could see them differently—especially after he had explained them so persuasively.

This session also marked Reagan's coming out with his favorite rhyming Russian proverb, *Doveryai, no proveryai.* By the summit's end, this proverb and the gas-mask analogy would be like fingernails on a chalkboard for the Soviet leader.

Finally, the session confirmed Reagan's determination to share SDI once it had become operational—for free; with everyone; even, or especially, with the Soviet Union. This splendidly naive notion only Reagan could have believed, much less conceived.

The president spoke of sharing it, even though SDI was not an "it," but rather a host of the most advanced technologies in cybernetics, early detection, miniaturization, firing mechanisms, etc., all bound together by the most advanced systems integration. To share all this would mean handing over the family jewels to our foremost enemy. The president kept blithely making this offer while his Pentagon was blocking the most marginal technology transfers to the U.S.S.R. and its allies.

Nonetheless, Reagan loved this idea of sharing SDI so much that he would keep repeating it. He brought it out every time Gorbachev complained that SDI threatened his country. How could that be, Reagan would ask to Gorbachev's rising exasperation, when we will share it with you?

IMMEDIATELY AFTER REAGAN AND Gorbachev left Hofdi House, the American team was summoned to the U.S. embassy to join Secretary Shultz in "the bubble."

Every American embassy around the world has a bubble—an impenetrable, unbuggable room-within-a-room for top-secret discussions. The Reykjavik bubble, like the others, had thick plastic walls on the inside and shiny aluminum sheets on the outside, thereby making it resemble an office cubicle encased in Reynolds Wrap. It rested on blocks to avoid touching any part of the embassy building itself.

Bubbles come in varied sizes and shapes. The one we had in Geneva held a conference table and comfortable seating for twenty-five or so of us. However, the resident Reykjavik bubble was the smallest ever made, befitting its placement in a country where not much ever happens and none of it ever classified.

That bubble contained four gray metal folding chairs, the cheapest money could buy, facing another four along the two side walls. Hence, at full capacity, eight people could sit comfortably secure that their secrets were protected while uncomfortably cramped knee to knee.

Seven of us were squeezed in to await Shultz. As soon as he maneuvered his sizable frame onto the one empty folding chair, two vault-like handles were turned from the outside to secure us in. As was his wont, Shultz began at the beginning and thoroughly summarized the morning's events. He recounted that Gorbachev and Reagan had met and posed for photographers on the steps of Hofdi House, that they had posed for further photos in the main sitting area, that they had stopped to sign the Hofdi House guestbook. He described how they then walked a few feet over to the small meeting room.

Thus far, he had used the high-security, low-comfort bubble to tell us what everyone around the world had already seen on TV.

With the caveat that his account could not be complete, since he and Shevardnadze had come somewhat after the meeting had begun, Shultz was slowly approaching the climax of his languid briefing when, surprisingly, he was interrupted by a rapid revolution of the vaultlike latches.

The door of the bubble swung open, and a Secret Service agent appeared at its entrance. He may have seen the startled look on our faces as he announced with flair: "The President of the United States!"

Everyone did what everyone does upon hearing these words. We all stood up straight. That respectful gesture put eight grown men face-to-face and belly-to-belly. The president paused at the portal to take in this singular scene and quipped, while stepping inside, that someone should fill the bubble with water and use it as an aquarium.

The president's arrival created an urgent and obvious problem. With his unexpected addition—and Reagan was not a small man— nine people were now crammed into our eight-seater. In this high-stakes game of musical chairs, one of us would be "out." The president was obviously going nowhere; he was in and would stay in. And the others in were also heavy hitters, not about to leave—Secretary of State Shultz; White House Chief of Staff Don Regan; National Security Adviser John Poindexter; arms negotiators Paul Nitze, Max Kampelman, and Edward Rowny; and Pentagon representative Richard Perle.

And then there was me. Although I wasn't exactly peripheral, neither was I at the top of this food chain. I knew that if I was going to stay—and, by God, I knew that I *was* going to stay—I would have to act fast. So I motioned to my gray folding chair and said, "Sit here, Mr. President."

Reagan smiled appreciatively and started to maneuver his big frame around to aim at my small chair. As he did so, I slithered to the floor and claimed a sliver of ground near his feet. As everyone sat down, I was facing eight sets of knees.

Luckily, the Secret Service agent was already locking us inside. The nine of us were so cramped that when one person moved, others had to shift their positions. Seated on the floor, I tried to sit up straight but ended up lightly leaning against the presidential knees.

The president opened by saying that his first session with Gorbachev had gone just fine. Rather than mentioning how Gorbachev had fiercely resisted his stance on SDI, Reagan focused on Gorbachev's accepting deep cuts in offensive arms. His news was appreciatively received by the rest of us.

But when the president began to report on the specific cuts Gorbachev had proposed, he slowed down. There was something about 4,600, but whether as limits on missile launchers or warheads was fuzzy. And something about 6,000, which could have been on strategic weapons or throw-weight. Moreover, Gorbachev mentioned 3,000, or 3,200, or 3,600 somethings or others.

When the president realized that his numbers were sketchy, at best, he looked over at Shultz. But the secretary was no better at clarifying what Gorbachev had in mind. The two of them weren't to blame, since arms control is a recondite field, laden with abbreviations and categories galore. Few people can keep all that straight and very, very few ever needed to.

Almost as an afterthought, the president reached into his breast pocket and pulled out a paper that Gorbachev had handed him. There, on a plain white sheet intimidatingly entitled *Directives for the Foreign Ministers of the USSR and USA to Prepare Agreements on Nuclear Disarmament*, was precisely what he was proposing. The president considered this a kindly gesture on Gorbachev's part. But to us, it was proof that Gorbachev knew his man.

The president then opened the floor—what little of it there was—for any suggestions. Unable to analyze the Soviet numbers, none of us could venture anything of substance. After an awkward silence, I urged that, in addition to arms control, the president push Gorbachev on human rights and key regional issues, including the upward of 120,000 Soviets troops occupying and brutalizing Afghanistan.

The president seemed to agree with that—or so it felt from the wiggling of his knees. He also liked the idea of asking Gorbachev to have arms experts meet that night to discuss his paper in detail. It wasn't clear to me why that was proposed for the night, since we weren't all that busy during the day, especially while the two leaders were meeting. Regardless, a nighttime meeting was the suggestion to Reagan and that would be his suggestion to Gorbachev.

After leaving the bubble, the president walked next door to the ambassador's residence, where he would have a quick lunch and nap, or perhaps read in an easy chair under Nick Ruwe's abundant antlers until the afternoon session began.

ON SATURDAY AFTERNOON, REYKJAVIK was pummeled by sporadic thunderstorms that approached biblical proportions.

The thousands of reporters and TV crews were forced indoors. After shaking off the water from their rain gear and blowing on their hands to warm them, they turned yet more restive. Thus far, the only summit news had been about Raisa Gorbachev's wardrobe and whereabouts, the only official government announcement that "Nancy is well!"

While this was disappointing for them, it was more so for their bosses, who were spending vast sums for them to write or broadcast "Live from Reykjavik." John Carmody's *Washington Post* column described the ABC schedule: "On Saturday, Jennings will provide two-and-a-half-minute updates hourly, starting at 8:30 a.m., through the day's sports coverage. That night, Jennings will anchor a half-hour special, starting at 11:30 p.m." How ABC was going to fill "two-and-a-half-minute updates" each hour, even during its popular *Wide World of Sports*, was unclear. How ABC's sports fans would react to the hourly Reykjavik updates interrupting their Saturday afternoon football games was clearer.

Saturday, October 11, 1986
The Afternoon Session

At 3:30 p.m., Reagan and Gorbachev returned to Hofdi House. While heading toward the conference room, they passed under a portal decorated with carved reliefs of Viking shields—a thousand-year-old strategic defense that Reagan wished to revive and update as SDI.

As the door was closed behind them, their briefcase-toting military officers resumed their places diagonally across from one another in the hallway. They were set to stand there, at the ready, for the rest of the afternoon.

Inside, Reagan and Gorbachev greeted each other, less ceremoniously this time, and assumed their places at each end of the table. Bjarni Benediktsson, larger than life, gazed down from the wall behind the president. On the wall to Gorbachev's right was a painting of wind-whipped waves crashing furiously onto rocks, an odd art object in such a setting.

The two foreign ministers were there from the session's start. Shultz was on the president's left because Reagan was nearly deaf in his right ear, after a pistol had been shot too close to it during a Hollywood filming. The two translators sat a bit back, each near his boss, while the notetakers—one American and one Soviet—lined the walls.

The small table had coffee cups and water glasses for the principals, while leaving some room for their papers to be spread about. The two translators rested their lined pads on their laps and took notes for consecutive translation.

Simultaneous translation would have been quicker, but was deemed less accurate. Tom Simons, the State Department notetaker for this second session, included in his notes some exchanges that either were missed, or misinterpreted, by his State Department colleague, Bill Hopkins. This was ungracious but unsurprising since fights within the State Department were legendary. In any case, Hopkins did no more translating at Reykjavik.

THE SECOND SESSION STARTED sluggishly but soon heated up, quickening the tempo of the weekend and darkening its tone.

Reagan began by claiming to be reacting to Gorbachev's morning proposals while actually reiterating long-standing American positions. Once Gorbachev realized that, he understandably got irritated. But the lively discussion that ensued made up for that wasted time. If the first session had been a warm-up with occasional sparring, the second became one of sparring with occasional letup.

After reading his paper, Reagan came alive. "You suggested that our defenses might be used to attack the Soviet Union. I assure you that SDI is not being developed for that purpose. I've heard it said that SDI will inevitably lead to space-based weapons with an offensive capability against earth. That's not true, either," and explained why.

"The quickest, surest, and most effective way to strike earth targets is with ballistic missiles," which both sides already have, in abundance. So why, Reagan asked rhetorically, would the United States build a costly new weapon in space to do what we can already do from land? Moreover, the two sides "already have agreements banning weapons of mass destruction in space. If you have additional concerns on this subject, I am prepared to work with you."

The president then addressed another of Gorbachev's concerns—that with SDI we could "launch a first strike against the Soviets and use our defenses to prevent retaliation." That, too, was wrong. "We don't have that capability, and that is not our objective."

Reagan then accused Gorbachev of violating the ABM Treaty by having built an illegal radar facility in Siberia. This was a matter not only of bad faith but also of hypocrisy. For while the Soviets were urging our greater devotion to the ABM Treaty, they were violating it. Gorbachev did not deny or rebut it. In fact, over the weekend, he never denied Reagan's accusation nor did he ever accuse the United States of breaking an arms pact.

Reagan explained why the U.S. proposal on strategic arms would leave both the Soviet and American "forces far more stable. Neither bombers nor cruise missiles are suitable for surprise attack. They are slow and vulnerable to your unconstrained air defenses." That's why the American proposal was "a very significant step. I'm convinced that it would give us our best chance to put the security of your nation and mine on a better, more stable long-term basis."

The president was baffled about what Gorbachev wanted. "I'm not clear what would be the subject of the negotiations you suggested." Would it include "what I have proposed, including sharing the benefits of defenses and the elimination of ballistic missiles?" Or something else?

"I'll let you know later," Gorbachev replied, evidently baffled by what Reagan was baffled about.

After a few more bafflements and several more repartees on nuclear weapons and one more Reagan accusation of Soviet cheating, the president said with typical optimism, "In conclusion, it appears that significant progress is possible." To facilitate that, he suggested that their arms experts meet in Hofdi House at 8:00 p.m. and enticed Gorbachev by naming the U.S. delegation: "Ambassador Nitze, Ambassador Kampelman, Mr. Perle, Ambassador Rowny, and Ken Adelman."

He paused for Gorbachev to react in kind, but Gorbachev wanted the president to sign off on his strategic proposal first. "The structure will remain the same, but the level will be lower, and this will be clear to everyone."

Reagan said he liked a 50 percent cut, which was, after all, his goal of five years' standing. Yet he wasn't ready to sign off on Gorbachev's strategic proposal, since it entailed the kind of detailed issues that "should be taken up by the experts, if you agree to my proposal" for their arms experts to meet.

"I myself don't know all these numbers," he admitted. "But I do know that you, the Soviets, outnumber us by a lot. So if we both cut by 50%, you would still have more than we do. Our number is smaller. But still, yours is an interesting idea."

"This is *not* a matter for the experts," Gorbachev said touchily. He then passed across the table a paper filled with numbers of various strategic arms categories.

"Here is the data," he said, pointing to his paper. "Let's just cut these numbers in half."

"I said before that I thought your ideas were interesting," Reagan replied. "You should now give the U.S. side a chance to study it."

"This is a bold idea, and we need bold ideas," Shultz said, adding to the atta-boys from the Americans.

"This is *just* what is needed," Gorbachev insisted. "Otherwise, the process goes back to Karpov and Kampelman. Let's not slurp the soup that these negotiators have been cooking for all these years," he said with a flourish to Reagan, who was one to appreciate a flourish. Gorbachev wanted to get things done by themselves, there at Reykjavik, and not to send anything to Geneva, which he regarded as the black hole of Calcutta for arms accords.

"Can I have this data sheet?" Reagan politely asked.

"Yes, I will give it to you," Gorbachev said graciously. Dealing with his numbers was the only way "out of this forest. Now you have all our secrets," he deadpanned before adding ominously, "If I ever felt the U.S. side was trying somehow to outsmart me, it would be the end of the negotiations."

"No, that will not happen," Reagan assured him. To get off that sour note, he again asked Gorbachev whether he would send arms experts to meet that night. Gorbachev agreed, although most reluctantly, and then returned to intermediate missiles. He reiterated how he could agree to limits on systems in Europe, but not those in Asia.

"I recall the time, after the war," the president reminisced in a stunning nonresponse, "when we were the only ones to have nuclear weapons. We offered to give them up, to turn them over to international control. We could have dictated to the whole world, but we didn't."

The president paused, waiting for some appreciation or curiosity, or even mild interest. Instead, he heard Gorbachev summarily say, "Next issue!"

That next issue was Gorbachev repeating what he had previously said on intermediate missiles. When that got nowhere, Gorbachev asked, "Why could the U.S. not take a single step to accommodate Soviet concerns?"

Eliciting no response, Gorbachev went on: "Our proposal is simple. Let's resolve the issue in Europe, and begin negotiations to resolve it in Asia later."

"Well, we have no ballistic missiles in Asia," Reagan said. "We have naval forces there, but you do too, and the Soviet Navy is bigger than ours."

"It matters little to us if a bomb is dropped on us from an aircraft carrier or a military base," Gorbachev countered. "And you have bases in the Philippines."

Blocked on intermediate missiles, Gorbachev returned to SDI, saying it must be confined "to the laboratories," much as he had said several times already and would five times more that afternoon. As always, Reagan let that proposal pass without comment.

AT THIS POINT, THE men found themselves deadlocked on the three key summit issues—strategic arms, intermediate missiles, and the SDI–ABM Treaty package. Each having said his piece, Reagan and Gorbachev looked at each other across the table. The tension rose, as their silence threatened to become ominous.

Shultz decided to step in. Long experienced at labor negotiations and mediation, he began by sounding helpful: "The problem is that . . ."

"I would like to hear the president's opinion!" Gorbachev said, cutting him off. The president, ignoring this Shultz-Gorbachev contretemps, offered his own perspective.

"Before we can get around to weapons," he said, after more than three hours of their discussing weapons, "we have to find out what causes mistrust between us. If we could only get to that mistrust, there would be no problem about what to do with the weapons."

"You are right," Gorbachev replied, and then reverted to talk about weapons. "I've already told you that our missiles in Asia cannot reach European targets. All the experts know that. Only *you* don't believe that." After that mild insult, he returned to his favorite topic.

"How, if we are beginning to reduce strategic missiles and eliminate intermediate missiles, could we two destroy the ABM Treaty? It's the only brake on very dangerous developments in a tense situation. How can we abandon it, when we should be strengthening it?"

Both nations needed to keep the treaty in existence for at least another ten years and to "limit work on SDI to laboratory research only." After hitting that crescendo, Gorbachev stopped so that Reagan could react.

NEGOTIATION MANUALS RECOMMEND THAT, when differences widen and tempers flare, the parties need to calm things down, to soften their arguments, to find common ground—no matter how far removed from the key matter of contention.

That self-styled master of negotiations, Ronald Reagan, now did exactly the opposite. He turned tougher than before.

"With regard to the ABM Treaty, we believe the Soviets have violated it already." The president then ramped up his defense of SDI in the most unabashed, in-your-face way imaginable. He told Gorbachev—who had just called SDI a grave threat to his nation's very existence—that "I myself think that SDI is the greatest opportunity for peace in the twentieth century." Before Gorbachev could react, Reagan wandered back in time.

"When I was growing up, a little before you were growing up, there had been rules of warfare that protected noncombatants, civilians. Now, with the ABM Treaty, we have horrible missiles whose principal victims are civilians. The only defense against them is the threat of slaughtering masses of other people."

"This is not civilized!" It needed to change. "SDI is something to be shared. It's not for one country only. It will protect people if a madman wanted to use such weapons. Take Gadhafi"—Muammar Gadhafi, the erratic, longtime ruler of Libya—"if he had nuclear weapons, he would certainly have used them.

"Think of us two, you and me, standing there and telling the world that we have SDI, and asking others to join us in getting rid of these terrible nuclear weapons."

"My remarks in reply will be less philosophical," Gorbachev said. "They are more prompted by the nature of what we have been discussing, which is practical."

Gorbachev then attempted a diplomatic pirouette. Having found that his barrage against SDI had failed to budge Reagan, he now dangled the prospect of shrugging it off. "The Soviet Union does not fear a 'three-echelon strategic defense,' if the U.S. decides that's what it wants."

This sudden stance must have struck everyone in the room, perhaps even himself, as unbelievable. Not that this stance was without merit—indeed, there was more merit to it than the panicked approach he had been taking—but it contradicted everything he had said over the previous three years, everything he said over the two-day Geneva Summit, and everything he said that very morning. Indeed, it contradicted everything he said two minutes before.

Gorbachev then let slip a key point he had made to the Politburo, that his country was in dire straits: "The U.S. has money and can do things the Soviets cannot do." Nonetheless, he could not "begin reductions" of nuclear weapons "while the ABM Treaty was being destroyed. This is not logical, and my people and our Allies would not understand it."

Reagan asserted that he was *not* destroying the ABM Treaty. Why could Gorbachev not understand that "here is something bigger that we want the world to have? We are not building it for superiority. We want all to have it."

Pleasing himself with good news, besides filling Gorbachev with bad news, he added, "With the progress we are making, we do not need ten years" to have SDI ready to deploy. "I could not have said that a few years ago, but now I can. We do not think it will take that long. Progress is being made."

"Regardless, we are not going to proceed with strategic defense ourselves," Gorbachev replied.

At this impasse, the American notetaker included an interesting sentence: *"He* [Gorbachev] *took note of the president's statement that less than 10 years would be needed."* There's nothing like it, in either the Soviet or American notes on either day of Reykjavik.

Reagan reposed his question: "Do you agree to hold a meeting this evening at the expert level?"

After mustering another weak assent, Gorbachev said, "As for who will participate in these groups for our side, I will tell you later," knowing full well that there wasn't much "later" left in that session.

"We've been so wrapped up that we haven't touched on regional or bilateral or human rights issues, to move them along," Reagan said, before naming the U.S. members on a second experts' group, in addition to the arms control experts' group. "They have to go to work tonight. Tomorrow will be our final day, to see if we can close on things."

With 100 percent of the unresolved issues between them still unresolved, Reagan suggested that they move the next morning's session forward a half hour from the scheduled 10:30 starting time. Gorbachev agreed, both to the 10:00 a.m. time and the additional experts' meeting that evening.

There was one thing more the president had to impart before they broke. "You said that the Soviets do not need SDI, that you have a better solution. Perhaps both sides should go ahead on a solution. And if the Soviets do better, you can give us your SDI."

"The Soviet solution," Gorbachev replied, "would not be better, but different. And I am sorry to say that, with regard to sharing SDI, I cannot take you seriously, speaking frankly. Your administration is unwilling to give us oil drilling equipment, automatic machinery, even milk factories. For the U.S. to give the products of high technology like SDI would cause a second American Revolution. It would never happen. It's better for us to be realistic."

"If I thought the benefits of SDI would not be given to others," Reagan insisted, "I'd give up the project myself."

"I do not think the president knows what the project contains," Gorbachev said cuttingly. He was having a hard time dealing with this latest Reagan idea. Gorbachev knew that he had neither the money nor the technical know-how to build an SDI. And that, if he somehow got an SDI of his own—his best chance probably being as a gift from the Icelandic gods—he *certainly* would never share it with the Americans. Nor could he believe the Americans would ever share it with him.

His mounting frustration led to his blurting out that, in essence, the president of the United States didn't know what he was talking about. (The Soviet notetaker did not include Gorbachev's slight in his notes.)

Reagan, ignoring Gorbachev's affront, then worsened the mood by reaching across the table to hand Gorbachev a long list of human rights abuses he wanted addressed, containing the names of dissidents he wanted liberated.

Meanwhile, as the men in Reykjavik were experiencing a veritable meltdown, Nancy Reagan was launching a zinger from Washington. Accepting an award at Catholic University for her anti-drug campaign, Mrs. Reagan told the audience in the hall, and those watching on television, "I feel fine, although I heard on the air that I wasn't fine."

After the laughter died down, she let loose: "The invitation that came from Mr. Gorbachev to my husband was for a business meeting between the two of them. I thought it was improper for me to go," she said sweetly.

. . . .

THE SECOND SESSION WAS markedly different in tone from the first. The more Reagan and Gorbachev discussed the issues, the franker they became—especially on their top-drawer issues of SDI and the ABM Treaty—and the clearer became the gulf between them. Each was genuinely dumbfounded by what the other believed.

In this second session, each man displayed his way of operating and his skills. Gorbachev sought to concentrate on practicalities. Besides being more focused, he was better than Reagan at pacing and timing. Reykjavik showed him to be a master of diplomatic choreography, a skill that would reach its height with stunning stage management the next day.

Although Reagan preferred to focus on grand topics, he nonetheless bettered Gorbachev at the nitty-gritty of negotiations. Throughout the weekend, Gorbachev constantly and correctly complained that *he* was making all the compromises, while Reagan was not budging.

Also intriguing were the back-and-forths on SDI and the ABM Treaty. Here ironies abound. Reagan was pledging to uphold a treaty he clearly despised—"This is not civilized!"—while Gorbachev was pleading to strengthen a treaty he was clearly violating.

Gorbachev's passionate plea to strengthen the treaty may have been influenced by a memo prepared for him by the Soviet Ministry of Foreign Affairs. The document, now declassified, states that maintaining the ABM Treaty "is necessary for us, as we seek to delay the creation by the U.S. of a multi-echeloned missile defense system, to gain time to conduct analogous work in our own country."

Hence, if he believed what the memo stated, Gorbachev was not opposed to missile defense per se. Rather, he was opposed to *our* missile defense. The Soviets could not match the U.S. program unless Gorbachev could somehow persuade Reagan to buy into an agreement that gave Soviet scientists the time they needed to catch up.

The leaders' intensity on SDI was likewise remarkable. Indeed, it was the most remarkable aspect of Reykjavik. Reagan's total faith in this chimerical defensive system still leaps off the pages of the official notes, whether written by the Russians or the Americans. His faith in SDI was heartfelt, almost transcendent, however misplaced. In October 1986, SDI wasn't much more than a presidential aspiration.

To many conservatives, strategic defense has been an idea worth trying. In fact, I had long before written an article for *Policy Review*, aptly titled "Beyond MAD-ness," making such an argument and predicting it would ruffle feathers. I wrote:

> The most politically volatile issue will be the push for defensive strategic systems. At present, the U.S. has no ballistic missile defense.... Largely because of the MAD doctrine, the strategic case for ballistic missile defense has not been considered on its merits for more than a decade.

The article recommended "serious consideration [be given to] scrapping the ABM treaty."

While the notion of advocating strategic defense in order to bolster traditional deterrence seemed bold to me and my dozen or so readers, it wasn't anything like what Reagan had in mind. He wanted strategic defense that would protect the entire nation and he wanted it fast. Granted, when his memoirs came out four years later, in 1990, he wrote that he did not view SDI as an "impenetrable shield—no defense could ever be expected to be 100% effective." But that was the latter-day wisdom of the president's, or, more likely, of his ghostwriter's. It was not how he felt about SDI, or what he said about it, while president.

To him, back in the day, SDI would do all the wonderful things he most wanted to do as president. It would help him rid the world of the nuclear threat and maybe even of nuclear weapons—just as gas masks, to his way of thinking, had helped rid the world of chemical weapons. SDI would protect the nation, after three dreadful decades of vulnerability to Soviet ballistic missiles.

With SDI, the former lifeguard would become America's lifeguard in chief. SDI would end that awful picture, so vivid in Reagan's mind, of two gunslingers holding pistols to each other's heads or, in the famous depiction by atomic bomb inventor in chief Robert Oppenheimer, "two scorpions in a bottle, each capable of killing the other, but only at the risk of his own life." SDI would end all that, as it would end MAD. Under SDI, as he told Gorbachev, they would share the shield instead of sharing the threat.

SDI had the other big advantage of playing into America's strength of technical proficiency in cybernetics, miniaturization, systems integration, and other areas—all areas of blatant Soviet weakness. Another pre-Reykjavik memo to Gorbachev admitted that their country suffered from "poorer technological quality (compared with the U.S.) of the basic critical elements required for multistage missile defense—optical-electronic systems, small high-performance computers, laser gyroscopes, cryogenic systems, etc." Only a far more extensive list could fill in the "etc." by identifying all the capabilities the Soviets then lacked.

Moreover, Reagan's SDI challenged the Soviets' comparative advantage of ballistic missiles by discounting their importance. These missiles were the backbone of the Soviet arsenal—the basket into which they had placed their strategic eggs—which, in turn, constituted the U.S.S.R.'s ticket to superpower status. The better our defenses against their missiles, the less important those missiles became, and thereby the less important the U.S.S.R. became.

Lastly, the advent of SDI would necessitate a massive shake-up of postwar strategic doctrine. This was a poignant, unwelcome challenge to the Kremlin. With its lumbering bureaucracy, it did not take well to shake-ups, massive or otherwise. It had not been able

even to adjust Gorbachev's arrival in Reykjavik by a few hours, once those plans had been set.

In sum, Reagan's concept of SDI took it far beyond a mere Pentagon research effort, as, amazingly, did Gorbachev's. Reagan wanted so badly to build it and Gorbachev wanted so badly to stop it, that it assumed for them, and practically only for them, a reality it actually lacked.

Near the close of this second session, Reagan suggested that each side eliminate ballistic missiles. This made some sense for Reagan to propose, but made no sense for Gorbachev to accept, since the Soviets were significantly ahead in this realm.

Here Reagan was conforming to a tradition in disarmament conferences, one already known in 1932 when the Spanish ambassador to the Geneva Conference on Disarmament, like Reagan decades later, broke out into storytelling:

When the animals had gathered, the lion looked at the eagle and said gravely, "We must abolish talons."

The elephant looked at the tiger and said, "We must abolish claws and jaws."

Thus each animal in turn proposed the abolition of the weapons he did not have, until at last the bear rose up and said, in tones of sweet reasonableness, "Comrades, let us abolish everything—everything but the great universal embrace."

While Reagan and Gorbachev were meeting at Hofdi House, the press was going stir-crazy outside. Armies of reporters, producers, and technicians were stuck in a stark place with nothing to report and next to nothing to do. Gray & Co.'s attempts to generate interest in Iceland's ancient legends or legions of gods failed. The media was there to cover the summit, not the sagas.

On that Saturday afternoon, while Reagan and Gorbachev were having it out in Hofdi House, I asked an embassy driver to show me something of interest. Our first stop was a small Gothic church surrounded by scaffolding. When I asked how long the church had been under construction, he replied, "Since 1946."

In Iceland the pace of everything is leisurely, if not downright languishing. The nineteenth-century explorer Richard Burton wrote that "the dawdling is worse in Iceland than in Peru," which, to his mind, was saying a lot.

As the driver headed out of town, I was able to see the countryside that had been shrouded in darkness when we arrived Thursday night. There was some, though limited, interest in the endless dark lava landscape, rising and falling in small hills, bereft of vegetation.

At one point, the driver pulled over and asked me to step out. He pointed to half a dozen houses on a hill in the far distance, so hard to spot that it took me a bit to catch sight of them.

"Just look there," he said, in a tone of unabashed Nordic pride. "In the 1950s, there was nothing on that hill!"

"Imagine that," I replied.

. . . .

A LITTLE AFTER 7:30 that night, when the American arms control team headed back to Hofdi House, it was a surprisingly moderate forty-two degrees. Most of the day had been overcast, but Reykjavik that Saturday enjoyed three and a half hours of sunshine, far more than usual for so late in autumn.

By this time, the reporters had climbed down from the wooden scaffolding on the huge Hofdi House lawn, packed up their equipment, and headed into town. Many would attend the People's Summit downtown, with a Joan Baez concert the featured attraction. The forty-five-year-old folksinger and activist had already given an afternoon concert in the Opera House, but her evening performance would be televised live nationwide.

Wearing a red silk blouse, she opened with an a cappella rendering of "The Times They Are A-Changin'" followed by a Russian folk song, "Soyuz Druzya" (Union of Friends), and a popular Icelandic ballad. Her press comments had been similarly even-handed, urging Gorbachev to release Andrey Sakharov and Reagan to disassociate himself from Chilean president Augusto Pinochet. Like many others, she was optimistic, saying that whenever Reagan and Gorbachev interact, "there is a lessening of international tension. It's a little room to move, but there has been so little room to move before this."

Hofdi House sat alone and isolated after the day's hubbub. With its white walls brilliantly lit by floodlights, Hofdi at night appeared even more magnificent than in daylight. Its square, solid silhouette of white wood showed off more starkly against the black of the vast sky, the endless sea, and the lava landscape.

We climbed the curved staircase with hearts carved into the white-painted wooden banister, up to the second floor, where a larger conference room was located. A few Soviet diplomats, who had been milling around their parlor, strolled over to greet us. In groups of two or three, the Americans and Russians began to walk over to the conference room for our session.

We were especially eager to meet the man Gorbachev had surprisingly chosen to lead his delegation. Until that afternoon, we had not known he was even in town.

President Reagan had chosen Paul Nitze, our most experienced negotiator, to head up our team. We expected Gorbachev to choose their most experienced negotiator, Victor Karpov. Indeed, the *New York Times* lead article, under the byline of ace reporter Bernard Weinraub, had stated as much. This was mistaken, but understandable. (Less understandable was Weinraub's repeating the error two days after the summit ended.)

Gorbachev had already mentioned Karpov to Reagan, though none too flatteringly. He would not appoint the old soup slurper to another big job.

Rather it would be a mystery guest, one who had not been mentioned by Gorbachev and had not been seen by most of us on Saturday. His surprise selection was Sergey Akhromeyev, a soldier who had fought outside of Leningrad in World War II, now with the exalted titles of field marshal and Hero of the Soviet Union, and with the position of chief of the General Staff, a post more powerful than that of the U.S. chairman of the Joint Chiefs of Staff.

While everyone in the American delegation knew who Akhromeyev was, none of us—including Ambassador Arthur Hartman, who had spent many years stationed in Moscow—had ever met him. Having mastered the military, Akhromeyev would now try his hand at diplomacy.

He was a compact and wiry man, maybe five feet six, obviously physically fit, with an attractive smile and firm handshake. To me, he most resembled Jimmy Carter, but without Carter's intensity or sanctimonious manner.

The marshal had obviously prepared for our session, as he had something personal and gracious to say to each of us when we introduced ourselves and shook his hand. The distinguished soldier wore a dark brown, poorly cut, rumpled suit with a dull brown tie.

Around 8:10 p.m. we took our seats at the long wooden conference table, which was bare. The meeting had been so hastily arranged that there were no name cards, water glasses, or pads of paper, as were customary in standard arms negotiations. Two modern chandeliers lighted the rectangular room with its polished wooden floors and white walls. Behind where the Soviet delegation was to sit were two curtained windows. Adorning the walls were modern abstract paintings of what may have been religious themes, every bit as odd as were all the paintings around. Hofdi House's beauty was in its structure, material, and proportions and certainly not in the art displayed inside.

On each side of the conference table were nine wooden chairs with rounded backs and, thankfully for what was in store for us, slight padding on the seats. While leaving the center chair for Nitze, we casually sat in no particular order. On the Soviet side, though, was some jockeying for the chairs on either side of Akhromeyev.

After the mini-shuffle, Georgi Arbatov, the Soviets' leading "Amerikanist," won the seat to the marshal's left. Having run the Institute for U.S. and Canadian Studies in Moscow since founding it in 1967, this wily survivor had advised a succession of general secretaries, Gorbachev being his fifth.

Arbatov, with excellent English and considerable media savvy, had become the go-to Soviet spokesman for American news operations. Well informed and always available, he became a familiar face on *Nightline* and even managed to charm no less an anti-Communist than the Reverend Billy Graham.

Arbatov called himself a scholar and journalist, and could win over an audience with an appearance of academic balance. But that was only an appearance. In actuality, he was an unyielding party propagandist and a powerful traditionalist on the Communist Party's Central

Committee. He had previously accused the Reagan administration of engaging in "a campaign of demonization" of the Soviet Union. Earlier that day, he had verged on breaking the news blackout by telling reporters that the summit "is not a symptom of improved relations, but a test for worsening relations," whatever that meant. But there was no doubt about his meaning that afternoon when replying to someone who identified himself as being with the National Council on Soviet Jewry. Arbatov rebuked him with, "You come from the Council on anti-Soviet Jewry."

Winning the seat to Akhromeyev's right was the soup slurper Karpov, whom no one could consider balanced, academic, or charming. Rather, he was cantankerous, bordering on brutish.

Karpov was the cross all American arms negotiators had had to bear for two decades running. He had been at the bargaining table during the Nixon administration's talks on SALT I. He was there during the Ford and Carter administrations' talks on SALT II. And he was there again for the Reagan administration's talks on START.

When a congressional delegation visited Geneva the year before Reykjavik, a senator pulled me aside to say that Ambassador Karpov had groped his wife's knee under the table during an embassy dinner. I was appalled but not surprised, and promised to protest angrily, which I did and which did no good. Ambassador Karpov was there to stay.

Several other Russians filled out their delegation—a diplomat, a soldier, a few KGB officers, and two others of particular note. Evgeny Velikhov was an accomplished physicist who headed the Soviets' crash program to develop their own SDI while serving as the top Soviet spokesman against our SDI. The other was Valentin Falin, a propagandist with few redeeming qualities, who worked both for *Izvestia* and the Central Committee Information Department. I was not surprised to learn later that some $600,000 in cash was found in his office following the 1991 coup attempt against Gorbachev, after which he left government service in disgrace.

. . . .

Across from them sat Paul Nitze, who was sophisticated, analytical, and precise. With white hair, a solid and symmetrical face, and a twinkle in his eyes, Nitze could have been cast for the role he would play over decades in government, capped by his service that night.

He hailed from that slice of America that had the formula for success down pat—come from old money, marry into old money, and make new money. He had done all three and, at seventy-nine, was still in top form.

One time in Washington, when the two of us were lunching together, Paul casually mentioned that his family once owned Chrysler. In an attempt to tighten the bonds between us, I replied that my parents, too, had once owned a Chrysler. No, he said gently, his parents had not owned *a* Chrysler. They had owned Chrysler.

It was in government that Nitze thrived most and served best. He was able to do it all—study the impact of World War II strategic bombing, help craft the Marshall Plan, create the post–Korean War strategy for America, advise President Kennedy during his Berlin and Cuba crises, serve as President Johnson's deputy secretary of defense, and negotiate Nixon's SALT I. His public opposition to SALT II impressed candidate Reagan, who later tagged him to lead the Geneva talks on intermediate missiles.

Sadly, though, Paul never got what he wanted most, a cabinet post. He would have made a fine secretary of state or secretary of defense instead of being relegated to one of their deputies, staff, or advisers.

Sitting beside Paul was Max Kampelman, a warm man from chilly Minneapolis. As a conscientious objector during World War II, Max worked for the government and volunteered for a grotesque but critical University of Minnesota experiment, simply entitled "On Human Starvation and Rehabilitation."

He later recalled the experience: "There were thirty-six of us and we were starved. For me it lasted for a year and a half. You ate minimal amounts. At one point, I was down to about 100 pounds," which must have been tough for a man over six feet tall. However, the results of this study helped safely rehabilitate emaciated victims of Nazi POW and concentration camps.

After being a conscientious objector—even during World War II, when the morality of fighting Hitler seemed evident to most Americans—Max earned a law degree and a doctorate, with a dissertation on the Communist infiltration of the CIO labor union, which helped turn him into a realist. His faculty adviser at the University of Minnesota was Evron Kirkpatrick, who would marry an Oklahoma girl named Jeane Jordan, decades later known as Ambassador Jeane Kirkpatrick.

A natural in politics, Max became good friends with the young, ambitious mayor of Minneapolis, Hubert Humphrey. When Humphrey was first elected to the Senate, he asked Max to come to Washington for three months to help him set up his Capitol Hill office. Max took a temporary leave from college teaching and moved to Washington, where he stayed for the rest of his life. At thirty-five, the former conscientious objector joined the Marine Corps as a reservist and served for seven years.

In 1977, along with Nitze and a few others, he founded the Committee on the Present Danger to oppose Carter's SALT II Treaty and advocate a U.S. military buildup. When the arms talks resumed in 1985, President Reagan chose him to serve as ambassador overseeing the Geneva arms talks.

Richard Perle, then forty-five, was a critical and powerful member of the U.S. delegation, not only because he represented the Pentagon but because he was so brilliant and knowledgeable.

Perle entered the nuclear business early, by chance. While still attending Hollywood High School, a classmate invited him for a swim one afternoon and introduced him to her father, Albert Wohlstetter. The brilliant theorist and historian was academic enough to think that some high school kid in a bathing suit might be interested in hearing his latest theories on the role of nuclear weapons in postwar U.S. security.

In this case, he was right. In fact, Perle became interested enough to specialize in strategic theory at the University of Southern California. After a year at the London School of Economics, he attended Princeton to earn a master's degree and was well on his way to a doctorate when Wohlstetter steered him to Nitze, then looking for a bright researcher.

Before long, the old boys' network kicked in again when Nitze introduced Perle to Senator Henry Jackson, who quickly hired him to focus on U.S. relations with the Soviet Union. Perle joined Scoop Jackson's staff in 1969, just after losing both of his parents. The senator became not only his boss but a father figure, with deep affection flowing both ways until Scoop's sudden death in 1983. The two constituted a formidable force against Presidents Nixon, Ford, and Carter when they pursued détente with the Soviet Union.

In 1981, with the advent of the Reagan administration, Richard left, being one of the most powerful Hill staffers to become one of the most powerful assistant secretaries of defense. Within months, he crafted and sold the "zero option" as an ideal solution for the intermediate missile talks. The idea was alluringly simple: The United States would defer deploying its intermediate missiles in Europe if the Soviet Union would scrap all the missiles it had already deployed there. Both sides would thus end up with zero.

President Reagan loved the notion, which appealed to his then-shrouded but deeply felt anti-nuclear proclivities. Yet the zero option met fierce opposition. It seemed too simple in the abstruse field of arms control to be credible. And it seemed too radical to be doable.

Indeed, arms control advocates claimed that Reagan and Perle championed the notion precisely because it was undoable. Again, the administration was asking too much of the Soviets—in this case, to dismantle some fifteen hundred intermediate- and related short-range missiles to preclude us from deploying any. The zero option was—like SDI, or asking for deep strategic cuts, or thinking that Communism would end up on the ash heap of history—dismissed as sheer pie in Ronald Reagan's sky.

Flagrantly hardline, Perle was dubbed by the press the "Prince of Darkness." Actually he is a king of kindness—sweet, willing to help a friend at any time, and eager to share his culinary skills to make a gourmet meal with the latest kitchen gadgets.

Besides being dedicated, gifted, and long-serving, these three key men of the Reagan administration—Nitze, Kampelman, and Perle, whose careers were so intertwined—shared one other element: all three were Democrats and would remain Democrats for the rest of their lives.

Given the toxic partisan politics that ensued, this becomes even more remarkable. Since Reagan, the two Republican presidencies—those of Bush 41 and Bush 43—and the two Democratic presidencies—those of Clinton and Obama—have made partisan fidelity a prerequisite for nearly all their top-level appointees. Each administration cared more about party ties than policy views.

The Reagan administration was the opposite, as it insisted upon ideological fidelity but showed acceptance, almost indifference, to party affiliation. Plenty of other Reagan Democrats filled other prominent positions, including Jeane Kirkpatrick, my boss at the United Nations, and Eugene Rostow, my predecessor at the Arms Control Agency.

Rounding out the experts on our side of the Hofdi House conference table were Ambassador Ed Rowny, Colonel Robert Linhard, the NSC representative, a colonel on the staff of the joint chiefs, and me.

AKHROMEYEV AND HIS SOVIET comrades were willing to have our nocturnal negotiations conducted in English, without interpreters.

This turned out to be a lucky break because, typical of this come-as-you-are summit, no one on either side had thought to arrange for translators that night. It also speeded up the process and was more comfortable, for us at least. Even with good language proficiency, as Akhromeyev and others had, it must have been tiring for them to speak and think in a foreign language during high-stakes negotiations all night long.

Because Reagan had suggested the session, Nitze opened it with the generic remarks expected on such an occasion—thanking the other side for coming, lamenting the current situation, urging progress, hoping both sides could break the deadlock, and finishing with a friendly comment or minor pleasantry. But before Nitze could get far on this diplomatic ritual, Akhromeyev nudged his way in to say, in a soft but commanding voice, that, unlike Ambassador Nitze, he was no gifted diplomat, merely a common soldier. As a soldier, he liked to get things done. So let's get started and see what we can get done. And what we can't get done, we will hand back to "our principals," as the president and general secretary were called.

His was a fresh, and refreshing, way to begin a fresh negotiation, one that set a friendly tone for the evening. The ensuing discussion was loose enough so that anyone with something to say would simply say it, without looking for the go-ahead from the delegation leader.

Someone suggested that we start with strategic weapons, which our principals sought to slice in half, but didn't know how to do so equitably. It was a good suggestion, clearly the place to start for those who wanted to get something done.

That, however, did not include everyone around the table. Within minutes, Karpov launched into a harangue against the American position on strategic arms. Then, just as Karpov was getting in his groove, Akhromeyev placed a hand on his arm and turned to stare at him. The diatribe sputtered midsentence. The marshal then lifted his hand and resumed the discussion, as if nothing had interrupted it.

Only a few more times did Karpov or Arbatov or Falin reload and attempt to refire, each time being dressed down by the same five-star stare. Over the all-night session, Akhromeyev grew increasingly exasperated whenever that happened, apparently not understanding that this was instinctual, or at least habitual, on their part. It was what they did, what they had been doing for years. It was, in fact, the modus operandi for Soviet arms negotiators over several decades.

But it was not, as Akhromeyev made glaringly clear, what they would be doing that night in Hofdi House. Instead, we engaged on key nuclear issues, narrowing the differences where we could and moving along where we could not.

We spent no time on SDI or the ABM Treaty because all of us—even the chief of staff of the mighty Soviet armed forces—considered that topic above our pay grades. Besides, the issues surrounding SDI were more philosophical than technical. Indeed, the fact that SDI did not exist precluded it from being too technical.

Besides, our mandate was to deal with issues our principals could not address. And if anything was clear from the two Saturday sessions, it was that Reagan and Gorbachev had no problem addressing SDI and the ABM Treaty. Indeed, they both relished doing so. We had nothing to contribute to that dialogue. President Reagan was already making the case stronger and clearer than we could have done. None of us would have thought of those 1920s gas masks.

Shortly after 2:00 a.m., when real progress was under way on strategic arms, a dispute arose within our delegation. Our Geneva negotiator for those weapons, Rowny, got steamed up about something that Nitze had deemed acceptable to us. Rather than slug it out in front of the Soviets, we proposed a brief break.

When we retired to our assigned parlor, Rowny let loose and Nitze lost his temper—two old rams going at each other with a vengeance. After calming things down, we managed to concoct an acceptable compromise. Rowny and Nitze collected themselves and we returned, ready to advance our new position the next time that particular issue arose. Which it never did—neither that night nor in the months of negotiations that followed. Like so much of arms control—and of government, perhaps even of life—what appears to be all-important and arouses passion at one moment can be conveniently forgotten the next.

AROUND 3:15 A.M. SOMEONE suggested a half-hour break, to which everyone heartily agreed. Akhromeyev said that such a break would allow him to check in with the general secretary. We took that cue and announced that it would give us a fine opportunity to consult the president.

In actuality, none of us wished to wake up the president to explain progress on sundry technical issues he had never heard of. At 3:20 a.m., he would be even less engrossed than usual in the recondite world of sublimits in various nuclear categories.

Admittedly, our reluctance to disturb the president's sleep cycle carried some political risk. Several years before, early on the morning of August 19, 1981, news had reached Washington that two of Colonel Gadhafi's Libyan attack planes had fired on two U.S. Air Force jets flying over the Gulf of Sidra. Ed Meese, then the White House deputy chief of staff, had been working at Reagan's side for many years and knew him as well as anyone except Nancy. He knew that the president would view the decision to order American retaliation for such an unprovoked attack as a no-brainer. So Meese gave the green light without arousing the chief executive, who was peacefully sleeping a few hundred feet away in the White House family quarters.

The Washington press went berserk when learning that Meese had issued the military order, and not the commander in chief. At Reagan's next public appearance, with journalists still raging, he calmly explained that he had already ordered that, in the future, any time such an incident arose while he was sleeping, the staff *had* to wake him up—even, he added with a smile, if it was in the middle of a cabinet meeting.

Unlike the Gulf of Sidra incident, however, the details of our strategic arms talks did not warrant presidential involvement. But Nitze and a few others did go to Holt Hotel to awaken Shultz. When filled in with the details and asked for guidance, the secretary said to carry on, and went back to sleep.

But some of us thought that more was needed, especially since Akhromeyev seemed so keen on accomplishing things that night. Back at Hofdi House, we caucused in our upstairs parlor and concocted a few big-ticket asks on nuclear arms.

When the meeting resumed, Nitze said that the president intended for us to focus on these particular items and began to explain them in order. Akhromeyev did not respond but said that he had something to tell us. He had consulted with Gorbachev and could now agree to 50 percent strategic cuts down to equal levels.

On our side of the table, we shot looks of amazement at one another. In his quiet, straightforward manner, Akhromeyev had just overturned key Soviet policies of many years' standing. In fact, he had just removed *the* major obstacle to realizing the president's goal of 50 percent strategic cuts. What previously had been deemed far too ambitious to be attainable had suddenly, in a half hour, not only become attainable, but had been attained.

WHILE WE WERE DIGESTING this stunning development in the main conference room, a smaller group in a smaller Hofdi House room was discussing human rights and regional issues. The president had requested that these issues—the fate of Russian Jews seeking to emigrate to Israel and of political prisoners in the gulag and the vast empire of KGB prisons—be addressed, along with Afghanistan, the Middle East, and other world hot spots.

Although they were no longer outside Hofdi at this hour, earlier on Saturday protestors from the National Council on Soviet Jewry, and others from Israel and Europe, had carried signs bearing witness to their cause. They had protested during the Geneva summit, where Avital Sharansky, the wife of dissident Natan Sharansky, had appealed to President Reagan to get her husband released from his decade-long gulag imprisonment. She had gotten a meeting with Secretary Shultz, who then told us admiringly of her dogged determination. He ended his brief by saying that he wondered whether any of *our* wives would show as much determination, if we had been carted off. That gave each of us something to mull over.

The sun was still several hours from rising when, at 5:00 a.m., we turned to deal with intermediate missiles.

So far, the Soviets had been flexible regarding Europe, but intransigent about not restricting them in Asia. We sought a global agreement while they wanted an accord confined to Europe.

Adopting Akhromeyev's mantra of accomplishing what we could and leaving the rest to our principals, we raised some less contentious, second-tier issues in that realm, making real progress on them.

But the night's big breakthrough had come already. The progress Akhromeyev made possible on strategic arms by itself would have made Reykjavik one of the most successful summits ever held.

As the skies outside began to brighten, the American team felt that we should tie down what we had achieved, particularly while Akhromeyev was still in the room. Otherwise, Soviet obstructionists—especially the two seated on either side of him—might well roll back, or even deny, what had been agreed over the night.

To our surprise and delight, summarizing the points of progress and getting the Soviets to agree turned out to be rather straightforward. This, too, was due to Akhromeyev's deft, if not authoritarian, management of his delegation.

All that was left was to put the agreed-upon points down on paper, along with marginal notes and explanations, and to make copies for each of us and for our bosses.

A massive copy machine had been hauled into Hofdi House that afternoon, but no one knew how the behemoth worked. The Hofdi caretaker and several members of each delegation fiddled with the darned thing, turning its several switches and pushing its many buttons. We kept plugging and unplugging it, but there was no reassuring hum in it and nothing lit up on it.

We were all flailing around—here, at last, an instance of American and Soviet cooperation, Cold War rivals working side by side to solve a common problem—when a Soviet colonel pulled out a pack of carbon paper from his briefcase, waved it about, and offered sheets around the table. In English, in a triumphant voice, he said: "Here—Soviet high tech!"

A member of each delegation then carefully wrote out the agreements in legible longhand, pushing hard on his ballpoint pen so that the words could come through clearly on subsequent sheets of paper under the layers of carbon paper.

WITH THE COPIES MADE, our work was now done. Akhromeyev smiled as he sauntered toward the door. He expressed satisfaction with the long night's work, as we all did.

Some of us spoke with him early the next morning, but he made no other noticeable contribution at Reykjavik. Gorbachev never once mentioned his name to Reagan. It was almost as if the marshal was part of Hofdi House's haunted history, appearing one Saturday night to cause bumps in the night and vanishing the next afternoon.

Nonetheless, Sergey Akhromeyev served nobly at Reykjavik. The arms control breakthroughs could not have happened with any other Soviet official in that center seat. Even the acerbic Arbatov mustered flattering words on his leadership, later recalling that the marshal "was very disciplined. As we stayed up through the night, others became emotional, but he stayed calm. Gorbachev relied on him."

At Reykjavik, Sergei Akhromeyev truly was a Hero of the Soviet Union.

It was 6:20 a.m., with the sky ever lightening, when he and members of the delegations bundled up and walked outside to a brisk breeze and chilly morning. There, we shook hands and went our separate ways.

CHAPTER 5

Sunday Morning in Reykjavik

Sunday, October 12, 1986
In the Bubble and Small Conference Room

After the Saturday night meeting broke up, I stood outside Hofdi House enjoying the cold air and welcome quiet. A few embassy cars were waiting to take us back to the Holt Hotel, but to clear my mind and get some exercise, I walked the twenty minutes through the sleeping town. I was elated but exhausted. I had somehow missed out on a college ritual, so this was my first all-nighter.

As I walked into town, I felt sorry for Paul Nitze, who was about to turn eighty; Ed Rowny, who was then nearly seventy; and Max Kampelman, who was sixty-six. At forty, I was dragging and could only imagine how they must be feeling.

A hot shower in my mini-room helped. As earlier instructed, I packed my bags and placed them in the hallway, to be picked up by the Air Force staff and loaded onto the plane later that morning. The summit would be ending at noon with the presidential party taking off right afterward.

I then used a handy trick learned from Ronald Reagan: When tired, change your shoes and you'll feel refreshed. A half hour later, showered and wearing my other pair of shoes, I walked over to the embassy, even with a bit of a bounce in my step.

At 8:00 a.m., we were back in the bubble, awaiting the president's arrival. This time, the gray metal chair in the middle was reserved for him and I had a folding chair all my own, since someone—I can't recall who—couldn't make the briefing.

While awaiting the president, we gave a snapshot summary of the night's triumphs to the top troika of George Shultz, Don Regan, and John Poindexter. None of them grasped the technical aspects of our accomplishment—none needed to—but each of them grasped its significance. Now, at last, we were on our way to achieving 50 percent cuts in strategic arms and possibly an agreement on intermediate missiles to boot.

The president soon joined us, this time absent the fanfare of a Secret Service announcement. Yet his less dramatic arrival was no less moving for me. I always felt awed to be in the presence of the president, let alone in a position of helping him in some slight manner. There, in the crowded and drab bubble, as in the spacious and decorous Cabinet Room, the Situation Room, and especially the Oval Office, I felt a tingle in the back of my neck.

Secretary Shultz, as usual, opened the briefing by placing developments in a grand context. He said that Gorbachev had proposed working on four issues—strategic arms, intermediate arms, the SDI-ABM Treaty bundle, and nuclear testing. On nuclear testing, which had received virtually no air time thus far, he reminded us that Gorbachev sought a treaty banning all tests. This, the Reagan administration opposed, though I personally supported it. With both countries nearing the end of their nuclear test programs anyway, why not have a ban? Advances in computer simulation had made such tests less important, if not obsolete. Besides, a comprehensive test ban (CTB) open to all nations would help imprint a new international norm—that countries must not test nuclear weapons. This might marginally discourage

North Korea or Pakistan or other countries from going nuclear, or give us a moral cane to use if, or when, they did.

Yet my logic, compelling to me, at least, was not as compelling to those in the Pentagon, or eventually in the White House. Thus did the president bob and weave whenever Gorbachev raised the matter at Reykjavik, which was neither often nor with much oomph.

Ensconced in the bubble, Shultz asked Paul Nitze to brief the president on our overnight progress. Nitze gave a precise, technical account, thereby inducing frowns of puzzlement down the two rows of gray folding chairs. I jumped in to help: As Paul just explained, Mr. President, last night here in Reykjavik we accomplished more to cut strategic arms than we have over the past seven years in Geneva.

Ah, so that's what happened, the nods and smiles seemed to say. Reagan had set ambitious goals and stayed the course, even in the face of harsh criticism over five and a half years. Saturday night had been his big reward.

But the day ahead would be his big challenge. What he would later call "one of the longest, most disappointing—and ultimately angriest—days of my presidency," would also be one of the weirdest. His morning, supposedly last session with Gorbachev would begin with the Marxist leader citing the Bible, later have the Leader of the Free World lecture on Marx and Lenin, and end with the world's two most powerful men discussing invitations to a birthday party.

Rain was pounding down as the presidential motorcade headed off to Hofdi House. By then, the weather had become a leading character in the summit drama, reflecting the mood swings of the humans below. Shultz later recalled the weekend as "alternating every half hour or so between dark, driving rain and brilliant sunshine, and the course of our work mirrored the weather. Round and round we went." During the first hour of the Sunday morning session, rain was beating against the Hofdi House windowpanes, an appropriate accompaniment to Gorbachev's stormy mood that morning.

THE PRESIDENT LOOKED CHIPPER as he greeted the general secretary with gusto inside the Hofdi House hallway. He said that he had slept well, for the first time since coming to Iceland, and was looking forward to this day.

As indeed he was. For five years, he had waited for a Soviet leader with whom to negotiate. This last session at Reykjavik would give him the opportunity of a lifetime. It was his best chance to get deep nuclear cuts, preserve SDI, and get Gorbachev to come to Washington the following year. Reagan would often speak to us of flying Gorbachev to California, pointing out that the private swimming pools below were owned by the workers of America. He'd beam with the prospect of showing, and showing off, America's success to the Soviet leader.

AS THE LEADERS APPROACHED the small meeting room, their two military officers again dutifully walked a few paces behind, clutching their deadly briefcases. They slowed their gait and took their accustomed positions kitty-corner from each other in the hallway, staring forward, seemingly with nary a glance at the other.

Reagan and Gorbachev wasted no time on diplomatic conventions. By the Saturday afternoon session, they had dispensed with beginning by themselves and then inviting in their foreign ministers. By this third session, they had dispensed with opening by presenting proposals to each other. Actually, they had none to present. Nothing had been prepared for either leader—no memos, no bulleted talking points, no background intelligence assessments.

Though they had no agenda, they knew what had to get done. Whether they *could* get it done was another matter. While the three thousand journalists outside—chafing under the two-day news blackout—were wondering what would happen, so were we on the inside. And so were the two men inside that small room.

"This is our third meeting, Mr. President," Gorbachev began. "The Bible says that first came the first day, then the second, etc. We are now on our second day, with still a long way before the seventh."

"We should instead be resting," the president said.

"Yes, as this is Sunday," Gorbachev added, completing the thought.

"With a few exceptions, I am disappointed with what had been achieved by the arms control group," Reagan began, perhaps having misunderstood us in the bubble, or having a momentary mind slip, or trying some negotiating ploy known to him alone. Regardless, a moment later he was back on message. "Both sides should be proud of their achievement" on strategic arms.

By then sensitive to Gorbachev's complaint that he was making no concessions to the Russians, the president attributed our overnight success to "give and take on both sides." While gracious of Reagan, Gorbachev must have realized that all the give had been on their side, all the take on ours.

"Despite the fact that the arms experts labored for ten hours last night, I too was very disappointed with the results," Gorbachev said, before once again complaining,

> We have made major concessions to the United States in the hope that it will be possible to get the arms control talks moving seriously on reducing nuclear weapons. Yet it is my impression that your side is not taking our position into account. Instead of seeking to give an impulse to the discussions, the U.S. is trying to drag things backwards.

That contradicted the reason Gorbachev had proposed Reykjavik. "The Geneva negotiations have reached an impasse. New approaches are needed, as is the political will and ability to think in broad terms, to escape this dead-end. I had expected the same from the Americans," he said sadly. On top of the one-sided American policies was the arrogant American attitude.

I have gotten the impression that your approach to arms control is proceeding from the false impression that the Soviet Union was more interested in nuclear disarmament than you are. Perhaps the U.S. feels it can use this leverage to force us to capitulate in certain areas. This is a dangerous illusion, as such a scenario will never occur.

Gorbachev had grounds for such fears, since just such a scenario *was* occurring. But this could have been expected, and was—in fact, by Gorbachev himself. He had explicitly told the Politburo that the Soviet Union needed an agreement to come out of Reykjavik in order to take the pressure off its economy. Moreover, he had realized that Reagan would have more leverage, given America's technological and financial superiority.

Reagan let Gorbachev's griping go without reacting. Half expecting this, Gorbachev let it be, and turned to intermediate missiles. Here, too, he faced disappointment since Reagan kept insisting on global limits, refusing to accept Gorbachev's deal on missiles in Europe free from restrictions on those in Asia.

The president gave several reasons for his stance. Soviet missiles in Asia threatened our allies there, particularly Japan and South Korea. Moreover, they had the range to target cities in Europe without being moved, or could be moved there.

"As these weapons are mobile," Reagan said, "they can be used in either Asia or Europe."

"The concerns you raise are not serious," Gorbachev said. "If you do not want any agreement, then you should just say so. In that case, we're just wasting our time."

Rather than console, Reagan reiterated his arguments once more, which annoyed Gorbachev once more.

"Seriously! We two are not at a press conference," Gorbachev huffed. "We both know the facts. So there is no reason to speak in banalities." Evidently the career party apparatchik regarded press conferences as ideal outlets for banalities.

Stuck again, Reagan once more painted a picture of the future. "If we could start reducing our own nuclear forces, down to zero, we could stand shoulder-to-shoulder and tell other nations that they too must eliminate their own nuclear weapons. It would be hard to think of a country that would not do so."

Gorbachev agreed and added,

In fact, the present opportunity here in Reykjavik might be our only one in this respect.

I was not in a position a year ago, to say nothing of two or three years ago, to make the kind of proposals I can make now. And I might not be able to make the same proposals in a year from now.

Time passes and things change. Reykjavik will become simply a memory.

"The two of us are in the same situation in that respect," Reagan offered. "Since either of us could soon be without authority, it's all the more important to use the time available to us to contribute something valuable to the world—to free the world from the nuclear threat."

"The proposals I've brought to Reykjavik leave my conscience clear," Gorbachev said with a tinge of fatalism. "I can look you right in the eye and say that—if it becomes impossible for us to reach agreements—that's all right." Failure would happen because "the U.S. did not feel obligated to take our concerns into account, while we met your concerns."

Having told why Reykjavik might end without progress, Gorbachev then gave Reykjavik great progress. Most matter of factly, the general secretary said, "In Asia, the Soviets *could* accept the U.S. formula— that there be 100 warheads on our systems and 100 warheads on your territory. We would accept this, even though it will require us to reduce several times, by an order of magnitude that I cannot even compute" more than the United States would have to reduce.

This huge concession was made more grudgingly than gracefully. Gorbachev said that he resented how the "U.S. had insisted on impos- ing an ultimatum," but nonetheless "the Soviet Union would accept this."

"I agree to the proposal you described," Reagan said, implying that it was, in some respects, Gorbachev's proposal.

"That's good," Gorbachev said before asking again: "When will the U.S. start making concessions of its own? We have gone through half the agenda already, and there has been no movement from the U.S. side."

With Reagan mum, Gorbachev warned, "This next issue of ours will test the U.S. readiness to meet us halfway." He was heading back toward SDI and the ABM Treaty.

WHILE THE TWO LEADERS were meeting downstairs, their delega- tions were milling upstairs, in the open area between the parlors.

This was truly a scene to behold—American and Soviet officials talking informally, asking each other about their families, sharing in- formation and impressions, even laughing together. And these were not your standard-fare Soviet officials, the type dispatched to attend embassy receptions and pick up political tidbits along with hors d'oeuvres. Rather, these were the men at the top of the Kremlin power structure—the likes of Anatoly Dobrynin, Georgi Arbatov, Anatoly Chernyaev, Alexander Yakovlev, and Sergei Akhromeyev. These were the men any U.S. ambassador would be dying to meet, much less talk with, in Moscow once every couple of years. And there they were—every leader who mattered under Gorbachev, all gathered in one small space with nothing else to do, nowhere else to go, willing, even eager to talk.

We in the arms control field first mingled with our counterparts. Just hours after finishing our all-nighter, we felt the special kinship of sharing a tense and intense experience together. After chatting up the Soviet arms team and hearing rousing tales of Washington from Tolya Dobrynin, then well into his anecdotage, I slid over to Marshal Akhromeyev. We talked about having two daughters, the delights and challenges that brings. Before long, John Poindexter joined us and remarked how much Akhromeyev resembled the past top U.S. military officer, Jack Vessey. That led Akhromeyev to say that someday he would like to meet the current chairman of the Joint Chiefs of Staff, Admiral Bill Crowe. I said that Crowe was a really good fellow, that they would take to each other if they ever did meet.

In the days following Reykjavik, CIA agents debriefed us for whatever information we had scooped up during this exceptional gathering. But its significance extended far beyond that. In a small way, it helped end the Cold War by helping to thaw the cold ways we dealt with one another.

In short, Reykjavik helped humanize officials, especially on their side. This was appreciated by a top Soviet aide at Reykjavik, Aleksandr Bessmertnykh. "I would agree that one of the major elements of changing the Cold War was changing ourselves," he reflected later. "We were products of the Cold War, all of us. But we became softened by the new realities," the most unexpected coming during that weekend.

Our Sunday morning milling lasted a few hours. We went about chatting in blissful ignorance of the bad turn of events on the floor below.

HAVING RESOLVED MAJOR ISSUES on offensive arms, the leaders returned to the prickly defensive systems. Gorbachev urged Reagan to uphold the ABM Treaty for ten years, which the president agreed to do, and to confine SDI research to laboratories during that decade, which he refused to do.

After thrashing about on that, Gorbachev revealed that he knew that SDI was far along. "The U.S. has scored breakthroughs in one or two areas—and Moscow knew just which they are." Perhaps Reagan was startled by Gorbachev's talk of "breakthroughs" on SDI. More likely, he believed that too. Regardless, there had been none and would be none for many years to come.

Their wrangling resumed, as they went round and round on SDI and the ABM Treaty with no new ground covered, no new arguments presented, and no new progress made—but with no less vitality in their discussion. The large painting of wind-whipped waves, to Gorbachev's right, seemed more appropriate than it did the day before.

"We have no intention of violating the ABM Treaty," the president said. "We have never done so, even though, as you know, we believe the Soviet Union has done more than is permitted by the Treaty.

"Now, with respect to SDI, I have made a pledge to the American people that SDI would constitute disarmament and peace, and not be an offensive weapon. I cannot retreat from that pledge." If Gorbachev was surprised by Reagan's reference to his pledge, he wasn't alone. None of us could recall it. In fact, none of us had even heard of it.

"The U.S. has proposed a binding treaty which provides for the sharing of research which demonstrates a potential for defensive applications," the president went on. "This would facilitate the elimination of nuclear weapons.

"I cannot retreat from my pledge. We would share the fruits of our research—out of our own self-interest. If everyone has access to the relevant SDI technology, nuclear weapons would be a threat to no one."

The president then sprang another new thought: "Personally, I don't see why SDI could not be made a part of the ABM Treaty." By this, he was suggesting that the treaty that existed *explicitly* to prohibit SDI be amended to encompass SDI.

Gorbachev passed over yet another Reagan brainstorm to return to his Reykjavik refrain: "We have taken into account your concerns. We know that you are bound by the pledge you have made to your own people and to the world," thus extending the president's nonexistent pledge to people of the whole world.

"Research could continue and show that SDI was alive," but nonetheless confined. "Such work would not go beyond laboratory research. There could be testing, even mock-ups in laboratories. And such efforts would ensure against the appearance of a nuclear madman of the type you have mentioned," Gorbachev added.

"No, in fact, it would not," the president replied, slapping down the claim that laboratory-tethered research could protect America, or anyone else, against a madman's nuclear launch.

At this point, the leaders had made their arguments on defensive systems many times, mentioning offensive systems often in passing. Neither had paid much attention to just which offensive arms might be cut—whether all strategic arms or all ballistic missiles or all of some other broad category—if they came to terms on defensive systems.

Yet gradually, perhaps imperceptively, each increasingly spoke of "eliminating nuclear weapons." Not some broad category of nuclear weapons, but all of them. This talk of nuclear elimination would be expounded and expanded later that day, with consequences reaching far beyond Reykjavik.

Sunday, October 12, 1986
The "American" Parlor in Hofdi House

At midday, while many of us were still mixing with the Soviets in the second-floor no-man's-land, Shultz summoned our team together. As usual, the secretary summarized the morning meeting—describing it as "a slugging match all the way"—before delivering the news headline, that Gorbachev had come around on intermediate missiles by agreeing to Reagan's global limits.

As after our 3:15 a.m. break the night before—when Akhromeyev announced the strategic arms breakthrough—we were taken aback by the Soviets' sudden volte-face. They had been so adamant for so long—starting five years back and continuing until thirty minutes back.

Gorbachev's concession meant that more than 90 percent of those deployed Soviet warheads would be destroyed. That was not bad for an arms accord. In fact, it was unprecedented.

Getting into particulars, Shultz related how the leaders had landed on one hundred systems in Europe and one hundred in Asia. He paused in anticipation of our appreciation for this fine turn of events. His moment of triumph was, however, marred by the State Department notetaker, Mark Parris. After clearing his throat, he told his boss that he had it a bit differently. His notes indicated that Gorbachev agreed to zero in Europe and one hundred in Asia.

The secretary, who prided himself on precision, was taken aback. He started flipping through his lined yellow pad to find just what Gorbachev had said. Finally, Shultz found the page he had been seeking. There! With great satisfaction, he pointed to the spot indicating one hundred, Europe, and one hundred, Asia.

Much to his credit, Mark toughed it out. *His* notes showed that Gorbachev agreed to zero in Europe and one hundred in Asia. This mini-drama within the larger drama of Reykjavik ended when Shultz looked up from his pad and, with a rare smile, proclaimed: "So be it!"

The rest of us thought: So much the better! Zero missiles in Europe moved Reagan's zero option that much closer to realization. Now, success loomed.

The moment Shultz uttered "So be it!" marked Reykjavik's high water mark for us in the arms control business. Before that weekend, arms talks had crept along "in this petty pace from day to day, to the last syllable of recorded time," as Macbeth put it. Suddenly to have two major breakthroughs, one on Saturday night and one on Sunday morning, was nothing short of miraculous.

Someone then came up with the fine idea of informing our NATO allies that, thanks to Western long steadfastness and Gorbachev's sudden concession, the alliance had succeeded. All of us had, since the Carter administration, wanted all such missiles removed from Europe. Together, we could savor the jubilation, relief, and gratitude of such startling news.

Shultz welcomed the idea and sent a staffer to the underutilized Iceland Executive Office Building (IEOB) to dispatch cables to American ambassadors across allied lands. They were directed to meet immediately, in person, with the head of government to relay such glad tidings from Reykjavik.

All this seemed too good to be true. And, as things go in life, it was.

Back in the small conference room, a bigger problem was looming, one that threatened to bring the summit crashing down. It began when the president came to feel that, as far as the ABM Treaty was concerned, enough was enough already.

The conservative cry of that era was: "Let Reagan be Reagan"—let him follow his conservative gut and not the namby-pamby counsel of his advisers. Here, at the most critical juncture of Reykjavik, Reagan himself let Reagan be Reagan.

What the Hell is it that we are defending here? The ABM Treaty says that we cannot defend ourselves, except by means of systems we have never deployed. The treaty says that if someone wants to blow us up, the other will retaliate. Such a regime does *not* give protection. It *limits* protection.

Why the Hell should the world have to live for another ten years under this threat of nuclear weapons? I fail to see the magic of the ABM regime, whose only assurance is the doctrine of Mutual Assured Destruction.

Instead, we should give the world a means of protection that would put the nuclear genie back in his bottle. The next generation would reap the benefits when we are no longer around.

The fact that Reagan's quasi-rant ran contrary to official U.S. policy of every administration since John F. Kennedy's, including his own, seemed not to bother him a bit. Instead, Reagan trashed the MAD doctrine with a ferocity rare in debates over strategic doctrine.

Gorbachev replied mildly that there was a "long and complicated history of the ABM Treaty. It had not come as a bolt from the blue, but after years of discussion by responsible leaders." That's why "no one in the Soviet leadership, including me personally, could agree to steps which would undercut the Treaty."

"From what you've been saying," Gorbachev claimed, "the U.S. is only considering its own interests. I cannot agree to a proposal which reflects only your interests. Our conversation has reached the point where it is time for the American side to make a move in the Soviet direction on the ABM Treaty.

"I've heard it said that the president did not like to make concessions." Getting no response, he pressed on: "I have heard an American expression which seemed apt—'It takes two to tango.'

"With respect to the major questions of arms control and nuclear disarmament, we two are the only partners in sight. So I ask: 'Are you prepared to dance?'"

Instead of responding to this invitation to dance, the president ran off the rails. "For three years during the late fifties, there had been a moratorium on nuclear tests. Then the Soviet Union broke the moratorium with a series of tests unprecedented in their number and scope." U.S. experts found that the Soviets "had been preparing that test series throughout the period of the moratorium. We were placed at a severe disadvantage. President Kennedy vowed we would never again be caught unprepared." That deceit gave the Soviets an edge that lasted right up to the present. "In fact, we are still behind."

Once embarked on this roll of Soviet duplicity, Ronald Reagan proved unstoppable. Consequently, at Reykjavik on that Sunday morning came the most remarkable debate over American and Soviet social and political systems, even exceeding the Nixon-Khrushchev "kitchen debate" in the summer of 1959.

The president identified the basic problem: "Each side has mistrusted the other." But each side has not been equally at fault. "The evidence is all on our side."

The mistrust started with Lenin. With growing unease at where this latest Reagan stream of consciousness was taking them, Gorbachev tried to divert it with a wisecrack about Reagan's previous talk of Karl Marx. "You've dropped Marx for Lenin," he said jocularly.

Reagan, focused on the tale he was about to tell, missed Gorbachev's stab at humor. So he informed the leader of world Communism, the husband of a professor of Marxist-Leninist philosophy, that "Marx said first much of what Lenin said later."

That clarified, Reagan resumed telling how Lenin had molded Communism to conquer the world. "Socialism has to be global in scope to succeed. The only morality is that which advances Socialism. And it has been a fact that every Soviet leader"—here, Reagan suddenly caught himself—"up to you, at least so far, has endorsed in speeches to Soviet Communist Party Congresses, the objective of establishing a world Communist state.

"Even when our two countries were Allies during World War II, Soviet suspicions had been such that Moscow had resisted U.S. shuttle bombing missions to and from Soviet territory. And after the war, the U.S. had proposed on nineteen separate occasions"—one wonders where Reagan got that number from!—"at a time when we had a monopoly on nuclear weapons, the elimination of such weapons. The Soviet Union not only rebuffed our offers, but placed nuclear missiles in Cuba in the sixties.

"I could go on," he said, until seeing that Gorbachev wanted anything but that. Then Reagan settled down and summed up.

"I wanted simply to make the point to you that such behavior gave us legitimate grounds to suspect Soviet motives." In contrast, "the Soviet Union has no grounds for believing that the U.S. ever wanted war." That Gorbachev would see with his own eyes when coming to the United States.

By this point, Gorbachev was desperate to change the channel. Hence the leader of world Communism said that he didn't really care to discuss Marx and Lenin. He advised Reagan "not to waste time and energy" attacking their philosophy. He personally was eager to "return to the present," to the topics of the Reykjavik agenda.

But first, Gorbachev had something to say. He had had quite enough of Reagan's litany of Soviet duplicity. Plus, he resented Reagan's assaults on his system, especially since the Soviets never questioned the legitimacy of the American system.

"We recognize the right of the U.S. people to their own values, and to choose their government and their president." Yet this spirit of tolerance wasn't being reciprocated.

Moving further into the land of no-holds-barred, Gorbachev said that he had been "surprised when I heard of a recent statement by you that you remained true to" calling the U.S.S.R. an "evil empire" and the "crusade against socialism in order to relegate it to the ash heap of history.

"I fail to understand how such statements could be considered an appropriate 'foreword' to this Reykjavik meeting." Having said his piece, Gorbachev calmed down but threw out the schoolyard "you started it" refrain, "I want to remind you that you initiated this discussion."

Again, rather than to adopt the natural reaction of a negotiator and excuse or explain his earlier rhetoric, Ronald Reagan doubled down:

Let me remind you that there is a Communist Party in the United States. Its members can, and do, organize and run for public office. They are free to try to persuade the people of the validity of their philosophy.

This is not true in your country. The Soviets enforce rather than persuade. Similarly, when Communist parties take power in Third World countries, they quickly eliminate other parties by force.

In the U.S., anyone could organize his own party. But there is only one party in the Soviet Union. Besides, a majority of the Soviet population is excluded from its membership.

There's a fundamental difference in our two societies' approaches. The United States believes that people should have the right to determine their own form of government, while the . . .

"I would be happy," Gorbachev broke in, "to have a wide-ranging conversation with you on the moral, philosophical, and ethical issues raised by your remarks"—but not just then. Only "at another time."

For now he "had no desire to quarrel." They had been finding a fine "man-to-man relationship between us possible." Reagan shouldn't ruin it by arguing their societies' differences.

Gorbachev's attempt to calm Reagan down finally worked. The president quipped, "I look forward to welcoming you at some point as a new member of the Republican Party."

Gorbachev could never resist getting in the last word: "There *had* been a profusion of parties in Russia, both before and after the Revolution. These things were the result of historical processes," he added in a convoluted attempt to explain what was palpably untrue. But Reagan let it lie.

MEANWHILE, RAISA GORBACHEV, UNDETERRED by the lack of anything further worth seeing or doing in Reykjavik, resumed her speed touring. On Sunday, she led her cavalcade thirty miles east of town to Thingvellir, where the country's parliament had first met more than a millennium before.

Icelandic officials had never suspected that the former professor of Marxism, which had nothing but disdain for genuine parliaments, would wish to visit the site of the world's first genuine parliament.

It wasn't much to see. In fact, there was nothing to see—nothing, except more big, black, barren lava. Yet on that site in AD 930 some Viking chiefs squatted down near a stream and selected a scribe to write down on a rock whatever they could agree upon. That was the legendary "law rock."

But no one knows just where those Vikings squatted, or which of the many rocks, which stretch as far as the eye can see, might have been that special rock.

After taking in the scene, not a terribly time-consuming activity, Mrs. Gorbachev headed back for her second lunch in two days at the prime minister's residence.

The highlight of her afternoon itinerary was a visit to a "working sheep farm." In the post-Reykjavik issue of *Time* magazine, Roger Rosenblatt described the visit: "Rain-shagged sheep, mops with four legs, pursue their ridiculous business of all-day eating." The tourist office spokesman announced that visiting the sheep farm had been Raisa's idea.

After stopping for coffee in Hvergerdi, a small town with lots of geysers and a few waterfalls, she visited its chapel. Again, no one in the Iceland government had suspected that a professor of godless Marxism would want to go visiting a church. And again, it wasn't much to see. The altar was plain, with some candles aflame on it. Standing in the church, she said: "I am an atheist . . . [but] I respect all faiths. It is after all a personal matter."

Back at Hofdi House, where a calm had followed the two men's outbursts, Shultz tried heroically to get things back on track.

They all needed, he reminded them, to think about a joint

statement, which the world expected at the summit's close. They could announce groundbreaking agreements on strategic and intermediate nuclear arms in such a statement. But what could they say about SDI and the ABM Treaty? Any agreed wording there would have to blend aspiration with obfuscation. Shultz opted for the former by suggesting wording on "a cooperative transition to advanced strategic defenses."

Gorbachev called that totally unacceptable. "It is the U.S. which intends to deploy SDI. The Soviets will not make such an arrangement possible." Reagan broke their tension in his own, distinct manner.

"As the oldest person in the room, I am the only one who could remember how, after World War I, poison gas had been outlawed. But people kept their gas masks." A collective groan must have filled the room, as the president told his gas mask tale, with the same expression and most of the same words, unabridged, yet again.

Gorbachev was becoming inconsolable. He was getting nowhere with this man. Maybe, he thought, he *could* get nowhere with this man.

"Our preceding conversation convinces me of the veracity of reports that you do not like to make concessions," he said. "You clearly do not want to give any concessions on the question of the ABM Treaty, its duration and strength."

Knowing that Gorbachev was quite right, Reagan let his statement lie. And so, again, they seemed stuck.

BUT THEN CAME ANOTHER Reykjavik surprise, one that shaped the summit's image that day and ever after.

"The Soviets have proposed a package," Gorbachev warned. "Individual elements of our proposals must be regarded as a package."

Back in Moscow on October 4, Gorbachev had told his Politburo that "we should not link" strategic arms to SDI, as strategic cuts were too imperative to be tied up. Yet, here at Reykjavik, less than a fortnight later, he was doing just that.

The president shot back: "There should be no such linkage!" They had already agreed to deep nuclear cuts. These should go forth, especially, Reagan added, since "the Soviet Union already [was] in violation of the Treaty."

"For my part," Gorbachev said, all but closing up shop, "I am sorry you and I have failed to provide a new impulse for arms control. This was unfortunate, and I regret it."

"I do, too," Reagan responded. He said that he welcomed the 50 percent strategic cuts and the deep cuts on intermediate missiles, and felt good progress had been made on SDI and the ABM Treaty.

"Is this not so? Are the two of us truly to depart with nothing?" he asked plaintively.

"That seems to be the case," Gorbachev responded, before circling back to their discussion of an hour before.

"Soviet public opinion," he said, with no irony over the oxymoron, "has been concerned about the state of human rights in the United States."

He then raised an issue the Soviets had previously addressed in a defensive crouch, their jamming of the Voice of America radio network. While VOA could broadcast successfully into Russia, Gorbachev said, Russia could not broadcast successfully into America. That's why they jammed the VOA signal, to level the playing field.

"Americans recognize the right of the individual to hear all points of views," Reagan replied and then predicted, "The press conference you will give after our meeting here will be carried by the American media. The same will not happen with Soviet media," which turned out to be exactly correct.

Gorbachev shifted from radio to cinema, another tilted playing field. "Half of the foreign films shown in the Soviet Union are American." Yet virtually no Soviet films were shown in the United States. "There is no equality in this arrangement."

Once he had heard mention of the film industry, Reagan perked up. "This is a function of the market rather than any attempt to ban

Soviet films. The U.S. government cannot dictate what films private entrepreneurs show," he said before mentioning, quite needlessly, that he knew of what he spoke since "I used to make films."

Reagan then offered an inside tip. Russian producers should hire an American film distributor "to convince local theaters to show its films." But they had to be good for this plan to work. "American audiences respond positively to quality Soviet performers," which is why a recent tour of the Kirov Ballet in the States succeeded.

Gorbachev moved along to a "humanitarian" issue. For thirty years, the United States had denied visas to Russian trade union representatives, while the U.S.S.R. automatically approved visas for U.S. labor leaders. "Again," he asked, "where is the equality of access?"

With the clock running down, Reagan refrained from mentioning that U.S. labor leaders represented laborers, while U.S.S.R. labor leaders represented the regime.

Instead, he brought up two quick, political hot topics. "I have to raise the Soviet failure to meet your obligations under the bilateral Long Term Grain Agreement to buy the minimum amount of American wheat."

"Tell your farmers," Gorbachev spoke, politician to politician, "that the money we had hoped to spend on grain is in America and Saudi Arabia as a result of lower oil prices." Having raised the issue dear to American farmers, Reagan left it at that.

Next, he mentioned the request of Mstislav Rostropovich that his relatives be allowed to leave Russia to attend his seventieth birthday party in Washington. The famous cellist and National Symphony Orchestra conductor was by then a Washington institution. After some confusion between Shevardnadze and Gorbachev as to who had Rostropovich's letter of request—whether it was in one or the other's in-box, had already been drafted, or signed, or even mailed off—Gorbachev assured the president, "The necessary instructions will be given to enable Rostropovich's relatives to attend the celebrations."

"Thank you very much," the president said amiably.

Then came an awkward moment as the superpower leaders, like two teenagers at the end of a great first date, didn't know how to end their time together. They sat in silence until Shevardnadze asked if he and Shultz "were to remain unemployed" or would be given a work assignment.

As if on cue, Shultz took yet another stab at outlining a joint statement. But once he reached SDI and the ABM Treaty, Gorbachev laid into him. "That is not acceptable to us," he said bullishly, before adding sarcastically, "What else do you want to write?"

Shultz, unruffled, turned to offer a statement on intermediate missiles, which Gorbachev dismissed with: "On that issue, everything is clear."

Having finished with Shultz, he turned to Reagan. "If you have no objections, our two foreign ministers might see what they can come up with while we two take a brief break. I don't mind waiting an hour or two." Reagan, not minding either, nodded appreciatively.

"Maybe we can slow down a little," Gorbachev said wisely. "After all, we do not want everything to end with a facade."

This statement is only found in the Russian notes of that session. Yet, it was true. Neither side wanted to end with a facade, or failure, or anything of the sort. Putting their impasse off by deciding to reconvene at 3:00 p.m. was, at least, not ending like that.

The president agreed and escorted Gorbachev from the room.

This Sunday morning session furnishes insights like none other at Reykjavik, and like few other summits in modern history. These hours revealed Reagan and Gorbachev always on their own and sometimes at their best.

Their discussion was of impressive depth and breadth, ranging from how Soviet intermediate missile deployments in Asia affected

European security, to the vast tapestry of comparative politics—of totalitarian Communism versus democratic capitalism. And, of course, the complete history of gas masks.

Reagan and Gorbachev handled these topics themselves. Neither turned to his foreign minister for either information or guidance during their three and a half hours of steady substance. During their dialogue that morning, Reagan and Gorbachev were most intensively active and alive. Each must have been feeling that "this is the real me."

The session also revealed how, and how much, the men differed. Gorbachev acted like a capitalistic CEO trying to analyze and solve the issues at hand. Reagan resembled a Russian artist, flitting here and there, following his imagination about.

Moreover, the president showed a wider range of interests than Gorbachev. He was willing, even eager to debate the great issue of their era, Marxism versus democracy, while Gorbachev kept yanking him back to the tasks at hand.

Sunday morning likewise revealed that even Communism's supreme leader could not justify its ways. By the end of 1986 the clock was already running down on Communist ideology and legitimacy. Gorbachev tried to respond to Reagan's attack on his system but did a poor job of it. His discourses on jamming VOA, Americans being unable to watch Soviet films, and the existence of multiple political parties under Communism were his weakest at Reykjavik. They may even have embarrassed him.

Gorbachev had no good response to Reagan's critique. A man that intelligent and clear-sighted had to have seen that. He had to have known that Reagan was basically right and that the path the Soviet Union had taken was basically wrong.

For sure, Reagan had the better case to make, but he made it boldly, pulling no punches. It's hard to think of any other U.S. president speaking as bluntly against the Soviet system to the head of that system as Reagan did that morning.

Not only what Reagan said, but the way he said it clearly frustrated Gorbachev. When they were debating arms proposals, Gorbachev pounded away—either at the issue or at the president for differing with him on it.

But Reagan would not respond in kind. Rather, he spoke in stories, almost in parables—extolling the wonders of the Baruch Plan, the shrewdness of making gas masks, the hostility of Russians denying U.S. pilots airfields, the duplicity of the Soviet test moratorium in the 1950s—really anything taken from the well-stocked shelves of his mental warehouse. Reagan's seemingly rambling stories did, though, come to a point. They had a message to convey, no matter how tortuous the pathway to arrive at that message.

In this critical third session, the two men revealed not only where they differed but what they shared. They both felt a deep sense of responsibility for the nuclear threat their gigantic arsenals posed to each other, and to the world. They shared a determination to reverse the nuclear buildup.

Both men repeated themselves constantly, Reagan in a manner that aggravated Gorbachev more than the reverse. True, Reagan would tell the same story in the same way many times. But while Reagan was bad on this, he wasn't as bad as Gorbachev made out. At one point when Reagan was relaunching his gas masks module, Gorbachev testily said, "That's the tenth time you talked about gas masks!" He exaggerated, as the record substantiates half that number of gas mask riffs.

But even had Reagan told that tale ten times, it wouldn't have been the indoor record at Reykjavik. Gorbachev complained that he was making all the concessions and Reagan none more than ten times that weekend. The overall Reykjavik record, however, was set by Gorbachev's insistence that SDI be confined to laboratories. He repeated it constantly during their first three sessions, and then a stunning *twenty-eight* times on Sunday afternoon, for an impressive clip of one mention every five minutes. Gorbachev was insisting on this condition, despite the fact (per Chernyaev's notes) that it had never been mentioned in any pre-summit meeting in the Kremlin.

Both men were courageous, willing to break with convention by disdaining nuclear weapons and extending the summit into overtime, something that had never happened before.

No general secretary before had agreed to scrap nuclear weapons that had already been built, paid for, and deployed, as Gorbachev agreed to do that Sunday morning. He acted boldly when springing linkage of the nuclear cuts with SDI constraints. Playing a weak hand, Gorbachev used whatever leverage he had well. His eleventh hour ploy would probably have worked with any other president.

Reagan likewise broke with convention, notably by assaulting the long-venerated ABM Treaty and championing SDI and being willing to share "it" with the Soviet Union. He had been bold when launching his delegitimization campaign, setting major nuclear cuts as his prime goal, and ordering a massive U.S. military buildup.

Their discussion, however, was not perfect nor was it perfectly truthful. Gorbachev claimed that confining SDI to the laboratories wouldn't crimp research on it, when it obviously would—which was precisely why Gorbachev kept insisting upon it. A week or so after Reykjavik, technical experts briefed me that some three-fourths of SDI planned tests would have to be scrapped, or greatly curtailed, if confined to laboratories. Moreover, Congress would never have funded a program so constrained in its infancy.

Gorbachev claimed that he was merely confining SDI in accordance with the ABM Treaty. That, too, was untrue. At one point on Sunday morning, Shevardnadze proposed they simply extend the ABM Treaty for ten more years, and dispense with all that SDI-in-laboratories business. Gorbachev swiftly shot down his foreign minister, insisting that "a much more rigid adherence to the Treaty" was instead needed.

Similarly, Reagan made a glaring error when he claimed that, after the two of them had eliminated all their nuclear weapons, "it would be hard to think of a country that would not do" likewise.

Actually, it would be hard for me to think of a country that *would* do likewise. No nation would scrap its nuclear weapons solely because Russia and America had eliminated theirs. In fact, such a move by the superpowers would prompt other nuclear powers to retain, even to enlarge, their nuclear arsenals in order to become a new powerhouse nation.

China would welcome Reagan's scenario as it would open the way for greater Chinese global prominence. Britain and France would keep, or increase, their nukes with the end of America's nuclear umbrella to help protect their security.

Superpower abolition would likely entice other states to go nuclear. Germany and Japan might seriously consider acquiring their own atomic weapons, once we ended our extended deterrence for their protection. Other nations, especially those endangered, like South Korea and Saudi Arabia, might well follow suit.

The size of superpower arsenals has little bearing on those of other nations. India and Pakistan went nuclear because of each other, not because of the amount of U.S. and U.S.S.R. weaponry. And they would stay nuclear, regardless of what we or the Soviets did. So would Israel, which developed nukes because of its hostile neighbors, not because of our weaponry.

History bears out the point. In the quarter century since Reykjavik, while the U.S. and Soviet/Russian nuclear arsenals have declined by some two-thirds, the nuclear arsenals of other nuclear states have increased. Since Reykjavik, Pakistan and North Korea have developed their own nuclear weapons.

On the other hand, both Reagan and Gorbachev made some excellent points. Reagan was right to question the perpetual threat of mutual annihilation with his "What the Hell are we defending?" diatribe. Gorbachev showed remarkable prescience when urging that they strike a deal while they still had the power to do so, since they "might not be able to make [or agree to] the same proposals in a year or so. Time passes and things change."

Indeed, time passed and things changed—far more and faster than either man ever anticipated.

Moreover, Gorbachev had offered Reagan a perfectly reasonable deal: compromise on SDI—a research program of dubious promise, which might or might not yield results at some distant time—in return for deep cuts in nuclear arms right away. Contrary to what Reagan claimed, such a deal would not have opened him up to criticism for going back on his solemn pledge. For despite what he thought, he had made no such pledge. Rather, Reagan's accepting Gorbachev's offer would have been heralded across America, and around the world, as a masterful diplomatic stroke on his part, precisely the kind rewarded by the Nobel Peace Prize.

As it happened, however—and however strangely it happened— Reagan's stubborn refusal to make this deal at Reykjavik reaped far greater benefits, unimaginable benefits.

CHAPTER 6

Sunday Afternoon and Evening in Reykjavik

Sunday, October 12, 1986
In the Embassy and at the Ambassador's Residence

Gorbachev's late morning linkage—tying the nuclear cuts to thwarting SDI—dampened our hopes for Reykjavik to end in heralded triumph. The euphoria of a few hours ago faded as we debated how to deal with Gorbachev's sudden-sprung trap.

The mood beyond Hofdi House turned just as bleak. U.S. ambassadors in key NATO capitals began reporting back that, far from celebrating the intermediate missile triumph, European leaders began fretting over it. While the allies had enthusiastically endorsed the zero option in 1978 and championed it since, they apparently had done so primarily because they were convinced it would never happen. This Margaret Thatcher admits in her memoirs: "I had gone along with it [the zero option] in the hope that the Soviets would never accept."

Now that the Soviets did accept it, the allies didn't. The U.S. missiles were already there, they explained to our ambassadors, so why not just leave them there? They'd become more or less accepted by the public and justified by defense intellectuals as part of "coupling"—reinforcing America's commitment to Europe's security. So instead of praise for

Reagan's negotiating skills, and huzzahs for Reykjavik, we got muffled grumbles. The summit in Iceland was coming to look as bleak and unpromising as its landscape.

Secretary of State George Shultz remained at Hofdi House to see what he could work out with Shevardnadze, while the president and the rest of us had lunch at the American ambassador's residence—absent, of course, the resident American ambassador.

When I entered the dining room, the White House chef took me aside to say that he had prepared a locally caught fish as a special treat. But even this delicacy failed to lift the president's spirits. Our usually ebullient leader was somber.

Having begun his day at 8:00 a.m. and engaged in constant verbal combat until then strained the seventy-five-year-old chief executive. Reagan wished to pocket the breakthroughs of the previous night and that morning, issue the expected joint statement, confirm the Washington summit the next year, shake Gorbachev's hand in departure, and be off for dinner with Nancy. Gorbachev had other ideas.

Reagan's native optimism revived some around dessert time. Gorbachev had bushwhacked him, but that was not necessarily the end of the story. All weekend long, Gorbachev had taken tough stances, adamantly stuck by them, and then yielded gracefully. Maybe that would happen again. Yet Reagan's instinct told him that, in this case, it might not.

At one point, Reagan said to us, "Hell, this isn't preparing for a summit. This is a summit!" He was awfully late in realizing that or perhaps in verbalizing it. Regardless, he faced the final round of a real summit with Gorbachev.

Sunday Afternoon, October 12, 1986
In Hofdi House

Shultz meanwhile was doing a diplomatic two-step with Eduard Shevardnadze. Each would write his principal's position, add diplomatic adornment, and proclaim this to be "compromise language," which the other should accept.

But there were big substantive differences between their write-ups. While Shevardnadze sought to eliminate all strategic weapons, Shultz sought to scrap only strategic ballistic missiles. This formulation left America's two strengths—strategic bombers and cruise missiles—outside the ban, and put the Soviets' main strength—ballistic missiles—inside it, on the chopping block.

Second, Shevardnadze's draft restricted SDI research to the laboratories, while Shultz's stated that "either side would be free to introduce defenses" after a decade of adhering to the ABM Treaty. Shevardnadze's draft left the treaty vibrant, while Shultz's turned the treaty into toast after that decade.

The two men traded and debated their drafts, which only highlighted the huge gaps between them. Their unpromising process delayed the opening of the Sunday afternoon session for a half hour.

It was well after three o'clock when the American president and the Soviet general secretary entered Hofdi House for the last time.

Absent all fanfare, Gorbachev began reading Shevardnadze's lunchtime draft, which he declared "incorporates the positions of the U.S. and Soviet Union, and it also strengthens the ABM Treaty while drastically reducing nuclear arms."

"This seems only slightly different from the U.S. position," Reagan said mistakenly. Indeed, Gorbachev claimed, the Soviet version *had* incorporated Reagan's positions.

They then discussed the alternative proposals, both either confused by or indifferent to just which offensive arms would be cut or eliminated. Reagan spoke interchangeably of "offensive missiles," "ballistic missiles," and "nuclear missiles." Gorbachev mentioned "nuclear forces" and "offensive weapons" without distinction. If confusion reigned with offensive arms, deception ruled on defensive systems.

"The Soviets are not trying to bury SDI," Gorbachev told the president, while trying hard to do just that. Reagan said time and again that he would make SDI "available to the Soviet side, if it wants it," when there was no way he ever would.

Reagan again asked Gorbachev why he was so attached to a treaty he was violating. Besides, "You have a big defense structure, and we have none. It is a peculiar fact that we do not have a single defense against a nuclear attack."

"If you would just read the Soviet proposal," Gorbachev said, trying to get Reagan to focus. "It incorporates both the U.S. and Soviet points of view. If it's acceptable to you, I'd be prepared to sign it right here," he finished temptingly.

"I think that the two sides are very close to an agreement," Reagan surmised, which led Gorbachev to extol the reasonableness of his paper. Just as he was hitting his stride, Reagan veered off again.

"Ten years from now, I will be a very old man. You and I could come to Iceland and each of us bring the last nuclear missile from our country with us. Then we will give a tremendous party for the whole world."

"I think the two sides are very close to reaching a common formula," Gorbachev broke in, before adding, "I do not think you should suspect the Soviet Union of having evil designs. If we had such designs, we would not have gone as far in proposing reductions of strategic and intermediate missiles."

The two men were then engaged in two different conversations, with Reagan still merrily strolling down memory lane. "Ten years from now, I will be very old and you would not recognize me. I would say, 'Hello Mikhail,' and you could say, 'Ron, is that you?' And then we will destroy our last missiles."

"I don't know if I will live another ten years," Gorbachev said, finally joining in Reagan's conversation.

"Well, I am counting on living that long," Reagan replied.

"Yes, but you are past the dangerous period, and will now live to be 100. In my case, I'm entering the most dangerous period of a man's life—especially after negotiating with the President, who is sapping all the strength I had!

"I had heard that you did not like to make concessions, and want only to come out a winner," he added righteously, "I think both sides ought to be winners."

"I will not live to 100 if I have to worry every day about being hit by a Soviet missile," Reagan quipped, finally bringing them somewhere close to the matters at hand. He then tried to nail down what he *really* wanted from Reykjavik. Why not, he suggested, just announce their agreed nuclear reductions now and sort out SDI and the ABM Treaty during their summit in Washington?

Gorbachev would have none of that, because of the tight "interrelationship between the issues" of offensive and defensive systems. It was all or nothing.

"We're not getting any place," the president said sadly. With nowhere to go then, Reagan proposed that they go to their parlors.

Would Gorbachev mind taking "a recess where we could each meet with our people, and see what is keeping us apart?"—as if that were a great mystery.

But Shultz thought they should stay, since the two sides seemed to be discussing "different categories." The secretary began this process of clarification by saying, "The President has talked about strategic offensive weapons." Except that he hadn't. That had been Gorbachev's category, not Reagan's.

With nothing clarified and everything confused, the leaders took a break to clear their minds, lift the mood, and see if they might sort things out.

. . . .

WHILE ALL THIS WAS happening on the ground floor, we were anxiously waiting on the second floor. The U.S.-Soviet conversational bazaar had closed down, with each side packing its tent and retreating to its parlor. The corridor resumed being a diplomatic DMZ.

Hofdi House felt quiet and somewhat dour. For relief, I wandered around, taking in its beauty and watching out for its spirits, of that young virgin or those incinerated Viking warriors.

After checking around the first floor, I headed down to the basement, where I witnessed a scene as strange as any spirits sighting. Half of the large, unfinished space was piled high with the latest communications equipment manned by the CIA and White House Office of Telecommunications technicians. The other half was filled with the same sort of gadgetry manned by KGB operatives.

Just as bizarre as the layout was the personnel. The KGB officers were evidently a most jovial bunch. According to the Hofdi House caretaker, a fine fellow named Magnus Oskarsson, they were laughing uproariously at *Tom and Jerry* cartoons shown on local television.

The Americans had a massive coffee maker in their half of the basement, the Soviets a more refined espresso machine in theirs. To accommodate drinkers of either sort were two bathrooms, one unfortunately larger than the other.

Unfortunately, since during the summit preparations, use of the facilities had become an issue. Caretaker Oskarsson tried to work out which delegation would get rights to which bathroom, since each sought the bigger loo. Poor Oskarsson—unaccustomed to negotiating between the world's nuclear superpowers on any subject, much less one as sensitive as privy privileges—faced a deadlock until the KGB station chief said, "This is ridiculous!" and suggested that both sides share both facilities.

Thus, while intelligence agencies normally operate on a need-to-know basis, for this weekend in Reykjavik, the world's two main intelligence agencies operated on a need-to-go basis.

Returning to the second-floor parlor, I rejoined our somber team, all wondering what would happen in the summit home stretch.

While I was staring at the parlor's painting of a barren Icelandic landscape, a work of art not created to lift human spirits, a Secret Service agent burst it and called out: "The President of the United States."

We stood as Reagan entered and stayed standing as he filled us in on the conversation downstairs—giving the discussion far more coherence than the written notes now indicate it had. The president said he was determined to find some way to salvage the summit and mused that maybe redrafting our position again might help.

Hence, the Pentagon's Richard Perle and the NSC's Robert Linhard went off to the parlor's bathroom to take Gorbachev's paper and fill it in with our substance. The Secret Service had placed a plywood board over the top of the old bathtub—evidently considering an uncovered tub a security risk to the president. Whatever the logic, their excess of protection proved useful, as Perle and Linhard sat and wrote on the board to revise Gorbachev's paper.

Meanwhile, the president was resting in the parlor corner armchair. We had fears of him fading at a critical juncture—something akin to what some historians claim happened with Franklin Roosevelt during the 1945 Yalta conference with Churchill and Stalin. Earlier that morning, Don Regan had told me that he was worried about the president's stamina.

But then, on second thought, he felt Reagan would be fine so long as Gorbachev stayed feisty. He would tire only if Gorbachev turned mild. Hearing that, I stopped worrying. There was no way Gorbachev could turn mild with SDI on the table.

The president was fatigued but never faded over that weekend, at least that I noticed. As a journeyman actor, he had been accustomed to staying alert during long and tiring shoots. At Reykjavik, he seemed ready for the next scene at every stage of the extended drama.

Nonetheless, he was antsy to leave. Reclining in that corner chair, he told us that, come what may, this would be it. This would be his last session, the end of Reykjavik.

"I told Nancy I'd be there, home for dinner. She'll be expecting me," he lamented, knowing that he wasn't going to fulfill his promise. We all nodded in empathy. I tried to offer consolation by saying that at least Mrs. Reagan would know where he was, that he wasn't up to no good. But the president was in no joking mood. He smiled faintly in my direction and repeated that he would go downstairs one time more. That would be it.

Years later, Ambassador Jack Matlock surmised that he personally made a big mistake by not insisting that Mrs. Reagan come to Reykjavik. With her there, he claimed, the president might have stayed another day or two, enabling the summit to end with a sweeping agreement.

While interesting, Matlock's argument presumes that the prime problem was one of time. It wasn't. The prime problem was one of substance—Gorbachev seeking to spike SDI, Reagan to protect or even enhance it. That gap would have remained, regardless of where Nancy Reagan happened to be.

ONCE PERLE AND LINHARD emerged with their bathtub redraft, we stood in a small circle, like in a Jewish minyan, while the president read it over.

He made one change in wording, which highlighted that extensive SDI research was *already* permitted under the ABM Treaty terms. This change budged the U.S. stance even further from Gorbachev's.

With that modification made, Reagan took another look. I offered that confining SDI to laboratories would kill it, mentioning—in a pedestrian way, at least it seems now—that no one would fly in a plane or drive in a car that had been limited to laboratory research. The president thanked me more warmly than my rather mundane comment merited.

Years later, as myths began to envelop Reykjavik, the claim arose in conservative circles that, at that crucial juncture, hard-liners surrounding Reagan argued with the pragmatists, and heroically kept him from caving on SDI. It's a nice story—more interesting than that of 1920s gas masks—but it didn't happen.

Some among us—including Matlock, as he stated years later—would have signed on to Gorbachev's deal in a jiffy. But no one suggested doing so, then or at any time over the weekend. We knew where the president stood. And the president knew where he stood—he wanted no further restrictions on SDI research, period; and would tolerate none, full stop—and that was all he needed to know.

Paper in hand, Reagan headed for the parlor door.

"Good luck, Mr. President," several of us called out, realizing that he was walking into a big moment in his life, in our lives, indeed in history.

After he closed the door behind him, we stood in silence for a moment, looking at one another, before resuming our seated places.

Almost immediately, however, the door was flung open and the president walked back in, stopping in the middle of the parlor. He said that he just wanted to make sure—to make *real* sure—that what we were proposing here, in this paper here, was good for the country.

Looking around at us, he asked something like: "Are each of you sure about this?" He looked at Shultz—"George?"—who nodded. The president proceeded along—John? Don? Ken? Richard?—finding no one with reservations. Reagan wrote of that moment in his diaries, "All our people thought I'd done exactly right."

For a decade afterward, I wondered what had prompted that

presidential U-turn. Then, in 1996, on the summit's tenth anniversary, I retraced his steps and noticed an oddly placed window a few steps outside our parlor. The president could have glanced through that window and seen the commotion outside, reminding him of the high stakes and high hopes of the minutes ahead.

Regardless of why he did it, it was a smart thing for him to have done. At such times, emotion can easily overwhelm reason. The desire for success can trump the benefits that may derive from a deal. Such risks get heightened within a group, with the shared emotions and collective adrenalin. By polling each of us individually, he was holding each of us accountable, thereby breaking down any groupthink. It took less than two minutes, but it has loomed large in my estimation of Reagan's leadership qualities over the past quarter century.

The roll call completed, the president again headed downstairs. There was nothing left for us to do but to wait and see how history would unfold.

THE SUNDAY-MORNING TV TALK shows were desperate. Broadcasting live from Reykjavik had incurred considerable expense and raised even higher expectations.

Because of the time difference, the summit was supposed to be over by the shows' air time. Hence there would be, finally, something real to report. *This Week with David Brinkley* promised its viewers "to keep up with developments," but there were no developments, besides another delay, to keep up with.

"There was plenty of excited speculation about what was going on behind closed white doors," reported Tom Shales of the *Washington Post* in his piece, "The Valleys and Peaks of Summit TV." Every one of the 3,117 accredited journalists wished they could be with us behind those closed white doors in order to end their excited speculation.

Yet those of us behind those doors didn't know any more than anyone on the other side. We were all excited, all speculating on just what might happen.

"I am sorry to have kept you so long," the president told Gorbachev as he took his seat across the small table. "But you know the trouble Americans have getting along with each other," he added with a smile.

"I've spent a long time trying very hard to meet your desires. This has to be my final effort," he told the general secretary and read the American redraft aloud.

"I notice that the reference to laboratory testing had disappeared," Gorbachev said sharply. Reagan finessed by explaining other parts of his paper, but Gorbachev interrupted.

"I will ask you again: Has the language on laboratory testing been omitted on purpose? I'm just trying to clarify the U.S. proposal."

"It has been left out on purpose," the president fessed up and again changed the subject by asking Gorbachev which offensive weapons he wanted eliminated. For several minutes, they tossed around different weapons categories.

"I'm ready to include all the nuclear weapons we can," Reagan said.

"Then we should include the whole triad," Gorbachev replied, matching the ante and raising it.

"Okay, let's take out 'strategic.'" Reagan crossed out the word on his paper. "Then all ballistic missiles would be eliminated." Gorbachev posed more questions and Reagan gave more confusing responses. Finally, he thought they were finished.

"Is that the only thing you object to in our proposal?"

"I do not think there will be a difference between the two sides," Gorbachev said optimistically, once they sorted out just which weapons to cut.

"If we add 'all offensive ballistic missiles,' then we can come to closure," Shultz figured, tossing in a new, and yet another nuclear category. For Reagan, who had his eye on the big prize, all such talk amounted to diving for the capillaries.

"All this can be sorted out later, when we do the paper" on just what's included—whether, he ran through, "cruise missiles, battlefield weapons, sub-launched or the like."

"It would be fine with me if we eliminated all nuclear weapons," was a bold move that then popped in Reagan's mind. Saying this aloud may have even startled himself, as he then scribbled on a piece of paper, "George, am I right?" and passed it to his left. Shultz leaned over and whispered in the good left ear: "Absolutely, yes."

"We can do that. We can eliminate them," Gorbachev said.

So charged was the moment that Shultz—nicknamed "Buddha" around Washington for his imperturbability—exclaimed "Let's do it!"

"If we can agree to eliminate all nuclear weapons," Reagan chimed in, "I think we can turn this over to our Geneva folks with that understanding, for them to draft up an agreement. Then you can come to the U.S. and sign it." The president's three fondest wishes in the world—scrapping nuclear weapons and getting Gorbachev to Washington while still preserving SDI—would be achieved in one fell swoop.

"Well, all right," the general secretary said. "Here we have a chance for an agreement."

AT THIS POINT, WE need to freeze the frame and consider what had just happened. Not only had the president of the United States and the general secretary of the Communist Party of the Soviet Union just agreed to dismiss the two officers standing there in the corridor, clinging to their deadly briefcases. They wished to dismiss them all, with all their blasted footballs, for all time. From this moment sprang one of the most enduring legacies of Reykjavik.

Of course, this outpouring of ecstasy, this tantalizing vision of a nonnuclear utopia, could not long endure.

"I now want to turn to the ABM Treaty," Gorbachev said before warning, "I am apprehensive about this. It is incomprehensible why research, development, and testing of SDI should go on and *not* be confined to the laboratories."

"I have promised the American people I would not give up SDI," Reagan said, again explaining that SDI did not entail weapons in space and again charging the Soviets with violating the ABM Treaty.

"I will not destroy the possibility of proceeding with SDI. I could not confine its work to the laboratory."

"If this your final position?" Gorbachev asked. "That you *could* not confine work to the laboratory?"

"Yes," Reagan said. "There is some research that can be done in the lab stage, but then you must go outdoors to try out what has been done in the lab."

When Gorbachev tried his argument again, Reagan shot back: "I cannot give in."

"Is that your last word?" Gorbachev asked.

"Yes," Reagan said and explained why. "I have a problem you do not have. If anyone criticizes you, they go to jail" he said to an increasingly uncomfortable Gorbachev.

"But I have people who were the most outspoken critics of the Soviet Union over the years, the so-called right-wing and esteemed journalists, who are the first to criticize me. In fact, they're kicking my brains out already."

"I assume you are addressing me from a position of equality, as a leader of another country, on a confidential basis," Gorbachev said and went on, "That's why I will be frank. I believe that you are three steps away from being a great president. If we signed what we have discussed and agreed to, these would be very major steps," so long as SDI was confined to laboratories.

"If this is not possible, then we can say goodbye and forget everything we've discussed," he warned. "Reykjavik is the last opportunity—at least, for me." They had "built a huge reservoir of constructive spirit." Now everything was up to Reagan. "With support from your side, we can solve very important problems. If we are able to do this, your critics would *not* open their mouths. The peoples of the U.S., of the Soviet Union, of the whole world would cheer. If, however, you cannot agree with our proposals, the people will say that what we have discussed will have to be left for another generation." And then Gorbachev added his usual swipe: "You have not made a single substantial, major step in my direction" all weekend long.

Shevardnadze then spoke up, breaking his long silence with a flourish, which the man from Hollywood must have admired.

"The two sides are so close to accomplishing a historic task, to decisions of such historic significance, that if future generations read the minutes of these meetings, and saw how close we have come, but how we did not use these opportunities, they will never forgive us."

After Shevardnadze's grand historical sweep, Reagan said that he would speak to Gorbachev "as one political leader to another political leader." He had "been attacked" for coming to Reykjavik, and had "given up a long span of time" to stay there. He now needed Gorbachev's help.

"I ask this one thing of you."

"I have said everything I have to say," Gorbachev replied.

"Listen once again to what I am proposing," Reagan urged and reread the U.S. position.

"It is a question of one word," he asserted, referring to "laboratories." The abolition of all nuclear weapons, indeed, the fate of the world, "should not be turned down over one word.

"We have the possibility of getting along as no two American and Soviet leaders have ever before," Reagan offered. "I'm asking you for a favor. And this is important to me, and what I can do with you in the future. But you're refusing to do me this one favor."

Indeed, Gorbachev was, since if he did not confine SDI's development to laboratories, he "would be permitting the U.S. to destroy the Soviet Union's offensive nuclear potential. And you would not like it, if I had asked that of you. It would cause nervousness and suspicion.

"Yours is not an acceptable request. It cannot be met. You're not asking me for a favor, but for giving up a point of principle."

"But you're asking me to give up the thing I've promised not to give up," Reagan countered, considering SDI itself on the block.

"I have met your requirements," he went on. "What more is needed than that? I am asking you to change your mind—as a favor to me. Hopefully we can then go and bring peace to the world."

"I would be called a dummy and not a leader," Gorbachev replied strongly. "No, I cannot do it. Yet if we could agree to ban research in space, I would sign in two minutes. The point of differences is not one of words, but of principle. I moved everywhere I could," Gorbachev said, before getting in the last word, as he was wont to do.

"I have tried. My conscience is clear before you, Mr. President, and my people. What had depended upon me, I have done."

With nothing left to say around their small conference table, the president and the general secretary stood and gathered up their papers. Slowly, almost in shock, and wordlessly, almost in disbelief, they left the room.

Having no idea what was happening on the floor below us, the American team anxiously lounged around our parlor until a Secret Service agent stuck his head in and said tersely, "They've broken!"

The news, announced in such an odd phrase, aroused us from our torpor. We exchanged startled looks and rushed to the door. Halfway down the wooden staircase, I saw a scene I will never forget. Below in the hallway I caught a glimpse of Reagan's face, uncharacteristically flushed and glowering. At that instant, I turned to Max Kampelman on the staircase beside me, and said, "It's no deal."

With iconic moments in history, it is often hard to reconstruct exactly what happened. Ronald Reagan and Mikhail Gorbachev leaving that small room—after more than ten and a half hours of what Gorbachev later called "debates that became very pointed in their last stage"—was such a moment.

Those there agree that Reagan stuffed his papers into a plain manila folder while Gorbachev put his in his brown briefcase. Beyond that, the two notetakers differ. The American account, put inside parentheses, is anodyne:

(At that point, the President stood, and both leaders gathered up their papers and left the room. As they stood together before departing, Gorbachev asked the President to pass on his regards to Nancy Reagan. . . . On the steps outside, they shook hands and parted.)

As befits its more epic literature, the Russian version presents a more dramatic finale:

REAGAN: It's too bad we have to part this way. We were so close to an agreement. I think you didn't want to achieve an agreement anyway. I'm very sorry.

GORBACHEV: I am also very sorry it's happened this way. I wanted an agreement and did everything I could, if not more.

REAGAN: I don't know when we'll ever have another chance like this and whether we will meet soon.

GORBACHEV: I don't either.

The two leaders lingered for a moment in the hallway, Reagan in his light raincoat and Gorbachev in his dark overcoat, exchanging a few more tart words before they headed for the doorway.

Meanwhile, upstairs Sergei Akhromeyev said to Paul Nitze, "I hope you will forgive me. I tried. I was not the one to let you down," implying that Gorbachev and not the military was fixated on SDI. "Someone must bear the responsibility," he said before walking away.

The two leaders went outside. By now, it was cold and pitch black, with a slight drizzle.

According to what I heard minutes later, Gorbachev tried to soothe the president by saying something like "I don't know what we could have done differently." Reagan then put a finger up to Gorbachev's chest and said, "You could have said 'yes!'" and ducked into his limo. The other version, as recalled by many Russians and some Americans, is less John Wayne and more Gregory Peck as the men parted with a few polite words and a quick handshake.

While it remains uncertain what they said, it is certain what they felt. Both were heartsick.

Each showed this in his own way. It was strange—as were most things at Reykjavik—how the two men did a role reversal. Gorbachev, who had flashed his iron-toothed temper repeatedly over the two days, was now cool and collected while Reagan, who had remained calm through their contentious debates—except once, on the ABM Treaty—got suddenly riled. "I was mad," he admitted in *The Reagan Diaries*. Gorbachev "tried to act jovial, but I acted mad and it showed."

It certainly showed to Reagan's personal assistant, James Kuhn, who said in an oral history:

I'd just never seen Ronald Reagan that way before, had never seen him with such a look. I mean, he looked distraught to me, very upset, extremely, very taken aback, upset, borderline distraught. The only other time I saw him kind of down, but not nearly that down, was when Nancy went in to have her surgery for breast cancer.

On a more mundane level, I was then searching frantically for the car and driver assigned to me.

A presidential caravan, I knew by then, moves out fast and unforgivingly once the president comes aboard. Anyone else gets left behind. Something similar happened earlier that day, when one of Mrs. Gorbachev's KGB agents was left at the working sheep farm, having then to find his way back to town from the middle of nowhere.

Nearly all presidential motorcades are meticulously scripted. But this one, reflecting the disintegration that had just unfolded inside, was chaotic. Desperate not to be left behind, I jumped into the nearest black embassy car at hand, a few vehicles behind the president's already-accelerating limo. As I flung myself in, I caught sight of a sign taped on the windshield: ADMIRAL POINDEXTER.

The admiral was startled at my hurtling into the seat beside him and none too pleased. But his displeasure could not last long, as we arrived at the ambassador's residence only minutes later. We rushed inside and spotted the president pacing the living room, too aggravated to sit down. Kuhn recalled the scene much as I do now: "He's just standing there, just looking with this forlorn look on his face. Everybody stayed away from him. They knew. Everybody could tell he was very upset. I just worried because I'd never seen him that way."

Shultz arrived and told us that an agreement had not been reached, despite progress on big issues over the weekend. Above all, he said that he was awfully proud of the president—in fact, never prouder. But that was all he said.

When the Reykjavik notes were declassified years later, Sunday of the summit became clearer and richer. It is impressive, even moving, to see how committed both men were to reaching an agreement. How hard they worked, how hard they worked one another. How they cajoled, wooed, pleaded with each other to make one more concession, to drop one line, even to change one word.

Especially impressive was how each master politician, during the summit's final hour, looked at the problem from the other's perspective. Each addressed the other's political predicament back home—with Gorbachev claiming that Reagan's critics would not lambast but laud the overall deal and Reagan claiming that Kremlin colleagues would come to see SDI as beneficial for their country and the whole world.

Nonetheless, each had a line he could not cross. The problem wasn't one of offensive arms—the weapons that existed with their immense power—but of defensive systems, specifically SDI—that did not yet exist and had uncertain prospects.

By that time, October 1986, critiques of Star Wars centered on a few arguments. One had it that Star Wars would kill off arms control. As the head of the Arms Control Association put it, SDI "won't shoot down any missile, but it certainly will shoot down arms control." Its infusion of new technology, new threat to the Russians, new approach to deterrence—all endangered arms control as practiced since the Nixon years.

Reykjavik obliterated this argument. There SDI dominated, yet there arms control flourished and progressed as never before.

Other attacks had it that Star Wars would gut the ABM Treaty, ignite an arms race in space, and upend tried and true postwar deterrence. All these Gorbachev trotted out at Reykjavik at one time or another and all these Reagan countered.

But the main argument against Star Wars was that it would never work. This, to me, seemed an odd argument for such fierce opponents as the Federation of Atomic Scientists to make, since Reagan put no time frame on the research. Hence, for any federation of scientists—whether atomic, or not—to claim that it would *never* work—no matter what the breakthroughs in science and technology, no matter how long the research allotted—seemed downright unscientific. After all, we live in a world filled with telephones, televisions, computers, and mobile devices which were once considered unimaginable but which work fine. Nonetheless, the critics' quip that SDI will never work became their most potent line of attack.

Gorbachev never bought it. Quite the contrary, in fact. Not only did he believe that it *would* work but he believed that it was on the brink of working. He, along with Reagan, spoke as if it were practically working already.

Among Reykjavik's many ironies is how Reagan and Gorbachev reinforced each other on this perspective. The more passionately each spoke of SDI—Reagan, as "the greatest opportunity for peace in the Twentieth Century," Gorbachev as some space gun aimed squarely at Red Square—the more real and potent SDI became to the other.

After Reykjavik, whenever we testified or gave a speech on SDI, we'd traipse out Gorbachev's zealous opposition as a convincing argument in support of the U.S. program. If he was so determined to stop it, there must be something to our proceeding with it.

Once the president cooled down, Shultz scrambled from the ambassador's residence to brief the world press at the international press center. As was his wont, he had thought carefully about what he would say. Unfortunately, he hadn't thought much about how he would look.

As one colleague quipped, he looked as if a horse had just kicked him in the stomach. "Weary, glassy-eyed, his voice strained, the Secretary of State imparted the grim news," was how *Time* put it. It was bad enough that Reykjavik had ended with no joint statement, no date set for the summit in Washington, no telegenic smiles or perfunctory pleasantries.

Now the secretary of state was embodying a "great sense of disappointment," as he said in his opening remarks. Asked if Reykjavik might end all superpower talks for all time, he said, "I hope this doesn't end the chances of an agreement, but I can't say for sure about that."

Sunday Evening, October 12, 1986
Keflavik Air Force Base

When Reagan arrived at the American-operated NATO air base that adjoined the Keflavik airport, the weather—freezing, wet, and dark—matched his mood. He wanted to get out of town, fast. After two days of adrenaline and absence, he was tired and longing to be back home with Nancy.

His motorcade had made a mad dash of the thirty miles to Keflavik, with sirens blaring and lights flashing. The commander in chief had planned to quickly thank the U.S. troops stationed at Keflavik and head off. Now, though, he had a more important reason for addressing them, as he had to say something about the summit's demise. Here, at least, he had the friendliest possible audience for this delicate, distasteful task.

In a black van several vehicles behind the presidential limo, speech-writer Pat Buchanan was scribbling as he rode. He had already written the planned thanks to the troops, but he now needed to add a paragraph up front on the summit. It had to be carefully crafted, since this would be the only part of the speech broadcast across America and around the world.

Things had moved so fast that neither Shultz nor the president had had a chance to tell Buchanan what had happened. All he knew—all any of us knew then—was that the herculean effort had ended in failure. And Pat knew that Ronald Reagan didn't do failure. Writing his remarks was thus a daunting task.

ONCE THE PRESIDENT WAS standing before the troops, his foul mood lifted. In the grand hangar, he began to become himself again—confident, smiling, at ease with the three thousand airmen and their families there with him.

This was a treat they never imagined having, especially being stationed in Iceland. Their having waited in the hangar for more than seven hours—due to the unscheduled, extended afternoon session—was soon forgotten.

"It's good to feel so at home," the president opened his remarks. He apologized "for being so late," explaining that he and Gorbachev felt "further discussions would be valuable."

"I called Nancy and told her I wouldn't be home for dinner." He paused, and added with a sly smile, "She said she understood." Then, after just a beat, the old actor produced a perfect worried-husband look before delivering his punch line: "In about six and a half hours, I'll find out!" Reagan basked in the laughter and warm applause.

He then explained that great progress had been made on cutting nuclear weapons until an obstacle arose. In his deepest voice, with his gravest expression, he said, "The Soviet Union insisted that we sign an agreement that would deny to me, and to all future presidents, for ten years"—Reagan shook his head slightly here, signaling the unacceptability of what was to come—"the right to develop, test, and deploy defenses against nuclear missiles for the people of the Free World." In full Clint Eastwood–Dirty Harry mode, he said: *"This we could not,"* paused, and added, *"and will not do."*

The troops and families greeted his words with cheers, while the TV cameras panned their admiring faces. While it sounded great, it was a bit off the mark. We *had* agreed to a ten-year extension of the ABM Treaty. The stumbling block had instead been confining SDI research to laboratories and Gorbachev's tying this provision to the offensive arm cuts previously agreed-upon. But no matter, as few noticed the misspeak.

The president then said that he had come to thank them all. "Ladies and gentlemen of our armed forces, on behalf of a grateful commander-in-chief, I salute you." Again the hangar shook with an ear-shattering roar.

In his free-associating mind, this mention of saluting led Reagan off script. "I can't resist telling you a little story . . . [which] has to do with saluting." When he "got this job" as president, and started flying aboard Air Force One and Marine One, he wanted to salute the soldiers as he boarded and disembarked. But he had been taught—when "a second lieutenant of the Horse Cavalry, back in the World War II days"—that it was improper for anyone not wearing a uniform to salute.

Then one evening at the marine commandant's quarters in Washington, he was "getting a couple of highballs and didn't know what to do," and so went over to the commandant and said, " 'Look, I know all the rules about saluting in civilian clothes and all, but if I am the commander-in-chief, there ought to be a regulation that would permit me to return a salute.' "

The commandant replied with "some words of wisdom. He said, 'I think that if you did, no one would say anything.'" And ever since that night, he happily saluted the troops.

With this tale told, he was now ready to close. "Well, it's time to go now. Nancy's waiting with dinner. [Laughter] After all, Congress is still in session, and I have to get back and keep an eye on them. [More laughter] Sometimes they get strange ideas about reducing pay rates for the military. But don't worry, I'll never let them. [Cheers and applause]." That somehow reminded him of another "little story" he then told, about some guys acting as stupidly as those military-pay-cutting congressmen.

What was billed as perfunctory departure remarks had now gone a half hour. Nonetheless, another story popped into his mind—this one about General George Marshall. When asked if America had a "secret weapon" during World War II, Marshall responded that we sure did—"the best blankety-blank kids in the world."

This, a favorite among the Reagan repertory of tales, had been told to us in private—many times, in fact—with Marshall's statement rendered as "the best God-damned kids in the world." But Reagan couldn't bring himself to curse in front of these fresh-faced kids.

"Well, I have to tell you," he said, looking left and right across the hangar, "we still got 'em—that secret weapon. God bless all of you! Thank you very much."

After still more cheers—reenlistments must have soared that year—he finally said good-bye and boarded Air Force One for the ride home to Nancy.

Early Sunday Evening, October 12, 1986
In Downtown Reykjavik

In his remarks at Keflavik, Reagan said of future dealings with the Soviet Union: "We will continue the effort." Unbeknownst to him, his chief of staff had said just the opposite an hour earlier.

Seated in the Holt Hotel lobby, Don Regan said during his live television interview, "No, there will not be another summit. . . . The Soviets are the ones who refused to make the deal. It shows them up for what they are. . . . They're not really interested in doing" a deal.

At about the same time, Gorbachev began speaking in a rented theater downtown. He was as energized at the outset of his remarks as the president had become at the conclusion of his, and became even more animated as he went on—and on. "There's Gonzo Gorby," someone on the delegation cracked.

Reagan had delivered two or three core sentences and then winged it for thirty minutes. Gorbachev carried on for an hour and forty minutes, without any core sentences. Mark Twain once quipped that few sinners are saved after the first twenty minutes of a sermon. Likewise, few reporters are convinced after the first twenty minutes of an explanation.

Gorbachev accused the president of coming to Reykjavik "empty-handed" or, worse, "empty-pocketed" (which must have sounded better in Russian). He condemned the United States for "surreptitiously developing a capability to give it an advantage." Of Reagan's insistence on testing SDI outside laboratories, Gorbachev asked rhetorically, "Who's going to accept that?" And he delivered the answer: "It would take a madman to accept that, and madmen are mainly in hospitals."

Gorbachev's discourse was more emotional than factual. For one thing, there was nothing "surreptitiously" happening on SDI. Indeed, more was being said about it in public than was being done on it in private. And as for what a madman would or would not accept, Gorbachev was complaining about something—allowing research on defensive systems outside of laboratories—that had been allowed under the ABM Treaty since 1972. All weekend long, he sought to impose that new restriction, never acknowledging that it applied already.

After reporters became bored by Gorbachev's talk, which did not take long, a few approached me to sit for interviews. I agreed, figuring that as long as I didn't look as bad as Shultz or come across as angry and misinformed as Regan, I would do okay.

I sat in a corner of the Holt Hotel lobby with the team from *CBS Morning News* and then went outside in the cold to speak with Peter Jennings. He opened his TV Special ominously: "After an extended session this morning—optimism, good cheer, and the suggestion by both sides that progress was being made at the Reykjavik summit. Tonight, when the summit was over, a somber mood. No banter, and no progress. The summit in Iceland was as much a failure this evening as it was thought to be a success this morning."

After breaking for an ad for Extra Strength Bufferin—"good for severe headaches during times of high stress"—Jennings turned to me. While sleep-deprived and drained by the emotional roller-coaster ride all weekend long, especially that day, I managed to appear perky, although unshaven.

I told Jennings that both sides had succeeded well in agreeing to cut nuclear weapons. But just as the president had been willing to sit down with the Soviets, he had to stand up to them when they proposed killing SDI. Jennings asked if the summit crash would trigger a new arms race, which I dismissed out of hand.

More interesting were Jennings's interviews with his ABC experts, who, he told his viewers, "had followed these negotiations in a very intimate way." Of course the only thing his reporters could have followed in any intimate way was the permutations of Raisa Gorbachev's wardrobe and wanderings about town.

The first intimate-negotiations follower was ABC's Moscow bureau chief, Walter Rogers, who claimed that Gorbachev "dealt President Reagan out of the arms control discussions." The view from Western Europe came from ABC's chief diplomatic correspondent, Barrie Dunsmore: "Certainly, in Western Europe . . . there will be *great* disappointment" now that the agreement to remove intermediate missiles from Europe was off. This was stated as fact, despite our hearing all afternoon that the Western European leaders would feel greater relief if the missiles stayed put.

Jennings then turned to his ace White House correspondent Sam Donaldson. By then, Donaldson had become something special in Washington, his aggressive manner being heralded in journalism schools and parodied on *Saturday Night Live*.

A merry pantomime had unfolded whenever the president came or went on the White House lawn. The press would be corralled behind barriers, from which Donaldson would yell out questions. The president would look in Donaldson's direction, cup his hand behind his ear, and shake his head sadly while shifting his gaze to the waiting chopper, indicating that he couldn't hear the question because of the loud, whirling blades. Years later, Donaldson told me that he once shouted to ask where Reagan had bought a new sports jacket he was then wearing. As usual, the chief executive finessed the question with the ritual. A half hour after the ear cupping and rotor pointing, a startled Donaldson got a call directly from the president, who had only two words for him: "At Bloomingdale's."

Now Donaldson declared that Reykjavik had been a "very bad setback for the president" with "the magic of the Reagan persona gone." He foresaw the end of the trail: "Time has just about run out on the Reagan presidency." Now the Kremlin leadership "will just wait him out." In short, "we're going nowhere."

Hearing that as part of a broadcast I had just done, I felt like taking some Extra Strength Bufferin.

AFTER SITTING FOR THE interviews, I gathered my bags and got ready to head for the airport. I couldn't wait to get on the plane and collapse. I had little sleep over the past three days, around ten or eleven hours in all. While being on the inside of a big-stakes, high-drama event like a superpower summit is exhilarating, at some point, exhilaration turns into exhaustion.

While waiting for my ride out to Keflavik, Don Regan asked me to ride back on the press plane in order to brief the news-starved journalists. I initially flattered myself by thinking that he asked me because I had ridden on the press plane back from the Geneva summit, with some favorable stories coming out. Or that he had just seen my interview with Jennings and thought that had gone okay. But Regan most surely asked me since I was standing within his line of sight just when he remembered that someone was needed on that plane.

Regardless, I declined. I was in neither the shape nor the mood to spend the next several hours schmoozing with the press, which had already proclaimed the summit a bust. I couldn't do it and wouldn't do it. This I told Regan firmly.

AN HOUR LATER, I was walking through the Keflavik airport, which was dark and dead. Air Force One and the official backup plane had already departed and all commercial flights had been canceled for that night, due to heightened security.

The press plane was scheduled to take off an hour after the president's, so that journalists could file their stories on Reagan's speech to the troops, Gorbachev's and Shultz's downtown performances, and whatever individual interviews they could get with members of either delegation.

It was depressing being there virtually alone in the night. Although I was as exhausted and tired as I had ever been—and would ever be—I still realized that this had been the most exciting and demanding days of my life. That it, in fact, had been the best weekend of my life—with its high stakes, constant challenges, and roller-coaster emotions.

With all this going on in my head, I walked across the wet, wind-swept tarmac and climbed the steps, onto the press plane.

CHAPTER 7

Departures and Immediate Fallout

Reagan's Flight Home
Aboard Air Force One

By the time Ronald Reagan settled in his aircraft that Sunday night, it was almost 10:00 p.m. It had been a long day, a frustrating day, a disappointing day, and now he was spent. The adrenaline that flowed during the heated bargaining was long gone, as was the kinetic energy between the soldiers and their commander in chief at Keflavik.

Alone in his cabin, the president perked up a bit when the Air Force steward offered him dinner. After finishing, the president ambled aft to the staff area to say hello, flash a smile, and tell a joke or two. He stayed long enough to be sociable and then returned to his cabin.

But he was too tired to sleep and he was haunted by one of the saddest phrases in any language: it might have been. How much different, how much better the world would have become, if only. The Reagan-Gorbachev Pact could have been the modern rendition of the Kellogg-Briand Pact, but one that stuck, one with real impact.

It might have been, if only Gorbachev hadn't raised all that business about laboratories. Why did he have to do that? Couldn't he see what was at stake? A new era of world peace . . . if only . . .

At least, the president had kept his pledge to the American people, and that was good. But better still would have been a nuclear-free world, forevermore. So much better . . . it might have been . . .

While the president was musing in the front of the plane, the press pool was laying siege to White House Press Secretary Larry Speakes in the back. Lacking any guidance and knowing nothing of the arms issues, Speakes resorted to what he did know, football. The summit was like a Super Bowl, where "the president stayed for overtime. He went 99 yards, but didn't get across the goal line."

Hence the "high Administration official" aboard Air Force One was portraying Reykjavik as much a defeat as George Shultz's morbid, postmortem briefing. We were not helping our own cause.

With the president closeted in his cabin, the staff was left to its own devices. This was nothing new. Few "action items"—as the military calls unwritten directives—emanated from the front cabin of Air Force One or the Oval Office of the White House. Although Reagan was always clear in his views and intentions, he was seldom clear in his instructions. Just as Horace Walpole once said of Prime Minister William Pitt, Reagan "kept aloof from all details, drew magnificent plans, and left others to find magnificent means."

After finishing their dinners, the senior staff aboard—Don Regan, John Poindexter, and Speakes—huddled in the conference area to devise some magnificent means for the president's magnificent plans. They realized that they first had to clean up the mess Shultz and Speakes had inadvertently made, before moving onto a higher plane. And they appreciated that the United States no longer had the PR field all to itself, with the Soviets being ham-handed.

Reykjavik had changed this, too. As *Time* reported, "The Soviet effort in Reykjavik [was] a far cry from their past stentorian sloganeering." Gorbachev's new-age PR team had opened its well-staffed media center with flourish. "'I welcome you with all my heart to this press center,' said the gray-haired Soviet propagandist Albert Vlasov, with perhaps a trifle too much earnestness," *Time* reported, and quoted a U.S. official who was perturbed "not at their side [since] that type of PR is perfectly within the rules. I'm perturbed by the lack of it from our own team."

There would no longer be that lack of it from our team. The airborne officials launched an all-out, no-holds-barred campaign to rescue Reykjavik and the administration's reputation, using the state-of-the-art Air Force One communications apparatus to gin up their staffs back in Washington.

After what felt like an awfully long flight, the big blue and white plane touched down at Andrews Air Force Base a bit after 10:30 p.m. Washington time.

Gorbachev's Flight Back
Aboard Aeroflot Ilyushin Il-62M

The Soviet first couple spent Sunday night aboard the *Georg Ots*. Perhaps because being afloat was, as Raisa put it, so romantic, Gorbachev wasn't taking the summit's failure as hard as Reagan.

After a good night, the Gorbachevs headed for the NATO air base to board their aircraft. The Soviet jet had a dozen ordinary seats up front and Gorbachev's wood-paneled sitting room, with its adjoining bedroom, in the center of the fuselage.

Crammed into that paneled sitting room with key aides, Gorbachev said he was more disappointed than depressed by the outcome. He was pleased that it was "quite easy to reach an understanding" on intermediate and strategic arms. His aides may have realized, even if he somehow didn't, that this had been made "quite easy" by Gorbachev conceding to the Americans.

Moving from policy to personality, Gorbachev cut Reagan considerable slack. The president had taken bad positions, all right, but that was because Reagan "was not free in making his decisions."

Although bighearted, this was wrongheaded, since Reagan at Reykjavik had been flying solo. He was free from his advisers' opinions, primarily because he didn't ask his advisers for their opinions much. Gorbachev never got that it was Reagan who concocted and revered SDI, not his advisers nor the right-wingers around him. SDI was *his* program. Only after he created and launched it did other conservatives buy into it.

Gorbachev urged patience, to give the president time to "think everything over, let him seek counsel." Then, after that pause to reflect, he, Gorbachev, would make "one more try." Meanwhile, "we can wait" and see what unfolds, while not taking "back the proposals we made at Reykjavik."

For Gorbachev, the Reykjavik glass was very much half full. "Everyone saw that agreement was possible. I am even more of an optimist after Reykjavik. In no sense would I call Reykjavik a failure."

Appreciative of the stagecraft of statecraft, Gorbachev said that he had enjoyed "the drama of Reykjavik." For the summit to take "quite dramatic shape," as it did, was a personal thrill.

Returning to Reagan—the topic that intrigued him most—Gorbachev complained that he had come "without a specific program, merely to pick the fruit and put it in his basket," thereby inadvertently reminding his colleagues again that Reagan had picked and basketed *his* fruit at Reykjavik, while he had picked nothing from Reagan's basket.

As the plane sped across Europe, Gorbachev reaffirmed that he had climbed aboard Reagan's goal of deep nuclear cuts. In words that could have come out of the president's mouth, Gorbachev said that before Reykjavik, "the conversation was only about limiting nuclear arms," but there it became "about reduction and liquidation."

In expounding such views, avoiding personal animosity, remaining upbeat, seeking deep nuclear cuts, loving the summit drama, and anticipating progress—Gorbachev was becoming distinctly Reaganesque.

After more conversation with his staff—which, with Gorbachev, largely if not entirely flowed one way—he excused himself and ducked into the adjoining cabin to enjoy lunch with Raisa, certainly not meatloaf.

Reagan's Arrival
Andrews Air Force Base and the White House

As Air Force One taxied into position, the president was thrilled to spot Nancy, vivid in one of her signature red suits, awaiting him on the tarmac. After the huge door swung open revealing the presidential seal on the inside, he bound down the stairs, gave the waiting U.S. Air Force general a snappy salute—of the kind he had described earlier that night—hugged his wife and kissed her on the lips.

They walked arm in arm toward the white-topped presidential helicopter, so engrossed in each other as to be oblivious to a group of reporters off to the side, waiting there to record the president's first words upon arriving back. This was to be the opening gambit of the administration's aggressive media ground game. But it didn't happen. The president may not have been informed, or had forgotten, or just chucked the plan once he spotted Nancy. The reporters, holding pen in one hand, pad in the other, were thus left standing on the tarmac, wondering why they had been assembled there for big breaking news.

Fifteen minutes later, Marine One came to rest on the South Lawn. The president was surprised to see that, even though it was near midnight, his daughter Maureen was there, along with Vice President George H. W. Bush, a dozen or so cabinet officers, and key White House staff members—all waving or clapping a welcome home.

There too were reporters, off to the side. Some shouted questions, Sam Donaldson–like, about Reykjavik's crash ending. The president, reverting to his ear-cupping pantomime, waved, smiled, and shouted back, "Tune in tomorrow night." He had remembered that the White House Press Office had reserved air time Monday night for "An Address to the Nation from the Oval Office" on the summit.

The president would have to review and rewrite those remarks, and begin briefing members of Congress, the press, and key foreign leaders the first thing the next morning. Meanwhile, though, he would enjoy being home with Nancy, sleeping soundly in what he liked to call "this public housing," at 1600 Pennsylvania Avenue.

Gorbachev's Arrival
Vnukovo Airport, Moscow, USSR

The rain falling on Moscow when the Aeroflot Ilyushin II-62M landed was heavier than the rain falling on Reykjavik when it had taken off and the temperature was colder.

While descending the stairs, Gorbachev pulled the gray fedora down over his head, just as he had done in Reykjavik four days earlier. A dozen stone-faced elders had been shuffling around arranging themselves in proper pecking order to welcome their leader home. Closest to the stairs was Andrei Gromyko, who might have been suppressing an "I could have told you so" smirk. Standing behind him was KGB chief Viktor Chebrikov, who was masking delight that all that business in Iceland had come to naught.

Gorbachev worked his way down the line of party elders, shaking hands and bestowing kisses. Near the end was one man who was not a member of the Central Committee, but had the honor of being there since he was effectively the mayor of Moscow. His name was Boris Yeltsin.

Two decades earlier, the Beatles had composed the song "Back in the U.S.S.R." to open their breakthrough 1968 LP *The Beatles*, popularly known as "The White Album." Now, at Vnukovo, life was imitating art, as the bundled-up officials who had seen Gorbachev off earlier were there to welcome him home: "Come and keep your comrade warm . . . back in the U.S.S.R. / Hey, you don't know how lucky you are!"

Gorbachev muttered some platitudes to his comrades, but made no arrival remarks. That was just as well, since he had talked plenty already. Soviet state television had broadcast his entire hundred-minute outburst from Reykjavik. In case anyone missed it—presumably not in response to public demand for its rerun—all one hundred minutes had been rebroadcast earlier that Monday evening. Then late on Monday would come new footage of Gorbachev's arrival accompanied by a *third* showing of his Reykjavik performance.

Meanwhile—just as Reagan had told Gorbachev would happen—the Soviet airwaves carried nothing of Shultz's press conference, nor of Reagan's remarks at Keflavik, nor of any other American's. It was an all-channels, all-hours, all-Gorbachev extravaganza for Soviet television viewers and radio listeners.

While her husband was going through the highly choreographed welcome ceremony, Raisa Gorbachev—who had just given the performance of a lifetime—walked off the plane through the back door to resume her life as a public nonperson named Raisa Maksimovna back in the U.S.S.R.

Airborne Agony
Aboard the Press Plane

There surely are worse things than being the "high administration official" on a White House press plane after a stunning summit. Most people would consider it a grand pleasure, if not a distinct honor.

But most people haven't done it. It isn't a barrel of fun, even in the best of times. Reporters are pushy, verging on rude, and often going beyond verging. Their deportment isn't improved by stewards passing through the aisles looking for half-filled glasses waiting to be replenished. The atmosphere is raucous.

Moreover, the working press plane has no good place to work the press on the plane. The briefer must stand in an aisle, shouting responses to shouted questions. That becomes awfully wearying awfully quickly.

Not fun in the best of times, post-Reykjavik was as far from the best of times as crashing. Granted, there was a sudden geyser of news with the post-summit remarks of Reagan, Gorbachev, Regan, Shultz, and others. But all these had spoken in black-and-white terms befitting superpower geopolitics, when the press wanted summit stories in full Technicolor.

I was airborne to give that color but did not do it well. My sentences came out convoluted, even more than usual. Worse still, I had not been in the room with Reagan and Gorbachev, and thus could not provide the you-are-there feel—"after pulling up his left sock, Gorbachev said sternly . . ."—which the press seeks.

I *had* been active in the bubble, during the nocturnal negotiations, at mealtimes and in the embassy parlor sessions with the president, but I didn't feel right about sharing these exchanges with the press. Aside from the strategic progress made on Saturday night, the experts' meetings had been arcane. And arcane wasn't what these reporters were after.

Besides, the press had already made up its collective mind: Reykjavik had been a bust. Reagan's crazy crush on Star Wars had blocked the dawn of a new era of world peace.

I argued, as I believed, that the summit had been a success, that we had accomplished more to cut nuclear arsenals in twelve hours at Reykjavik than negotiators had accomplished in seven years at Geneva.

Granted, the counterargument had some merit—that such cuts remained theoretical, since the summit ended without an agreement on anything. I countered their counter by saying: Quite right, but that was just for now. The Soviet stall would be temporary. So, before long, we'd resume the bargaining on the strong foundation established at Reykjavik. How long? No telling.

Moreover, I claimed that the prevailing press narrative—that SDI sank the summit—was wrong. It was Gorbachev who sank the summit—by tying SDI to nuclear cuts. It was nothing he had to do, nothing that anyone had ever expected him to do. And damaging for him to have done it.

Admittedly, it was a tough sell—to be honest, no sell. Still, I gave it my all, for more than five awful hours. My focus was on what had been accomplished; theirs on what might have been accomplished. Mine on the future value of SDI; theirs on the present blockage by SDI. Mine on the strength of Reagan; theirs on his obstinacy.

Amidst this tug of war, a reporter asked for a private minute with me. The others balked at any individual interview during a press pool opportunity, but she assured her colleagues that our conversation would have nothing whatsoever to do with Reykjavik.

After grudging nods, we headed for the only quasi-private spot on the plane, just outside the malodorous lavatories. Our conversation would have been memorable, even without that.

The reporter asked me about a weird rumor she had heard, something out of the Middle East somewhere, but wasn't sure. Something about Americans and/or Israelis supplying arms to Iran, maybe even missiles, she ventured.

Okay, she admitted that all this sounded crazy. But she felt that she had to ask about it. Could I comment on it? Could I guide her on the story? What had I heard of it?

I agreed that it sounded wacko and said that my responses to her questions were: No, no, and nothing.

Nothing like that could have happened, I told her, but added that she shouldn't take my word for it. While I didn't know anything about it, I wouldn't—even if it were true, which it couldn't be. She, too, doubted it, but felt the need to check it out.

I apologized for not being more helpful; she thanked me for the time; and I walked away from the lavatories area thinking, "Boy, you hear the craziest stuff on the press plane!"

The reporter was still checking it out a few weeks later when a Lebanese newspaper, *Al-Shiraa*, broke a story about the craziest stuff.

As the facts came out, one month before Reykjavik, Reagan's former national security adviser Bud McFarlane, along with four other Americans, had traveled to Iran on Irish passports, carrying a Bible signed by the president and a cake baked in the shape of a key—the edible embodiment of our unlocking the relationship with the so-fashioned Iranian moderates. The very morning we landed back from Reykjavik, after CIA director William Casey called me at home, he told Colonel Oliver North that "this whole thing was coming unraveled, and that things ought to be 'cleaned up.'" This Colonel North took to mean that he should shred every document he could lay his hands on. And this he duly did, with the able assistance of his attractive secretary, Fawn Hall.

For the Reagan administration, the worst of times lay ahead.

Monday, October 13, 1986
Reykjavik, Iceland

All around town, yellow wooden sawhorses were being broken down and removed. Piles of communications gear in the international press center were being packed up, so that grammar school could resume on Wednesday morning. Plenty of hotel rooms were available at reasonable rates. Taxis were easy to hail and the traffic again flowed smoothly. The Wednesday ban on alcohol sales and the Thursday TV blackout were in effect.

Protective screens around Hofdi House were taken down and loaded onto flatbed trucks, along with the planks of the wooden bleachers on the front lawn. The top-secret, high-tech equipment in the basement was unplugged and packed off by U.S. and Soviet technicians to CIA and KGB headquarters. Hólmfríður Karlsdóttir resumed her goodwill tour in Asia as Miss World and Miss Young Iceland resumed her normal after-school activities.

By nightfall, there was but one reminder that Reykjavik had been the epicenter of world attention the day before. A line of local citizens formed in front of Hofdi House. Two by two, they passed through what had been the world's most photographed front door. And, for a moment or so, they could file into the small conference room and, beneath the slyly smiling portrait of Bjarni Benediktsson, sit in the chairs they might have imagined were still warm from Reagan and Gorbachev.

Early Monday, October 13, 1986
Arlington, Virginia

It was after 2:00 a.m. by the time I arrived home in Virginia. In five hours, I was booked to appear live on NBC's *Today* show—at the same time that *CBS Morning News* would be broadcasting the interview taped in Reykjavik on Sunday afternoon.

Unfortunately, the White House press staffer who booked me for *Today* had neglected to arrange a car to take me from the house to the NBC studios. Normally, this would have been no problem—I had driven myself there many times—but there was no "normal" where Reykjavik was concerned. Upon arriving home, I learned that our family car—purchased third-hand from my brother years before—had, after months on life support, chosen this weekend to expire. Perhaps in sympathy, the deep freeze in our garage also gave out.

Despite the ungodly hour, I awakened a neighbor, who helped me load the packets that were, literally, sweating blood, onto our daughters' wagon. We wheeled the red meat in the red wagon over to his house and stuffed the oozing packets into his freezer. He offered me his car to get to the NBC studio in a few hours.

The interview went well enough, considering. After the airborne hours, my message was pretty well honed, even if not particularly well-delivered. When the interviewer led with failure, I countered with success. While he looked back, I looked forward. When he claimed that SDI had been an obstacle to reaching an agreement, I countered that SDI drove the Soviets to bargain more seriously than ever before. When he pointed out that no further arms talks were scheduled, I predicted they would be and then go forth on the basis of the Reykjavik breakthroughs.

Back from the studio, I was looking forward to desperately needed rest and recuperation. But after I returned the neighbor's car, the phone started ringing off the hook.

First was Bill Casey. Without any identification or greeting—Casey was not one for formalities or small talk—he mumbled, "What the hell happened there, Ken?" I recognized the gruff voice and knew where "there" was. I gave him the highlights, low points, and bottom line. He was delighted that the president had walked away from, well, whatever it was he walked away from, and had refused to give Gorbachev whatever it was that he wanted. Having obtained this intelligence, Bill emitted a mumble and a grunt which I took to mean "thank you" and "good-bye."

Sitting back down at the kitchen table, I reflected on how the head of the multi-billion-dollar-a-year intelligence empire had just called me to get intelligence about the foremost topic in the world then.

The phone rang again. This time it was Bill Crowe, chairman of the Joint Chiefs of Staff, calling from the Pentagon. Unlike the grave and mumbling Casey, Admiral Crowe was a naturally jolly fellow, with an endless repository of jokes, most ribbing his fellow Oklahomans.

On this morning, though, Crowe was not a jolly fellow. He had heard that his Soviet counterpart, Marshal Sergei Akhromeyev, had been at Reykjavik. Was this true? Had he participated in the meetings? What did he say? What did he do?

Akhromeyev was a mystery in Washington and Crowe's nose was clearly out of joint. The top Soviet military officer had come to Iceland and headed its delegation, while the top American military officer had been sitting home.

But worse was to come. Crowe asked if, as he just heard, the president had actually proposed eliminating all ballistic missiles—or even all nuclear weapons. Could either of those be right?

Even my muffled confirmation sent the chairman of the Joint Chiefs into DEFCON 1, the highest national state of military crisis.

How could this be? Bill demanded angrily. What the hell was *his* man, the joint chiefs' representative, doing when this was happening? Why didn't he stop such madness? I wasn't too comforting when saying that I had not heard "his man" utter a word all weekend and in fact had barely seen him at Reykjavik.

More calls came from Dick Cheney, then a close friend and the third-ranking Republican in Congress; Ambassador Jeane Kirkpatrick, my boss at the United Nations; and Don Rumsfeld, my boss at the anti-poverty program in the 1960s, in the Pentagon in the 1970s, as special presidential envoy in the 1980s, and friend for decades.

While Casey was delighted that Reagan had resisted all Soviet proposals, these callers were distinctly undelighted by what Reagan had proposed to the Soviets.

What had got into the Gipper? Didn't he realize that scrapping ballistic missiles would knock out two legs of the strategic triad, which constituted the foundation of postwar deterrence? That eliminating our strategic weapons would end extended deterrence, which had protected our allies for generations? That this would encourage them to go nuclear? Did Asia want a nuclear Japan? Did we? Would Europe like a nuclear Germany? Would we?

And if Reagan was actually serious about eliminating all nuclear weapons—egads! that was even worse.

While Reagan and Gorbachev embracing the elimination of nuclear weapons sounded mighty noble, doing so would be mighty dumb. And these comments were coming from our friends!

I understood their points well, having made most of them inside the administration, many even to the president. So I didn't need any convincing. But neither was I doing any convincing. I could not get them to consider Reykjavik in any sense a success.

After more than an hour of telephonic torture, I became aware of a wonderful irony, assuming anything could have been wonderful then. The president extolled SDI as giving the West strategic protection against the threat of Soviet missiles. At Reykjavik, however, SDI gave the West strategic protection against the threat of Reagan proposals. It blocked his proposals for eliminating ballistic missiles or even all nuclear weapons. Hence SDI had already provided strategic defense, though not in any way Reagan wanted.

But I wasn't trying to fill these friends with irony or win them over with convincing arguments. I was trying simply to get them off the phone—as quickly as possible, though with a modicum of manners.

For by now I was past exhaustion. I needed peace and quiet. I needed an hour without saying the words "SDI," "Reykjavik," or "nuclear," an hour without hearing the word "failure."

Just as I was wrapping up these calls, an operator broke in—I hadn't known that operators could do such a thing—to say, somewhat breathlessly, that "the White House needed" to speak with me, immediately. Before moving to Washington in 1967, I hadn't known that a building could speak. And now I was learning that it could have needs, as well.

The operator read off a phone number and repeated that I should end my call and dial it immediately. I did so, and heard a secretary answer with, "Office of the White House Chief of Staff." After identifying myself, I was told that Don Regan wished to speak with me, immediately.

Despite the urgency, I was kept holding for the requisite time to remind me of his higher elevation in the Washington status-sphere. Once on the line, Regan was in his typical hurried-hearty mode. He asked how it had gone with the press on the flight back and how I was doing. After my rapid-fire responses—I knew that he wasn't calling for that—he came to "the ask."

Would I do him a favor?

That was a bad sign. The White House chief of staff calling me directly, rather than going through staff channels, was bad enough. His asking me for a favor indicated something worse.

Then he upped the ask to: Would you do the president a big favor?

I braced myself for the worst possible.

Then it came. "The president would like you to go to Australia to brief Bob Hawke."

Apparently the president had just hung up with the Australian prime minister, who came from the party of the left but was a staunch U.S. ally. He had recently taken political flak from his party's big anti-nuclear wing for allowing American technicians to monitor MX missile test flights from Australian ground stations. Hawke had stood firmly with the president, which won him a coveted spot on the president's call list of foreign leaders to be briefed about Reykjavik on the very morning of his return.

But unlike the others on that list—Britain's Margaret Thatcher, Germany's Helmut Kohl, and the like—who thanked the president and went about their day, Hawke asked if someone could come there quickly to explain and defend what had happened in Iceland. Having sided with the hawks on the MX issue, Hawke needed to show the doves his deep devotion to arms control. With Reykjavik dominating the news, he sought to seize the opportunity.

All this made perfect sense—for someone else to do. When I demurred and suggested another emissary, Regan said that the president had told the prime minister that Ken Adelman, his arms control director who had been at his side in Iceland, would be there soon. I listened to this story realizing that it was coming from Regan, but accepting that part of it might nonetheless be true.

Still, enough had become more than enough already. Without even saying that I was flattered by the president's confidence in me, I told Regan I could not do it. I was in no condition to travel anywhere, let alone halfway around the world. The president surely intended for the prime minister to be briefed by someone alert, articulate, and alive. And that would not be me.

Besides, the ACDA staff had already scheduled several post-Reykjavik briefings on Capitol Hill for me. I had piles of catch-up work on my desk. I threw in everything that popped in my mind—everything, that is, except what was uppermost in my mind, namely getting some sleep, fixing the car, and replacing the freezer.

Regan listened silently to my whining, which may have struck him as awfully self-centered, especially given all the flack he was constantly taking in his job. Finally, after hearing me out, he said that a White House limo was on its way to take me to Dulles Airport. The driver had my ticket to Los Angeles and then on to Sydney and the capital at Canberra. The first flight, to LAX, was scheduled to depart in about five hours, at 4:00 p.m.

Regan thanked me and wished me bon voyage, which made me feel even less bon about my voyage than before.

While down, I was not completely out, as I asked Regan for a favor in return. Now, I could tell by the changed tone in his voice, I was speaking his language.

I asked if he could make sure the president would not hold a meeting on post-Reykjavik planning until I got back. He said he could and would.

Monday, October 13, 1986
Washington, DC

Because this was Columbus Day and thus a federal holiday, and because of clear skies and unseasonably mild temperatures, Washingtonians flocked to the National Mall. They pushed strollers alongside the Reflecting Pool, played Frisbee at the foot of Capitol Hill, and generally enjoyed glorious fall weather.

Congress was in recess, but reporters and cameras had little trouble finding members eager for the media spotlight. Reykjavik was the topic of the day and every politician formed a quick reaction to its outcome and was eager to expound it for the media. The complexity of the issues and the absence of hard information on what actually happened in Iceland were no deterrents. Their interest was not educational but presentational, to be pithy or witty enough to make it on the air or front page of the leading papers.

Claiborne Pell, the ranking Democrat on the Senate Foreign Relations Committee, called this "a sad day for mankind" and hoped that "second thoughts may persuade our President . . . [to take] a bird in the hand . . . for two in the bush." Sam Nunn, chairman of the Senate Armed Services Committee, said he was sure that SDI would lose its support after Reykjavik (in fact, support for SDI jumped, to 64 percent of Americans in favor, the highest level ever attained). Speaking from the departure lounge at Dulles airport, Nunn urged the administration to "immediately pull [Reagan's] proposal off the table before the Soviets accept it."

Freshman Senator Al Gore trashed Reagan's performance as "bumbling . . . a fiasco" and blamed the conservative president for being too radical, as he "departed from arms control to the less-charted waters of disarmament." The ever-inflated Senator Ted Kennedy concluded that, "A grand and historic opportunity was there in Iceland, but it has been sacrificed . . . on the uncertain altar of SDI." And the ever-sensible Senator Daniel Patrick Moynihan cautioned that it would "make anyone suspicious if they could negotiate agreements in eleven hours at Reykjavik that the two countries have been arguing about for thirty years."

On the House side, the chairman of the House Armed Services Committee, Les Aspin, called the anti-nuclear discussion at Reykjavik "cuckoo." Winner of the best quip went to liberal Democratic congressman Edward J. Markey, who said that Reagan had missed "a chance to cash in Star Wars for the best deal the Russians have offered us since they sold us Alaska." The winner for the wisest comment went to liberal Republican congressman Jim Leach, who called Reykjavik "the most significant discussions that have ever taken place between heads of state in peacetime."

Adding to the cacophony were voices of the foreign policy establishment. In a grand display of bipartisanship, these were all critical. Preeminent Democratic wise man George Ball said dismissively, "SDI is not only fantasy, it is fraud. If the president persists in his SDI fantasy, there is no possibility of success in arms control." On the Republican side, Reagan's first secretary of state, Al Haig, called the summit "ill-prepared" and said, without knowing what had happened over the weekend, that "the U.S. side did not have an opportunity to weigh the proposals that were being offered." And former secretary of defense James Schlesinger, another Republican, pronounced Reagan's "position at Reykjavik . . . little informed" since he treated SDI "as if it were a reality instead of a collection of technical experiments and distant hopes. . . . Unlike Aladdin with his lamp, we have no way to force the nuclear genie back into the bottle."

Monday, October 13, 1986—The President Addresses the Nation
The Oval Office

President Reagan loved being in the Oval Office. Some of his predecessors found it too formal and preferred working in a smaller, less officious space next door in the Old Executive Office Building. But Ronald Reagan couldn't feel more comfortable anywhere else—except at his real hideaway, the small spread he named Rancho del Cielo outside Santa Barbara.

Nancy did a fine job redecorating "the Oval," as the staff called it. While she kept it stately—it can hardly be otherwise, with its grand history, distinctive proportions, and eighteen-and-a-half-foot ceiling— she also made it friendlier, with earth tones suggestive of the Southwest. Her husband made it personal, with a revolving parade of family photos on his credenza, and with favorite art pieces, especially bronze sculptures of cowboys and bucking broncos by Frederic Remington. The president was always eager to show them off to visitors, which helped ease the tension upon entering what Reagan called "this sacred ground."

The Oval's centerpiece was the *Resolute* desk. The desk's name was not to flaunt presidential determination, but to indicate its origins. The handsome desk had been made from timbers of the *HMS Resolute,* a British frigate that had been abandoned in Arctic waters by its desperate crew in 1852. Americans sailors came across the vessel three years later, extricated it from the ice, and returned it to the Royal Navy. This gesture was so appreciated that, when the ship was decommissioned twenty years later, Queen Victoria ordered two desks to be made from its hull. She kept one for her use at Windsor Castle, and sent the other to the White House as a gift to President Rutherford B. Hayes in 1880.

This Victorian treasure was used by subsequent presidents. Franklin Roosevelt had carpenters carve the presidential seal on its front, making it even more of a showpiece. As part of her White House revitalization, Jacqueline Kennedy had the desk restored in 1961. Photos of John-John and Caroline crawling beneath and peering out from its kneehole, the president grinning as he watched them, became iconic.

JFK's successor, Lyndon Johnson, never sat at the desk because, after the Kennedy assassination, it toured the country as the centerpiece of a traveling memorial exhibit. When the tour ended, the desk landed in the Smithsonian Institution. There it stayed, since President Nixon preferred the Wilson desk, which he had used in the 1950s as vice president. Yet when Jimmy Carter took office in 1977, he requested the *Resolute* desk be returned to the Oval Office, where it has remained ever since.

President Reagan loved the desk, with its noble proportions and fetching history. But, being a big fellow of six feet two inches, he asked if it might somehow be raised, so that his knees wouldn't keep knocking up against its drawer. White House restorers did such a fine job lifting it two inches that the new base seemed part of the original.

Reagan kept the desktop clean. He had a jar of jelly beans and two plaques prominently displayed on it. One, in gold letters on a red leather background, said "It CAN Be Done." Alongside it was a plaque reading "There is no limit to what a man can do or where he can go if he doesn't mind who gets the credit."

Reagan loved talking to the American people from behind the *Resolute* desk, which he did more times than any president in history.

He was behind the desk at 9:00 p.m. Monday night when he began telling upward of 20 million Americans about Reykjavik. Even Reagan's critics couldn't begrudge him being called the Great

Communicator. Only he denied it, claiming that he was merely communicating great ideas.

That night he looked grand, in a dark suit and red tie, surrounded by ranks of family photos, with stately gold curtains behind him opened for a glimpse of the greenery in the South Lawn, made visible by the garden floodlights.

Early in the address, Reagan made a prescient comment when saying that "the implications of these talks are enormous, and only just beginning to be understood." Both parts of this remark were true, and became truer over the ensuing years. The president said that he had gone the "extra mile" at Reykjavik—even though he really hadn't budged all that much, if at all, over the weekend.

For a speech designed to show him as a peacemaker, it was awfully tough. He called the Soviet radar in Siberia "a violation of the ABM Treaty," and threw in that "the Soviet Union is violating another agreement—the Helsinki Accords they had signed in 1975." He refrained from mentioning that he had harshly condemned those accords as a symbol of weak-kneed détente when President Gerald R. Ford signed them back then.

Reagan repeated what he had told Gorbachev—that the postwar policy of mutually assured destruction was "uncivilized" and should be scrapped. As before, he vastly exaggerated SDI's promise by claiming that "our scientists . . . [are] convinced it is practical," so much so that within a very few years, "we can have such a system ready to deploy." If this optimistically inaccurate statement caused consternation among some American scientists, it must have caused heartburn in Gorbachev, as it confirmed his worst fears.

The president kindly acknowledged "with respect and gratitude" our all-night negotiating session and explained that Reykjavik had not succeeded since Gorbachev was intent on "killing SDI," which to him was unthinkable. "I had pledged to the American people that I would not trade away SDI," he went on. "There was no way I could tell our people their government would not protect them against nuclear destruction," even though that was the case that evening, as it had been since the 1950s.

Nonetheless, the president was "still optimistic that a way will be found" to succeed on arms control. "The door is open, and the opportunity to begin eliminating the nuclear threat is within reach."

I watched the address in a lounge at LAX, sipping a glass of wine amidst many whiskey-guzzling travelers. Just as I began thinking that the only thing missing was any mention of gas masks, it came. Reagan likened building SDI to "our keeping our gas masks, even though the nations of the world had outlawed poison gas after World War I."

The speech ended with typical Reagan themes of strength and hope. Our side was in fine shape. "Because the American people stood guard at the critical hours [of the Cold War], freedom has gathered its forces, regained its strength, and is on the march." That's why we were "dealing from a position of strength." All in all, "there's reason, good reason, for hope."

The president closed his address looking through the camera into America's living rooms, even into airport lounges, as he said quietly, "Thank you, and God bless you."

Tuesday, October 14, 1986—The General Secretary Addresses the Nation
The Kremlin

The next night, October 14, was Gorbachev's turn. Though heightened of late, Soviet PR had still not risen to anywhere near the Reagan level. Gorbachev read his bland speech rather blandly from his desk with a bland background, devoid of any family photos and without any impressive gold curtains. And whereas Reagan, aware of his audience's limited attention span, spoke for less than twenty minutes, Gorbachev read on for more than an hour.

Nonetheless, this was the first nationwide address by any Soviet leader on a meeting abroad. It showed Gorbachev's sensitivity to public opinion in his own country, and especially in the world beyond.

The general secretary opened with customary tributes to such a fine Politburo and such a wise Central Committee of the Communist Party. That dispensed with, he proved prescient when calling Reykjavik a "major political event, the consequences of which, we are convinced, will be felt in international relations for a long time to come."

Then, with Reaganesque simplicity, he ticked off "what everybody wants to know" about Reykjavik—to wit, "What happened? What results did it produce? What will the world be like after it?"

But those three crisp questions yielded no three crisp answers. Before even beginning his windy explanations, Gorbachev wanted to refute Reagan's "thesis . . . that the Soviet Union will ultimately be unable to endure the arms race economically." This he refuted to the nation on terms just as strong as he had confirmed it to the Politburo before heading out for Reykjavik. The very notion that "one needs only squeeze the Soviet Union harder and step up the position of strength" to win the Cold War—a fair summary of Reagan's views—was "built on air" since "the strength of our society will be growing." And later in the speech, he boasted of that strength—4.3 percent to 5.2 percent growth in Soviet industrial production, labor, and income.

Having rebutted Reagan on that score, Gorbachev concurred with him that their "talk was no longer about limiting nuclear arms, as was the case with SALT I and SALT II and other treaties, but about the elimination of nuclear weapons." He admitted to making "major concessions" on nuclear arms, while the Americans "were offering us the same old moth-eaten trash." He then again drew on terms familiar from his days as agriculture chief, saying that the Americans had "come there empty-handed to gather fruits in their basket."

Despite the president's refusal to "meet the Soviet side halfway," the two sides had achieved "breakthroughs" on nuclear weapons. Gorbachev acknowledged progress in our all-night session, dismissed Reagan's notion of sharing SDI, and shrugged off their geostrategic debate, due to Reagan's "inability to understand the Socialist world." He, Gorbachev, wanted to steer clear of debating "ideological differences, [and] persistently drew [the president] back to the subject that had brought us to Reykjavik," as indeed he had.

It was when Gorbachev turned to SDI that his address turned better than bland. He told the nation that "the entire 'Star Wars' undertaking is purely militaristic in nature and is directed at obtaining military superiority over the Soviet Union." During their "nearly eight hours of nonstop and intense discussions" on Sunday, the United States sought "to defeat the ABM Treaty."

Gorbachev then gave SDI greater importance and more power than it ever had, or would ever have again. Not only was it "the main snag" at Reykjavik, but SDI was "a matter concerning the security of our country, the security of the entire world, all peoples and all continents." Even a little child in southern Africa or isolated Eskimo in northern Alaska had something to fear from SDI. To Gorbachev, "the most important lesson of the Reykjavik meeting" was clear—that SDI was "the epitome of obstructing peace, a strong expression of militaristic designs, and an unwillingness to get rid of the nuclear threat looming over mankind. It is impossible to perceive this program in any other way."

Despite the dire threat posed by SDI to everyone, everywhere, forevermore, meeting Reagan at Reykjavik had still been useful. It might lead to progress "if we do not slam the door and give vent to our emotions, although there is more than enough reason for this." He, however, would neither slam nor vent.

The speech closed, as it opened, with prescience. Reykjavik, he called "a major event," during which "a qualitatively new situation developed in that no one can continue to act as he acted before."

On this, Gorbachev showed keen insight. Those forty-eight hours in Iceland changed the relationship between the two men and their two superpowers. As "a major event," it resulted in helping end the Cold War.

Reykjavik Media Blitz
Washington, DC

As planned aboard Air Force One, the administration's assault to redeem Reykjavik was formidable. The top administration troika of Shultz, Regan, and Poindexter canceled all other appointments for the next several days to explain what happened over the weekend.

209

Don Regan, in the first of his stunning twenty-three post-Reykjavik press sessions, attended the Breakfast Group, which was hosted by the veteran *Christian Science Monitor* Washington correspondent Godfrey Sperling. For more than two decades, these on-the-record "Sperling breakfasts" had brought the capital's most influential print journalists together with the city's newsmakers over scrambled eggs and rolls.

Before Regan could even refill his coffee, he was asked about the president's reaction on the ride out to Keflavik, after the summit ended. The chief of staff said: "There were only two of us, and I will never reveal what he said in the car."

He then revealed the president's reaction by holding his thumb and index finger a quarter inch apart and saying: "How would you like to be the chief executive that came *that close* to wiping out nuclear weapons forever?"

After that dramatic overstatement, Regan revealed that he was still piqued. Reykjavik, he said with revived anger, "shows the Russians up for what they are" and what they are up to, which was no good.

Secretary Shultz made a determined effort, even though he was still somewhat uncertain over just what had happened. Reagan, he told the press, had proposed that "all offensive strategic arms . . . be eliminated." Actually, that was Gorbachev's proposal, not Reagan's. We opposed that, wanting all ballistic missiles eliminated instead.

The *New York Times* quoted Shultz as saying that "all offensive strategic arms and ballistic missiles would be eliminated" under Reagan's proposal, which was better since it was half true.

Nonetheless, the secretary was giving it his all. On Tuesday—his first day back from briefing the NATO allies in Brussels, straight after Reykjavik—Shultz appeared at 7:00 a.m. on the *CBS Morning News*, joined the president at the White House for a briefing to the network anchors, lunched with the *Washington Post* editorial board, held an afternoon press conference at the State Department, and appeared live in late afternoon on CNN's *Crossfire* and later on Ted Koppel's *Nightline*, which ran to midnight. The next day, at a standing-room-only luncheon at the National Press Club, he was asked why he had looked so angry and tired at his Sunday briefing in Reykjavik. The answer was vintage Shultz: "Probably because I was angry and tired."

Shultz, Regan, and Poindexter held an impressive forty-four on-the-record sessions with the press that week. Meanwhile, their aides fanned out to fifteen cities across the nation.

Having no comparable trouble with, or questioning from his domestic press, Gorbachev sent all his spinners abroad. Fifteen Soviet spokesmen traveled to thirty-five countries, spanning Austria to Zimbabwe, to shape the Soviet story of Reykjavik.

Tuesday, October 14, 1986—Touching Down Down Under
Canberra, Australia

I slept soundly for the bulk of the fifteen-hour flight from Los Angeles to Sydney. Among my fellow passengers was the legendary CBS news anchor Walter Cronkite and his wife, Betsy. The "most trusted man in America" couldn't help but ask the question I least wanted to answer: "What happened at Reykjavik?" He listened intently while I gave him a hurried response in that most unhurried of settings. He asked a few follow-up questions, but soon sensed that I would prefer discussing any other topic. So he filled me in on their sailing plans in Australia.

In Sydney, I bid the Cronkites happy times at sea and flew on to Canberra, where the American ambassador, Reagan's horseback-riding buddy Laurence William Lane, was waiting for me at the modest airport. When we reached his red brick, colonial-style residence, he told me that I had only half an hour to shower, shave, and suit up. He apologized for the rush, but the prime minister was anxiously waiting. Hawke, Bill Lane said knowingly, was eager to hear everything about Reykjavik.

As we approached the big, white Parliament Building—with the flags of Australia's six states and two territories fluttering in front—we spotted a crowd of reporters milling around the main entrance. Even in Canberra, so far from any Cold War ground zero, and even farther from Iceland, at the opposite longitude of the world, Reykjavik reigned as the topic of the day.

We no-commented our way through the rowdy reporters—and, to me anyway, all Australian reporters seemed rowdy. The ambassador's explanation, that the prime minister's office had arranged a briefing later on, only turned them rowdier.

I had met Prime Minister Hawke a few times before, during his annual trips to Washington. But now, as I entered his office, he greeted me like a long-lost friend. He ushered me into his big wood-paneled office and invited me to sit on one of the two large white chairs against the wall. He sat facing me. His personal aide and a notetaker pulled up similar white chairs to form a square.

The prime minister thanked me for coming and asked me to tell him what happened at Reykjavik. By this point, my summit spiel came in various sizes—from the Cronkite mini-pack to the Casey expanded package.

Because Hawke had been so keen on having someone come so far to fill him in, my initial instinct was to give him the full monty. But it didn't take long to realize that Hawke's interest in the intricacies of arms control was less than extensive.

So after describing the colorful atmosphere, I summarized the weekend's mega-events and supplied a bottom line. I then paused to await his questions.

After a moment's thought, he nodded his head and asked: "How is the president?"

Everyone in that era was intrigued by Ronald Reagan, especially his fellow politicians. He was, after all, the Leader of the Free World. Besides, he had been stunningly successful, having revived both the

American economy and the American spirit. Everything he touched seemed to have turned to gold. Nothing thrown at him stuck; he was indeed "the Teflon president."

The cause of their greater interest, and some jealousy, was his extraordinary popularity. Reagan had won reelection by a landslide, taking all but one of his country's fifty states. Most mysterious—and most intriguing to his counterparts—was how he did all this while seeming so detached and lightly informed. Reagan was unique among world leaders, and they knew it.

I told the prime minister of the president's tenacity and mental agility at Reykjavik. I walked him through what the president had said and done, both with Gorbachev and with us in the bubble, over lunch, and upstairs in our parlor-bedroom. After expounding for some fifteen minutes, I wrapped it up and waited for another question.

This time I did not have to wait long. Prime Minister Hawke leaned forward and asked earnestly: "Do you sail, Ken?"

My first thought was that he had some wonderful metaphor in mind—Reagan and Gorbachev sailing on the turbulent ocean of history, bobbing on the sea of fate, or some such. But I quickly learned that he had just bought a new sailboat.

With that, he stood up, grabbed a big picture book from the coffee table between us, and pulled his white chair around to be next to mine. He pointed to different photos to show what masts he had ordered, spoke lovingly about its sleek lines and his fast hull. He couldn't wait to take it out for a maiden sail on Friday afternoon. My smiles and nods were enough to keep him going joyously on, as he paged through the book.

After he closed it, we had another cup of coffee. Then, much as President Reagan would show guests his Remingtons, Hawke escorted me around the office to show off his porcelains. After telling of these wonders of China, he said that we should go out to brief the reporters.

The prime minister opened the press conference by saying that he had a long phone call with President Reagan on the very morning of his return from Reykjavik, and was grateful that the president had sent the head of the U.S. arms control agency to Canberra for a further briefing. That showed their personal friendship, and the close ties between the two allies.

Hawke added that, due to the press of other business, he had been able to schedule only an hour to meet with me. But because of the importance of nuclear weapons and world peace, he had extended our meeting far beyond that.

He then opened the session for questions. Any having to do with Australian-American relations, Ronald Reagan, or the ANZUS Alliance, he took for himself. Any on the summit, he turned over to me. We made a good team.

After the press conference, we ducked back into his office, where we thanked each other. He urged me to give the president his best, which I promised to do. He asked what my plans were. When I told him that I would be returning to Washington the very next morning, he looked a bit startled—perhaps believing that there might *really* be something to all this talk of close relations between the two countries and its leaders.

He thanked me again, this time even more warmly. As I took my leave, I said, "Good sailing, Prime Minister." He smiled his winning politician's smile.

By the time I landed back in Washington three airports later, I felt a bit like Phileas Fogg in *Around the World in Eighty Days*. It was Wednesday morning, and the staff-level meetings to follow up on Reykjavik and the extensive Capitol Hill briefings scheduled for me were to begin at 11:00 a.m.

Press Reactions
Washington, DC

My twenty-thousand-mile trip back and forth between the two capitals took less than forty-eight hours. When landing at Dulles, I found the weather in Washington better and the fallout from Reykjavik worse than when I had left.

The *New York Times* ran the first of its three critical editorials on Reykjavik. It said that "if the President's purpose" at Reykjavik "was finally to cash in [SDI] for great arms control gains, he failed." For the blundering president, "cool-handed turned into empty-handed." Of course, it had been the *Times*'s purpose to "cash in" SDI, never Reagan's.

The *Times*'s second editorial, a few days later, described "the widespread impression"—at least among the New York commentariat—"that SDI is a harebrained adventure that will induce a ruinous race in both offensive and defensive arms." At least with its third editorial, the nation's newspaper of record finally got the record right: "Reykjavik produced a roller coaster, first of hope, then disappointment, and now confusion." It went on to say that since the summit ended it had become "increasingly clear that Mr. Reagan erred in Iceland," as if that had not been clear to the *Times*'s editorial board the moment Reagan left Reykjavik.

The cover of *Time* magazine's post-summit issue featured a striking photograph by ace photographer David Hume Kennerly showing a downcast Reagan and a confident Gorbachev leaving Hofdi House. Above them in gigantic bold letters was NO DEAL and beneath that STAR WARS SINKS THE SUMMIT—not SDI but Star Wars, not Gorbachev's linkage of Star Wars that sinks the summit, but SDI/Star Wars in and of itself.

Time's issue appeared on newsstands nationwide one day after the summit ended, making it as much of a stunning editorial, printing, and distribution feat for the newsweekly as it was a PR disaster for the administration. Its main story, written by Strobe Talbott, missed the new dynamic in the Reagan-Gorbachev relationship. At Reykjavik, he wrote, the leaders came at each other "with their dukes up" and headed "for the back alley of rhetorical scrapping and unbridled competition." As usual, he lambasted Reagan most for missing the glaring truth that "neither side can gain a decisive advantage over the other in the nuclear age."

Reykjavik sparked emotional reactions from those across the political spectrum. Conservatives were upset by Reagan's proposals to scrap ballistic missiles, even all nuclear weapons, and liberals were enraged by Reagan's SDI blocking the greatest arms control accord in history.

The foreign policy establishment—at work in Foggy Bottom and at home and play in Georgetown—concluded that Reykjavik had been ill-conceived and ill-prepared. This stood in sharp contrast to the Geneva summit, which, as a wholly owned State Department operation, had run so smoothly and produced so little—pretty much the way, they figured, a summit ought to go.

And the Pentagon was upset by everything. The military didn't support Reagan's proposals, actively opposed Gorbachev's policies, and resented the exclusion of their JCS chairman. You name it on Reykjavik, and the brass disliked it.

Despite such trashing, Reagan's Oval Office address produced a solid bump in public opinion. Polls showed that three times as many Americans blamed Gorbachev than Reagan for the summit's failure, and 63 percent considered Reagan more committed to arms control than Gorbachev, who had only 9 percent.

Monday, October 27, 1986
The White House Situation Room

Over the years, I have taught *Things Fall Apart*, the masterful 1958 novel by the late Nigerian author Chinua Achebe. But I never experienced the phenomenon until these months.

Eager for the quickly planned event, Reagan and Gorbachev greet each other at Hofdi House on Saturday, October 11, 1986. Neither imagined what was in store for him that weekend. (*Ronald Reagan Library*)

Reykjavik was the second summit for Reagan and Gorbachev, after their meeting at Geneva the year before, in November 1985. At their first session on a chilly Swiss morning, a sprightly, coatless Reagan assisted the younger, overcoated Gorbachev up the steps of the villa. "I felt that we lost the game during these first movements," grumbled a Soviet spokesman after watching the opening play. (*Ronald Reagan Library*)

Billed as a low-key business meeting, Reykjavik was anything but. A hastily summoned Summit Preparatory Committee met on October 3 with forty-five representatives from various U.S. government agencies (*on the left*), Soviet agencies (*right*), and Icelandic officials (*behind the photographers*) to prepare for the unexpected superpower summit just one week away.
(© *Ljósmyndasafn Reykjavíkur/Kristjan Ari Einarsson*)

The government called back the newly crowned Miss World—Iceland's own Hólmfríður Karlsdóttir—from a goodwill tour of Asia to be available in Reykjavik for press interviews over the weekend.
(*David Hume Kennerly/Getty Images*)

A stylish Raisa Gorbachev stayed aboard the *Georg Ots*, a Soviet ship named for a pop singer dubbed "the Soviet Sinatra." When asked why the Gorbachevs lodged there rather than in a Reykjavik hotel, Raisa responded that it was "very romantic."
(© *Ljósmyndasafn Reykjavíkur/Kristjan Ari Einarsson*)

On their stroll, Iceland's president, former actor Vigdís Finnbogadóttir, told President Reagan that since there was no school to teach anyone how to be a president, "the best place you could learn that was at the theater, where you were defining life and society all the time." Reagan liked that so much he called her "my old colleague" afterward. (*Ragnar Axelsson/Morgunbladid*)

Against the wishes of the Iceland government, the U.S. Secret Service and the KGB chose Hofdi House for the summit meetings because its isolation provided greater security. Built in 1909, the modest wooden structure is called "the haunted house" by locals because spirits are thought to inhabit it.
(*David Hume Kennerly/Getty Images*)

Iceland officials made themselves readily available to the flood of press requests. Interrupting his daily dip in Reykjavik's thermal springs, Prime Minister Steingrímur Hermannsson had a presummit interview with Tom Brokaw. If there were ghosts in Hofdi House, he told the NBC anchor during that interview, they were most welcome there.
(© *Ljósmyndasafn Reykjavíkur/Brynjar Gauti Sveinsson*)

Raisa Gorbachev, dressed to the nines, changed outfits four times on the first day of the Reykjavik summit. She hit all the tourist sites of Reykjavik—and then some. With Nancy Reagan back in Washington and a summit news blackout imposed, she had the world stage to herself. She used, and relished, every minute of it. (*AP/Jeff Widener*)

This photo-op—after the photo-op at the front door of Hofdi House—was stage-managed by Reykjavik's mayor to show off his flag, ferns, sculptures, and seaside. (*Ronald Reagan Library*)

During her speedy tour around Reykjavik, Raisa visited eight sites in under seven hours. In a silver fox jacket, she clapped in delight at bathers paddling around an enormous thermal springs pool, and then extended a fox-clad arm to shake the bathers' hands.

(© *Ljósmyndasafn Reykjavíkur/Kristjan Ari Einarsson*)

Meanwhile, the leaders met in a small conference room under the watchful eye of Bjarni Benediktsson in the portrait above Reagan. After an initial chat, they invited in Foreign Minister Shevardnadze, taking his seat on the left; and Secretary of State George Shultz, on the right where Reagan could hear him. Translators sat at the corners, and two note takers sat behind them, out of the photo. (*Ronald Reagan Library*)

On the Saturday night of the summit weekend there was a grand gathering—
part peace rally, part street festival—in downtown Reykjavik, before a live
Joan Baez concert. (*Ólafur K. Magnússon/Morgunbladid*)

Marshal Sergei Akhromeyev, chief of staff of the Soviet armed forces,
and President Reagan eye each other warily, as Gorbachev and others look on.
The five-star general made a surprise appearance in Reykjavik and led
the Soviet arms team in making unprecedented concessions during an all-
night Saturday session. (*Ronald Reagan Library*)

The official U.S. residence in Reykjavik, which the ambassador had to vacate for the president's stay, was filled with the antlers of assorted animals the ambassador had shot. Amid all the antlers, the president frequently called Nancy back home, calls that always cheered him up. (*Ronald Reagan Library*)

Downtime for the U.S. team in Reykjavik came only at the outset of meals. Here Reagan was joking while, to his right, Shultz and Poindexter prepared a paper to present over lunch. To the president's left is Don Regan. Nearest the camera are Max Kampelman on the left and the author on the right.
(*Ronald Reagan Library*)

Late Sunday afternoon on the second floor of Hofdi House, Reagan read over the U.S. final offer. He was eager to finish and get back to Nancy. From left, Paul Nitze, nearly eighty, straining to keep awake after the all-nighter on Saturday; Don Regan; the president; George Shultz; John Poindexter; and the author—watching and waiting. (*Ronald Reagan Library*)

When Reagan left the room to return to the sudden-death overtime session Sunday afternoon, we all called out, "Good luck, Mr. President." A moment later he was back, wanting to ask each of us there—(*clockwise from Reagan*) Poindexter, the author, Richard Perle (*back of his head*), Shultz, NSC staffer Bob Linhard, and Don Regan—to make absolutely sure that we hadn't succumbed to summit fever, but were doing right by America. (*Ronald Reagan Library*)

Reagan and Gorbachev squaring off in the Hofdi House hallway on what
Reagan called "one of the longest, most disappointing—and ultimately
angriest—days of my presidency." Outside, they had one final exchange, but
its content remains uncertain. According to one report, Gorbachev sought
to soothe the president, saying, "I don't know what we could have done
differently." Unsoothed, Reagan responded defiantly, "Well, you could have
said yes!" What's certain is that Reagan was angry and frustrated when
leaving Gorbachev. (*Ronald Reagan Library*)

Failure filled Shultz's face as he met the world's press in downtown Reykjavik
to announce his "great sense of disappointment" at the summit's outcome.
One colleague said he looked as though a horse had just kicked him in the
stomach. His appearance reinforced the growing impression that Reykjavik
was an utter failure. (© *Ljósmyndasafn Reykjavíkur/Brynjar Gauti Sveinsson*)

President Reagan was always happiest when addressing the troops. Speaking to three thousand airmen and support staff at the NATO airbase before he left Reykjavik boosted his sunken spirits. He told a (rather long) story of how, as commander-in-chief, he thought he could not salute, since he wasn't in uniform. But after the president got official "permission" to do so, he loved saluting the troops. (*Ronald Reagan Library*)

What *Time* called "the four most famous words of the Reagan presidency" were almost not spoken, owing to opposition from nearly all of Reagan's aides. But he spoke them anyway, on June 12, 1987, at the Brandenburg Gate, a short distance from the Berlin Wall. Screens had been set up to protect him against any East German sniper. The president called out, "Mr. Gorbachev," paused, and then repeated the name for emphasis—"Mr. Gorbachev—tear down this Wall!" It had an electrifying effect that day, and was evoked again when the Wall fell two years later. (*Ronald Reagan Library*)

Raisa Gorbachev and Nancy Reagan were mostly just tolerating each other by the time of the welcoming ceremonies for the Gorbachevs' arrival at the Washington Summit on December 7, 1987. (*Dirck Halstead/Time Life Pictures/Getty Images*)

When Reagan repeated his favorite Russian adage, *Doveryai, no proveryai*—"Trust but verify"—during the signing ceremonies for the most sweeping arms accord in history, held on December 8, 1987, in the East Room of the White House, Gorbachev ribbed him. Watching in the front row are the two first ladies; Vice President George Bush and his wife, Barbara; Shultz and Shevardnadze; and congressional leaders. Two rows back, behind the protective Secret Service and KGB, were members of the arms control team, including the author. (*Top: Copyright Bettmann/Corbis/AP Images. Bottom: © Bettmann/CORBIS*)

"I never expected to be here," Reagan cracked in May 1988 in Moscow, the epicenter of what he had called "the evil empire." Nobody would have expected him to deliver a major address on the blessings of freedom at Moscow State University beneath a hammer and sickle and a gigantic bust of Lenin. The students gave him thunderous applause and a standing ovation—"the most enthusiastic," said U.S. Ambassador Jack Matlock, "since his nomination at the Republican convention." (*Ronald Reagan Library*)

The president took time out from proselytizing around Moscow to visit Red Square, first with Gorbachev. On that visit he was asked if he still regarded the Soviet Union as an evil empire. Slowly shaking his head, Reagan said, "No. That was another time, another place." Gorbachev, standing beside him, flashed an appreciative grin. Reagan later took Nancy to see the spectacular site. "We've leaving tomorrow," he explained to a reporter, "and I didn't want her to miss it." (*Ronald Reagan Library*)

Gorbachev, in East Berlin for the fortieth anniversary of the German Democratic Republic in October 1988, bestows a kiss—more passionate than dictated by comradely protocol—on the East German tyrant Erich Honecker, then into his eighteenth year of Stalinist rule. During their days together, thousands of East German protesters chanted, "Gorby, Gorby." Their efforts to overthrow Honecker succeeded just a few weeks later. It was the last anniversary of East Germany, which joined West Germany in a unified nation. (*Chris Niedenthal//Time Life Pictures/Getty Images*)

Mstislav Rostropovich, the celebrated Russian cellist and conductor, whose birthday party Reagan and Gorbachev had discussed at Reykjavik, rushed to the Wall when it fell on November 9, 1989. "Voilà! All I need is a chair," he said. A chair was produced, and the maestro sat, expressing his profound feelings through profound music: Bach's *Suites for Unaccompanied Cello.* (© *Stringer/Reuters*)

The next month, an ailing Leonard Bernstein, in his last year of life, came to the Wall to lead the West Berlin Philharmonic in Beethoven's triumphant Ninth Symphony. In the soaring choral conclusion, "Ode to Joy," Bernstein substituted *Freiheit* (freedom) for *Freude* (joy). The performance was followed by the roar of the standing audience and the ringing of church bells across Berlin. Bernstein called it "a historic moment sent from above."
(*Zentralbild ADN/picture-alliance/dpa/AP Images*)

On June 10, 2004, Mikhail Gorbachev unexpectedly appeared in the Rotunda of the U.S. Capitol to pay his last tribute to Ronald Reagan, lying in state. After standing a few feet away from the casket for a moment of reflection, Gorbachev approached and at first patted and then rubbed his hand along the red and white stripes of the American flag that decorated the coffin of the fortieth president of the United States. (*Roberto Schmidt/AFP/Getty Images*)

Everyone was eager for an NSC meeting to follow up the summit, but the president had been heavily scheduled to campaign for Republicans running in the midterm elections, and the top staff was full blast with its media blitz, which Shultz deemed successful: "Our efforts with the press have turned the story around," he wrote the president, though I had my doubts about the degree of turnaround (if any).

Regardless, Don Regan found an hour to schedule the session in the Situation Room, located in the White House basement. The president sat, as always, at the head of the mahogany table in the wood-paneled room. On the wall behind him hung the presidential seal, below which was a framed copy of the World War II poster depicting Winston Churchill, backed up by tanks and planes, with a quote from his first speech as prime minister: "Let us go forward together."

The president relished that poster and that quote. He would have been less delighted had the poster instead featured a quote from Churchill's last address to the U.S. Congress warning: "Be careful, above all things, not to let go of the atomic weapon until you are sure, and more than sure, that other means of preserving the peace are in your hands."

Vice President George H. W. Bush sat to the president's right and Shultz to his left. Admiral Poindexter, who would open the meeting and frame its discussion, sat facing the president. I was at the end, kitty-corner from Poindexter, seated next to Regan.

After Poindexter called the meeting to order and gave as its purpose to help the president plan post-Reykjavik arms control, Weinberger and Shultz proceeded to face off over the ABM Treaty. The defense secretary denounced the ten-year pledge to uphold the treaty, claiming it would delay SDI deployment. The fact that Weinberger had opposed the president's announcing SDI in March 1983 only heightened his fervor afterward, as he championed it with the passion of a convert.

Shultz considered SDI more a reasonable research program than a holy crusade. He believed SDI would need a decade of research, or more, before it could be deployed.

Such secretarial squabbles weren't unusual in the Situation Room. The president would sit passively through their verbal combat, turning his head left and right as if taking in a tennis match, while his senior cabinet officers duked it out. This one, however, was unusual in its ferocity.

When a break came, I jumped in to suggest that we steer future U.S. policy away from the ballistic missile ban and toward the reductions of intermediate and strategic nuclear arms, as had been agreed at Reykjavik. I reasoned that the Soviets would never buy a ballistic missile ban, but if they ever did, it would be expensive and unwise for us to sign it.

Poindexter summarily cut me off, saying that the president had already proposed the ban. As official U.S. policy, it was not open to further review or discussion. Undeterred, I turned to the president and explained that U.S. ballistic missiles had been, for a generation, a relatively low-cost way to balance the Soviets' conventional superiority.

With that, Shultz objected, saying that the public would gladly pay whatever the cost to end such a threat. The president then added that the American people stood with us on SDI.

I was not getting favorable reviews from my superiors.

Yes, I plunged on, the public *did* support us—for now. But the public might not support us later, once it became clear that the greatest disarmament accord ever concluded would require the greatest peacetime budget hike ever allocated.

Shultz again took exception. He had done some back-of-the-envelope calculations and figured that the $280 billion annual defense budget would *only* need to rise to, say, $400 billion a year under such a ban. That, he offered, would be no problem, economically or politically. Congress would readily concur.

In no uncertain terms, Weinberger reminded everyone that he, as secretary of defense, would handle the Pentagon budget, thank you very much, and no one but him and the president.

In his sparkling white uniform with admiral gold stripes, Chairman of the Joint Chiefs of Staff William Crowe then joined the unseemly fray. Still piqued with the mere mention of Reykjavik, Crowe said that he, too, questioned the ballistic missile ban.

As he began to explain why, Poindexter figuratively threw another yellow flag on the table to indicate a foul. Again, he said sternly, the president had already decided that issue.

The battle of the admirals ended by Crowe simply ignoring Poindexter and delivering a brief and cogent tutorial on the role of ballistic missiles in protecting the nation and its allies for the past half century. He wrapped his tutorial up with a zinger.

"Mr. President," he said, looking directly across the table at him, "your Joint Chiefs of Staff have concluded that the proposal to eliminate ballistic missiles in ten years' time would pose high risks to the security of the nation."

This was as stunning a remark as ever heard around the Situation Room table. For here was America's top military leader stating that his commander in chief's own policy would endanger the nation. The chairman's stance posed serious substantive and political problems for the president. Substantively, because any unanimous conclusion of the joint chiefs on military matters had to be taken seriously. Politically, because the chairman would undoubtedly say the same thing to the Congress—and thus to the public, when asked. This would be devastating.

Fearing he might have gone a bit far, Crowe added that, should, however, a ballistic missile ban be imposed, the Pentagon would need upward of $200 billion added to its budget—beyond its already scheduled, already hefty increases—each year for the next ten years. And even with that additional $2 trillion, he said, U.S. security would still be worse off than before.

At some point, I went back to suggesting that we build on what the president had achieved at Reykjavik, the nuclear arms cuts. If we and the Soviets could get organized and became nimble enough, we might just conclude an arms accord in the limited time remaining of the Reagan presidency. That would take some doing, but it would be worth doing.

Everyone around the table looked at me like they were listening, but no one was reacting. Their minds clearly were elsewhere—perhaps on the more dramatic and important words of Crowe, which were bad enough, but more probably on what was never said, which was much worse.

With the exception of me and possibly Crowe, everyone else around that table—the president, Shultz, Weinberger, Regan, Casey, and Poindexter—sensed the tsunami about to engulf them. They knew that five hundred missile systems were at that very hour in transport from Israel to Iran, scheduled for delivery the next day—all with White House approval. Hence, while their words were about Reykjavik, their minds must have been on Tehran.

After most White House meetings, I would leave with a sense of where the president would come out on the issues under consideration. But leaving this White House meeting, I wasn't sure even what issues were under consideration.

As I walked out of the West Wing toward the northwest gate, I thought how sad, but fitting, for the follow-up session on Reykjavik to have been as disjointed as Reykjavik itself had been.

Early the next morning, Crowe's action officer called to invite me to a meeting in the tank, the windowless conference room deep within the Pentagon where the joint chiefs hold their most sensitive sessions. They were scheduled to discuss the future of arms control. Evidently the chairman considered me a kindred soul and wanted me in on that discussion.

Word travels fast around Washington and before long my phone rang. It was Poindexter calling from Air Force One to forbid me from attending the meeting in the tank. My going would, he said clearly, constitute insubordination.

I objected in the strongest terms possible, to no avail. I then said a reluctant okay, not because I considered what Poindexter ordered proper—it wasn't—but because I didn't want to cause yet another Reykjavik problem. There were enough of them piling up already.

Consequently, I called the JCS action officer to beg off and apologize, giving no reason for my unusual, and rather rude, cancellation.

The post-Reykjavik free fall continued. After returning from his Brussels briefing (as he repeated in his memoirs), Shultz concluded that the NATO foreign ministers "felt Reykjavik was an astounding achievement." Be that as it may, the foreign ministers' bosses considered it simply astounding. German Chancellor Helmut Kohl hastened to Washington in a desperate attempt to block the intermediate missile part of Reykjavik. England's Margaret Thatcher came in November to express her iron-willed opposition during a tense session at Camp David, and France's François Mitterrand was having conniptions over Reagan's coming out so starkly as a nuclear abolitionist. The other NATO allies were even more nervous than their usual state of acute if not clinical nervousness.

While allied relations headed south, superpower relations went worse. The Soviet Union then expelled five U.S. diplomats accused of being spies and we booted out fifty-five Soviet "diplomats" known to be spies. It was like *Mad* magazine's "Spy vs. Spy" cartoon series come to life.

Soon thereafter, Congress erupted when learning that listening devices had been planted deep within the walls of the astronomically expensive U.S. embassy under construction in Moscow. As if that wasn't enough, a U.S. marine sergeant was found escorting KGB officials around secure embassy offices in the middle of the night.

Relationships within the administration, the policies of the president, our ties with the allies, and our relations with the Russians—all were plummeting. Things were falling apart.

I gained momentary comfort from thinking of that old adage, "The darkest hour is just before dawn." But, as that dismal winter of 1986 began to set in, I couldn't help but wonder: What if there *is* no dawn?

CHAPTER 8

From the Worst to the Best of Times

B y the week's end, Reykjavik was yesterday's news. It had been a failure, and could be conveniently forgotten. Only the *New York Times* still cared, as it ran more editorials critical of Reagan.

Washington returned to its default mode, which was politics. That fall, GOP prospects were dim. In 1980 and 1984 Reagan's coattails pulled along even the most pedestrian of Republican candidates. But by 1986 those coattails had shortened, most recently by the perceived failure of Reykjavik.

Election night was bad. Democrats kept the House and picked up eight Senate seats, for a solid 55-to-45 majority. With both chambers in Democratic hands, Reagan legislation would be dead on arrival. Any life left in the Reagan presidency had to come in foreign policy.

Yet the world wasn't looking great either. Relations with the allies were frayed and those with the Soviets as bad as ever in Reagan's presidency. Plus, there was the Middle East.

Two days before the election, the president adamantly denied the *Al-Shiraa* story that the U.S. approved arms sales to Iran. A week later, Reagan added categorically: "We did not—repeat, *did not*—trade weapons or anything else for hostages. Nor will we." Six days later, he angrily denied any Israeli involvement. All those assurances were adamant, all were iron tight, and all were wrong.

In a *Time* interview in late November, Reagan was still complaining that "this wasn't a failure until the press got a tip from that rag in Beirut." While the president was denying any involvement in one part of the White House complex, Oliver North and Fawn Hall were in another part shredding documents that showed such involvement. Meanwhile, Poindexter and Casey were telling the two congressional intelligence committees, in secret sessions, that the United States had *dis*approved of the Israeli arms sales to Iran. That too was wrong.

As these machinations became known—in typical Washington scandal mode, with juicy tidbits dribbling out by the hour—the image of Reagan's foreign policy turned from failure over Reykjavik to disaster over Iran. To stop the drip, drip, drip of revelations, the president asked Attorney General Ed Meese, his longtime Mr. Fix-It, to get to the bottom of this strange business.

On November 24 Meese found the bottom blacker and stranger. It was bad enough that the administration had approved of Israeli arms sales to Iran. It was worse that the administration had directly sold arms to the terrorist regime. It was worst of all that the money from such illegal sales had been shifted over to the Contras fighting the Nicaraguan government. The U.S. Constitution stipulates that *only* Congress can appropriate federal funds. The morning after Meese made this discovery, he informed the president.

By chance, I happened to be in a White House meeting that Tuesday, the 25th. When the president dropped by, I was stunned by his appearance. He looked even worse than George Shultz had in Reykjavik. His look of total shock and dismay convinced me that he had just learned about the Iran-Contra diversion and knew nothing about it before then. I still believe that.

. . . .

The Iran-Contra revelation caused a firestorm, the likes of which Washington had not seen—or, for many in Washington, enjoyed—since Watergate. Administration officials watched their lives pass before their eyes. With two years to go in office, the Reagan legacy, if not presidency, hung in the balance, as an epidemic of investigations broke out. The president established a commission led by former senator John Tower; the Senate created a select committee; the House named a special committee; and the attorney general appointed an independent counsel. Plus, a thousand investigative reporters started scurrying about, with visions of Pulitzer Prizes dancing in their heads.

People were jumping, or tossed, overboard. On November 22, North was fired and Poindexter quit. The next month, Casey, at the crosshairs of every investigation, was hospitalized with brain cancer one day before he was to testify; he resigned in early February. A week later, former National Security adviser Bud McFarlane attempted to commit suicide but was rescued at the last minute. In May, Casey died. When sorrows come, as the Bard put it, they come not as single spies but in battalions.

Amidst all these sorrows, Reagan became unmoored. He had, as he was the first to realize, lost his touch with the American people. Try as he might, the Great Communicator was failing to communicate greatly. He staunchly maintained that he had not—repeat not—traded arms for seven American hostages being held by terrorist groups in Iran, yet U.S. or Israeli arms had been shipped around the times hostages were released. He spoke of reaching out to "Iranian moderates," yet the Iranian mullahs appearing nightly on TV seemed positively unhinged. He called North "an American hero," yet he fired him.

Coming right after the failed summit, these revelations reinforced the Washington trope that his administration was, at best, sloppy on foreign affairs. Letting Reagan be Reagan was deemed dangerous.

Even his ardent supporters were asking one another: What happened to our guy?

This battalion of sorrows did not just hurt Reagan. It devastated him. It was, according to his son Ron Reagan, the lowest point of his life, except perhaps for his divorce from Jane Wyman. Getting through the funk was especially tough for someone unfamiliar with "the black dog" of depression, as Winston Churchill called it.

Iran-Contra was so threatening that nothing else was getting done at the top of the administration. For nothing else mattered as much in the White House as saving its occupant.

Just the month before, at Reykjavik, Reagan had been at his best—alert, informed, engaged, and exceptionally effective. In fact, the now-declassified notes of his Hofdi House debates with Gorbachev reveal that he was even better than we knew at the time. But Iran-Contra showed Reagan at his worst—all instinct with little thinking; all improv with little formal decision making; all emotion with little logic.

To be fair to the president, his key advisers in the White House, current and past—Poindexter and his predecessor, McFarlane—were vigorously pushing him forward. Meanwhile, his two top advisers outside the White House—Shultz and Weinberger—were gently pulling him back. While tough as nails when disagreeing over arms control, they proved timid when agreeing on these machinations.

Neither threatened to resign over policies that clearly warranted it. Shultz had made such a threat the year before, on an issue of far less importance, and Reagan had relented. Another Shultz threat would most likely have brought Reagan back to his senses, back to his core beliefs. But Shultz did not do so. Nor did Weinberger. Their timidity did a real disservice to the president they so admired, even loved.

WASHINGTON, DC, IN THE late fall of 1986 resembled a kids' soccer match, with all the players scrambling to where the ball was at any instant.

The capital's fickle attention fastened first on Reykjavik, then pivoted to the midterm elections, and then turned full blast on Iran-Contra. Washington pundits began relegating, not Communism, but the Reagan administration to the ash heap of history. It seemed unlikely that anything could come out of the last year of a spent, acrimonious, and besieged presidency.

All hands were on deck for the crisis. Although I was head of the arms control agency, my head was not into arms control during this time.

After Poindexter left, the president chose as his new national security adviser Frank Carlucci, the only person around agreeable to both Shultz and Weinberger. As Reagan's fifth NSC adviser in less than six years, Carlucci was a fine choice. We had worked together in the 1970s when Don Rumsfeld headed the anti-poverty agency and had been close ever since.

Frank asked if I might head up his transition team. Because of previous business obligations, he could not take office until January 2, 1987. During the intervening six weeks, might I get the NSC ready for him? This, I came to see, was a nice euphemism for clearing the place out before he got there.

Thus began the worst job of my life. Our tiny team had to replace one-third of the NSC's some 120 staff members and hire their replacements. Firing is always a tricky business and hiring even trickier, especially in government. And I personally hate firing anyone, especially fellow conservatives, most of whom had served the president well but stayed too long or stumbled into some mischief.

Worse yet, it was the blessed time of year, the weeks before Christmas and Hanukah, the time to hand out gifts and cards and not pink slips. But the NSC needed a swift and dramatic makeover, partly to convince the press that the Reagan presidency was not on life support, but starting anew. Days before Christmas, we told dozens of staffers the bad news with sounds of carolers joyfully filling the EOB hallways outside our transition quarters.

. . . .

SOON AFTER REYKJAVIK, GORBACHEV, like Reagan, was immersed in a crisis endangering his survival. But, unlike Reagan's crisis, his was neither sudden nor unexpected. It was the crisis he and Shevardnadze had discussed years before, while walking through Pitsunda Woods, the ongoing crisis that led them to conclude that "everything's rotten [and] has to be changed." It was the crisis that Gorbachev had warned the Politburo would grow worse should Reykjavik fail. "We will [in that case] be pulled into an arms race beyond our power, and we will lose this race as we are presently at the limit of our capabilities." For Gorbachev, a breakthrough at Reykjavik was needed.

But there had been no breakthrough at Reykjavik—at least none evident then. If anything, Reykjavik had worsened Gorbachev's problems. It showed Reagan moving full steam ahead on SDI and claiming great progress on the program.

Hence, there was no time to spare. Gorbachev had to push reforms—hard, everywhere, and at once. Consequently, just weeks after Reykjavik, he called a special session of the Party's Central Committee to meet in Moscow in January 1987, and asked the committee to adopt his package of political changes, known as *glasnost,* and economic reforms, dubbed *perestroika*. It was, he told his colleagues, adapt or die for the Soviet system.

While his proposed reforms were extensive, they were still only reforms. They would modify, not replace, the system Lenin had created and Stalin had expanded. Gorbachev—like Lenin with his New Economic Policy in 1921—wanted an upgrade and not a replacement to the existing system.

Consequently, his reforms became discombobulated. Gorbachev spoke of greater freedom, but would not release most political prisoners nor allow many Jews to emigrate. He permitted the printing of long-banned books, including *Doctor Zhivago* and *Nineteen Eighty-Four*, but would not relinquish state control over all television, radio, and print media. He allowed elections between competing candidates, but not competing parties. All candidates came from the Communist Party and only competed for local posts. Gorbachev never allowed anyone to run against himself.

Even such baby steps, however, posed grave dangers. Candidates soon learned that they could garner support by tearing down Moscow and boosting up local pride. This posed a mortal danger to a centrally controlled, multiethnic empire like the Soviet Union.

Gorbachev's economic reforms were similarly confused. A CIA report at the time concluded that he advocated " 'profound' changes in the area of economic reform, while strongly supporting the need to maintain central control." He allowed firms to determine their own products and set their own outputs, but only after they had fulfilled their state quotas. He allowed them to sell their products in the open market, but only at a price set by the state, after fulfilling state orders. Firms could raise their own funds and operate as they wished, but still had to be owned and answer to the state. While some firms could be privately owned, none could own private property. All had to pay high taxes and get state permission to hire or fire employees. Soviet products could compete internationally, yet the ruble would stay nonconvertible.

Even the most adept executive—of which there were few then— had to slap his forehead at such convoluted restrictions. And even the most experienced executive—of which there were none then—was destined to fail if he followed the rules.

Adding to the gloom was a suddenly sprung jihad against drinking. This, too, was well-intended and right-minded, as drunkenness had become a Russian pandemic. But Gorbachev's crusade did nothing to lessen alcohol consumption and much to heighten popular resentment.

Before long, a joke began circulating around Moscow—allegedly told to Gorbachev himself—about some fellow who, after hours of waiting in line for bread, goes berserk and tells others in line that he's going to find and shoot Gorbachev. He leaves the bread line but soon returns, quietly resumes his place, and explains that he's back because the other line, the line to shoot Gorbachev, was even longer.

Among Gorbachev's galaxy of reforms was one unique in the annals of history—the defeat of an unopposed candidate. All key party officials ran unopposed. Nonetheless, voters could draw an *X* across the name of someone they *really* opposed. Whenever the *X*'s outnumbered the ballots in support or left blank, that candidate would lose his post. Hence the advent of an unopposed, defeated candidate—a new phenomenon in political science, although one which became increasingly familiar in subsequent Soviet elections.

Gorbachev was forced into sundry compromises, which made the reform package eventually approved by the bickering Supreme Soviet even less coherent. Before long, party stalwarts were spouting an old Russian proverb, that it is better to turn back than to lose your way.

But there was no turning back. The genie of economic liberalization and political democratization had been let loose. The Soviet edifice, impenetrable for going on seventy years, was creaking and set to crumble. Gorbachev was about to lose his way.

WHILE ALL THIS WAS happening on many fronts in the United States and the U.S.S.R., nothing was happening on the arms control front. All eyes looked elsewhere, except in the arms control agency. There, the professionals acted like they still believed that something could get finished, something historic, in the brief time remaining in the Reagan era.

No one else believed that, until January 1987. That's when Victor Karpov—who habitually opposed everything in sight, especially in sight of the negotiating table—said during an interview in London that the Soviets *could* resume talks on nuclear weapons apart from SDI or the ABM Treaty.

Skeptical that Karpov, of all people, was signaling an end to

Gorbachev's linkage, we quickly checked the quote and found that he had spoken clearly and in English. Our upbeat mood lasted less than a day, until the Foreign Ministry spokesman in Moscow slapped Karpov down and denied what he had declared.

Yet when Karpov returned to Geneva, he began bargaining seriously on intermediate missiles without regard to SDI or the ABM Treaty. A bit later—during an interview in Indonesia, of all places—Gorbachev dropped linkage as casually as Karpov had.

Hence, in the period of a few weeks, the Soviet insistence on linkage—which had wrecked the Reykjavik summit—was quietly scrapped and quickly forgotten. Throughout its history, Soviet rulers had airbrushed out disfavored past leaders. Now Gorbachev was airbrushing out his own past policy.

The U.S. team greeted this good news by asking for more. Nitze pressed Karpov to zero out the remaining hundred intermediate missiles in Asia. The advantages of that zero option—simplicity, verifiability, and security—were compelling, at least to us. But Karpov, having gone very far, said he could go no farther.

That's how things stood for weeks—zero intermediate missiles in Europe and one hundred in Asia—until one fine day, Karpov, in a Russian version of a deadpan, said he was fine with zero missiles in Asia.

All at once, a historic arms accord became possible in the time left of the Reagan administration.

In arms control, the devil lies in the details—each one needing to be identified, discussed, negotiated, and settled in a document which ended up to be more than a thousand pages long. Ambassador Nitze in his memoirs wrote, "At one point, Karpov and I estimated the number of remaining issues at about thirty. Two weeks later, Mike Glitman [Nitze's deputy] told me the list had grown to more than a hundred." Some were minor, but even a minor matter could prove a deal buster.

A cable from the White House said that, while the president was pleased by our progress under way, he'd be more pleased if everything could be wrapped up by December. He was eager to get Gorbachev in Washington by the year's end and go to Moscow the following year.

We hadn't planned on such an accelerated schedule, and didn't have all we needed to meet it. Shultz was still wading around the Iran-Contra swamp and couldn't be back at work any time soon. Impatient for progress, I came to believe that the main diversion of Iran-Contra was not that of the funds going to Nicaraguan guerillas but the diversion of top executive time from serious future matters to foolish past deeds.

At the end of February, the Tower Commission issued its final report, which strongly criticized both Reagan and Regan. One investigation down but many to go.

THE ANNUAL ECONOMIC SUMMITS of the industrialized democracies—known then as the G-7—was a must-attend event for presidents, no matter how embroiled in matters at home.

The thirteenth such session had long been scheduled for June 8 to 10 in Venice. Chancellor Helmut Kohl asked the president to stop by Berlin afterward to help celebrate the city's anniversary. Reagan had already been to Berlin twice before as president and didn't need to go again. But Kohl was a friend and faithful ally, and a 750th anniversary didn't come around all that often. So Reagan accepted.

In mid-May, White House speechwriters were given a few minutes in the Oval to discuss remarks the president might need for the trip. With their allotted time running out, speechwriter Tony Dolan asked if the president had anything in mind for the Berlin anniversary. Dolan later recalled what happened next: "He made the well-known nod of the head, said the equally familiar 'Well,' and then added in his soft but resonant intonation, while lifting his hand and letting it fall: 'Tear down the Wall.'" Dolan, who headed the small shop of conservative wordsmiths, was ecstatic.

"Tear down the Wall" was what Ronald Reagan wanted to say, but not many in his administration wanted him to say it. State Department officials claimed it would damage the president's relationship with Gorbachev, which was a bad thing to do at any time and worse to do when serious arms talks were at a critical stage, as they were. Howard Baker, the new White House chief of staff—Don Regan having by then finally departed, amidst much drama—deemed it unpresidential. Frank Carlucci's NSC deputy, General Colin Powell, considered it extreme.

As the speech went through many drafts, the White House speechwriters kept shoving the phrase back in, while other White House officials, backed by the State Department, kept yanking it out. The issue became more polarizing as the speechwriters' words became more offensive, especially by adding Gorbachev's name to the admonition.

This exercise became a ritual which only an anthropologist could have described, or appreciated. As Dolan recalled, "With a fervor and relentlessness I hadn't seen . . . even during disputes about the 'ash heap of history' or 'evil empire,' they kept up the pressure until the morning Reagan spoke."

On that memorable Friday morning—June 12, 1987—Berlin enjoyed clear skies and bright sun as it began its 751st year. The president and Mrs. Reagan came into town from Venice that morning, and headed straight to the Reichstag, the old parliament building, where they climbed up to the balcony to look out at the Wall. "I think it's an ugly scar," Reagan said.

No battle in government gets resolved until it must. But with the speech hours away, must was fast approaching.

Twenty years later, *Time* noted that "the four most famous words of the Reagan presidency almost were never uttered." Deputy White House chief of staff Ken Duberstein rode in the presidential limousine to the speech and raised the wording once again. "It's the right thing to do," the president said quietly, as he resumed gazing out the window.

Reagan was wearing a dark suit and a red striped tie when he mounted the large wooden stage constructed near the iconic Brandenburg Gate, about a hundred yards from where the Wall divided the city. Behind him, as he began speaking at 2:00 p.m. on that picture-perfect afternoon, were two panes of bulletproof glass to protect him from any possible East German sniper. Some forty-five thousand people, many waving small American and West German flags, stood before him.

The president opened in a folksy manner by quoting a popular German song: "I come here today because wherever I go, whatever I do, '*Ich hab noch einen Koffer in Berlin,*' I still have a suitcase in Berlin."

Before long, he got to the meat of his message: "There is one sign the Soviets can make that would be unmistakable, that would advance dramatically the cause of freedom and peace." Then, after a dramatic pause, he let loose: "General Secretary Gorbachev, if you seek peace, if you seek prosperity for the Soviet Union and Eastern Europe, if you seek liberalization, come here to this gate." Another pause, and then: "Mr. Gorbachev, open this gate," which was greeted by an outburst of applause.

The president waited until it died down before he went on. "Mr. Gorbachev"—he then repeated the name, as if intentionally to defy the doubters—"Mr. Gorbachev, tear down this Wall!"

The crowd erupted in wild cheers and shouts. Everyone there knew they had just witnessed something special, something memorable.

The rest of the speech, subsequently overshadowed by that powerful passage, was likewise hard-hitting. Having long believed that the Cold War would end soon, Reagan asserted that the Wall would end sooner: "Yes, across Europe, this Wall will fall. For it cannot withstand faith. It cannot withstand truth. The Wall cannot withstand freedom."

The president said that he wanted a new arms accord and replayed Gorbachev's theme of adapt or die: "In this age of redoubled economic growth of information and innovation, the Soviet Union faces a choice. It must make fundamental changes or it will become obsolete."

Chancellor Helmut Kohl would never forget what was said there and who said it. He later called Reagan "a stroke of luck for the world, especially for Europe."

But some traditional diplomats, even gifted ones, never grasped the power of public diplomacy nor the role that Reagan's campaign to delegitimize the Soviet system played in bending history. George Shultz, in his thousand-plus-page memoir, *Turmoil and Triumph: My Years as Secretary of State*, makes no mention of Reagan's speech that day. Nor does Jack Matlock in his book, *Reagan and Gorbachev: How the Cold War Ended*. Nor did Paul Nitze in his five-hundred-page memoir. Nonetheless, "Mr. Gorbachev, tear down this Wall" became the hallmark, if not the highlight, of Reagan's foreign policy, and, as *Time* declared twenty years later, the most famous words of his presidency.

Unlike the American diplomats, top Soviet officials immediately grasped the power of Reagan's challenge, which was broadcast live across Europe, including into the Eastern bloc and U.S.S.R. The Soviet news agency Tass, obviously with Gorbachev's approval, accused Reagan of giving an "openly provocative, war-mongering speech." The KGB ordered its agents across Eastern Europe to step up their monitoring of "subversives," who might be attracted to such foreign notions. One of those agents stationed in East Germany was a thirty-five-year-old up-and-comer named Vladimir Putin.

THE PRESIDENT WAS PLEASED that his speech showed him to be more than a lame duck, running out the clock of his time in office.

Having boldly challenged Gorbachev where he was most vulnerable, Reagan wanted to work with him where he might be most helpful. He wanted an arms agreement based on what they had agreed to at Reykjavik yet one which trusted but verified. Any acceptable accord had to have tight verification, despite the Soviets' historic opposition to foreign inspectors on their land.

After Karpov misspoke the truth about ending linkage—perhaps the only way he could speak truth—the American negotiators reiterated our Reykjavik request for on-site inspection. By early spring, Karpov broke decades of precedent and agreed. We had, by then, been subject to so many Soviet surprises that we were no longer surprised by them.

Consequently, we devised a tight verification regime, one eased by learning from intelligence sources that all Soviet intermediate missiles were being built at one factory in the town of Votkinsk, Russia. So we would not need to send teams of Americans scrambling across their country. We would need only to monitor that one factory.

Votkinsk is an isolated, mostly snowbound town, some seven hundred miles east of Moscow at the foot of the Ural Mountains, known to music aficionados as the birthplace of Pyotr Ilich Tchaikovsky. Because of its isolation, it has been a major weapons producing center since the reign of Peter the Great. The composer's father had been manager of its ironworks.

Besides producing the intermediate nuclear missiles, Votkinsk's plants also put out drilling equipment, washing machines, dairy equipment, auto bumpers, and massive machinery for construction. Our verification challenge was to distinguish the banned missiles, or their key components, from all the other machinery shipped out of the plant. This was made possible by a radiographic imaging system, duly named CargoScan, to show us if they were sneaking out a missile in a crate marked "washing machine" or "tractor."

We devised a scheme, known as perimeter and portal monitoring, which entailed fencing the whole facility and monitoring its few portals. We presented the scheme to Karpov, expecting strong resistance yet receiving the Russian equivalent of "*nyet* big deal."

That, as it happened, was the easy part. The tough part came when the Soviets asked us for Russian inspectors at our facilities. This was a request we should have anticipated but hadn't.

Instead of our heads nodding in agreement, spines stiffened at the very thought of it. The tables had turned at the bargaining table, with them now all for openness and us spouting arguments against foreign inspectors on our turf. We pointed out that, as an open society, information on American arms production was reported in our newspapers and congressional hearings. Plus, unlike in their case where all such missiles were being made in a single plant, our intermediate missiles were made in many different plants.

That's what we argued. Left unargued was that we were no longer making them. But this the Soviets didn't ask and we didn't tell. Gorbachev had showed at Reykjavik that he *really* wanted our missiles gone from Europe forever. We could use that desire to get their missiles gone forever, from both Europe and Asia.

There the issue sat, but couldn't sit for long. Our argument was unsustainable, and, after a bit, unsustained. If the president was going to get his zero option signed during a Washington summit that year, we needed to move along.

And so we did, after much pulling and hauling within the administration. Once we consented to Russian on-site inspection at an American facility, the natural question became "Which facility?" Someone concocted a scheme—unnecessarily complex, as befits arms control— which ended up with the Soviets being able to inspect the Longhorn Army Ammunition Plant in Waskom, Texas.

With the Washington summit fast approaching, Shultz and Shevardnadze, along with their arms experts, met in Geneva in November to resolve outstanding issues, the inspection site foremost among them.

Rather than being accepted, this choice was met with furrowed brows. "Why the Longhorn facility?" a skeptical Shevardnadze asked. No parts for intermediate missiles were being built there, he asserted.

Well, yes, but then again they weren't being built anywhere, we thought but did not say. Shultz pointed out that Longhorn had been on a list of possible sites that the Soviets had accepted. Shevardnadze couldn't deny this but couldn't accept Longhorn either.

After a flurry of frantic calls back to Washington, a new winner emerged—the Hercules Plant #1 in Magna, Utah. Its big advantage was that it actually had made key components of U.S. intermediate missiles. Its big disadvantage was that it also had made, and in fact was still making, key components for U.S. strategic missiles, which we sure didn't want the Soviets to know about, much less to inspect.

This problem, typical for government, was solved by throwing a lot of money at it. With supplemental funding, the Pentagon could move the sensitive strategic work from Magna to some other facility.

This mini-tale, so stressful at the time, had a happy ending. In fact, it had several happy endings. The Soviets got their U.S. on-site inspections. The Pentagon got its additional funding. Reagan and Gorbachev got their arms agreement. And the thirty or so Soviet inspectors sent to Hercules Plant #1 got a good life then and perhaps in the afterlife.

For the sixty churches and wards of the Church of Jesus Christ of Latter-day Saints, which served the 115,000 souls of Magna and neighboring West Jordan, outdid each other in hosting the Russian inspectors of our nonexistent missile manufacturing. They enjoyed fine dining—albeit without accompanying vodka or even wine—and were showered with invitations to family gatherings, confirmations, and weddings. They were welcomed into homes and given gifts, including Russian translations of the *Book of Mormon*. West Jordan and Votkinsk became official sister cities, which they remain to this day.

Hence while thirty American inspectors were shivering and bored out of their minds in Votkinsk, Russia—you can only visit Tchaikovsky's birthplace so many times—the thirty Soviet inspectors were finding a bit of heaven in Magna and West Jordan.

TRUTH BE TOLD, WE were finding a bit of heaven too. Working on a complicated issue is always fascinating, and crafting a nuclear arms accord sure fits that bill.

Plus, we were making real progress. For years, we had devised solutions to every conceivable arms control problem—at times, even devising solutions to nonproblems—only to find that nothing ever got concluded. Suddenly, thanks to the post-Reykjavik Soviet attitude, all that changed, and arms control became satisfying. As Teddy Roosevelt said, the best prize life has to offer is the chance to perform work worth doing. Here clearly was work worth doing.

All this was happening in the realm of nuclear arms negotiations, which was exciting enough. Even more exciting, though, was all that was happening in the geostrategic realm.

Reagan's speech at the Brandenburg Gate had taken the sheen off Gorbachev's star quality, once everyone realized that he was not about to "tear down this Wall." Nonetheless, he pushed for *glasnost* and *perestroika* harder than before, despite their having the types of contradictions that Marx told presaged revolution. Gorbachev also pushed his anti-alcohol campaign just when the turmoil of his reforms drove citizens to reach for the bottle as never before.

At the end of October 1987 Gorbachev celebrated the Soviet Union's seventieth anniversary with a major address. It was as long and mundane as most of his and his predecessors' speeches were on such occasions, with one major exception. Gorbachev touched the third rail of Soviet politics by taking on the man who had ruled the country for nearly half of those seventy celebrated years, Joseph Stalin. "The guilt of Stalin is enormous and unforgivable," he told his citizens.

In 1956, while the tyrant's body was still nearly warm in the Red Square mausoleum, Nikita Khrushchev had denounced Stalin in his "Secret Speech" to the Twentieth Party Congress. But that speech was, as its name says, delivered in secret and kept a secret. Gorbachev's denunciation was delivered and debated in public.

Before this address, Gorbachev had told his Central Committee that he "understood the impatience of the public wishing to take a look at the closed pages of our past." Among the documents published soon thereafter was Khrushchev's Secret Speech, for the first time ever.

The parliament took Gorbachev's words to heart and opened the closed pages of the 1930s and 1940s. Members of the Duma vigorously debated whether Stalin had murdered more people than Hitler (he had) and whether it was Stalin, or Lenin, who had created the reign of terror (Lenin started it and Stalin extended it). Historians, freed from their ideological shackles, examined how Stalin's henchmen starved and worked to death millions of loyal peasants and slaughtered tens of thousands of patriotic plant managers, military officers, and intelligentsia.

Citizen associations began identifying and marking the pits into which thousands of bodies had been tossed. They put up plaques to honor the unknown victims of such horrendous crimes.

By opening the closed pages of Communism's past seventy years, Gorbachev was endangering the next seventy years of Communist rule.

The precipitous decline in legitimacy prompted pushes for faster and deeper reforms than anything Gorbachev had proposed. He was accused of having what Lincoln lamented in his generals, a bad case of the slows. During one volatile Central Committee meeting, Boris Yeltsin—Moscow's rambunctious mayor, whose ambitions extended beyond the city's boundaries—attacked Gorbachev on this basis. Such an outburst would previously have had him banished or, under Lenin or Stalin, even liquidated. Now it got him expelled from the Politburo. Based on past experience, that would be the end of Boris Yeltsin. It wasn't.

For all its audacity at the time, Reagan's six-year assault on the legitimacy of the Soviet system suddenly seemed like small potatoes. Ronald Reagan was no longer the main person undermining the regime's foundations. Mikhail Gorbachev was.

. . . .

WHILE TENSIONS WERE WAXING in Moscow, they were waning in Washington. Iran-Contra had stripped Ronald Reagan of the sparkle he had in the first half of his second term. But at least he was coming through the gauntlet of investigations in one piece.

At the end of August, he gave his final speech on the scandal. Half explaining and half excusing, he said, "Our original initiative got all tangled up in the sale of arms, and the sale of arms got tangled up with the hostages." Sympathy had trumped responsibility: "I let my preoccupation with the hostages intrude into areas where it didn't belong."

In mid-November, one year after the Lebanese "rag" broke the story, the congressional committees issued their final reports. Although they differed in many ways, they all blamed the president for poor management and, in the words of one report, his administration for "secrecy, deception, and disdain for the law." It was bad, but it was over.

Both Reagan and Gorbachev now desired—in fact, both were now desperate for—a superpower summit. That seemed the only thing around to help them go from failures at home to successes abroad, from being deemed stumbling politicians to being portrayed as global statesmen. In short, they felt that the best way to counter the prevailing narratives in Washington and Moscow was to build on Reykjavik.

FOR THAT TO HAPPEN, however, several different and undependable elements had to fall in place. The Soviet negotiators would have to stay cooperative. Secretary Shultz would have to reemerge from Iran-Contra and reengage in arms negotiations. And the arms experts would have to find acceptable solutions to the endless problems that arose.

Over the past year, Shultz had been not only distracted but also discounted in the Washington power meter. He had disparaged the Iran-Contra freelancers in the White House and the president for, at best, failing to control them and, at worse, for egging them on. But Shultz was too able and Reagan too decent to keep the two of them apart for long. Their relationship healed but did so, as do most human relationships, all too slowly and incompletely. They resumed working together, although never with the same mutual trust and admiration so evident at Reykjavik.

Though Shultz's relationship with the president had been strained, his ties sideways—with Eduard Shevardnadze—and downward—with representatives of sundry U.S. government agencies—held strong. Shultz was a workmanlike negotiator and he was dogged. The ex-marine would storm any hill, tackle any issue to accomplish his mission. The arms agreement would not have happened without him or without Shevardnadze across the table from him. Don Oberdorfer counted thirty-three Shultz-Shevardnadze sessions during the forty months they overlapped in office.

They met in different cities to nail down the arms control deal. In April 1987 Shultz and his team spent two days negotiating with Shevardnadze and his team in Moscow. At the end of the first day, several of us attended an unforgettable seder hosted by Ambassador Jack Matlock at Spaso House, the U.S. ambassador's historic home. When we read the Haggadah, which tells of a people seeking to escape from bondage into a land of freedom, the story held special meaning.

After the service, Shultz and I, adorned with white yarmulkes, circled the room to greet the fifty or so Soviet dissidents and their families attending. They had been denied permission, many for several years, to leave for a land of freedom.

One wrought, bearded academic described how he had been fired from his university post, his kids expelled from their preferred school, and his wife downgraded in her bureaucratic position after the family applied for an exit visa to Israel. He was sweating profusely and shook some, so I asked if he was ill. No, he explained. He had been on a hunger strike for days, as a desperate attempt to get the family visas approved.

Before we parted, he asked me to thank President Reagan and to tell him that he and the United States of America were the main things going for him—and for all those living in bondage who wished to escape to a land of freedom. I promised him I would tell the president that and, when I did, he loved hearing it.

After that April meeting, Shultz and Shevardnadze met more frequently. They held sidebar meetings at international gatherings over the summer. Then in September Shevardnadze came to Washington, where Reagan welcomed him into the Oval Office and hosted a working lunch for him in the White House, to which he graciously invited several of us along. In mid-October Shultz and his team traveled to Moscow for two more days of meetings. A few weeks later, as the sprint to the summit began, Shevardnadze was back in Washington for another two days of bargaining. A fortnight later, the two teams met in Geneva for two days. By then, only weeks remained until the summit was due to begin.

While the issues were most vital then, the personalities are most vivid now. The last Geneva trip was the first for Colin Powell to join our traveling troupe. Colin had been Frank Carlucci's deputy at the NSC. When Frank became secretary of defense, Colin replaced him as national security adviser.

My fondest memory came from that Geneva trip. Like so many of the best experiences in life, this one came unexpectedly.

After a long day of bargaining, Shevardnadze was hosting a dinner at the Soviet chancellery for the two delegations. The dinner began unexceptionally—with the usual mutual appreciation for each side's efforts during the day and expressions of mutual determination to resolve outstanding issues the following day.

The ever-tenacious Shultz teed up several issues that needed more work, but even those of us who lived and breathed arms control quietly groaned. By then, we had arms control coming out our ears. We needed a break, if only for the few hours of a lovely dinner.

Looking across the lavishly set dining table at Marshal Akhromeyev, I said that many of us had read of his background with interest. I was saying in diplomat speak that the thick CIA dossier on him made fascinating reading. It told how he had grown up outside of Moscow in poverty, raised by a single mom, and escaped into the army in 1940, at the age of seventeen. Over the next forty-six years, he had gone from the very bottom of the heap to the very top, remaining humble throughout. He polished his own boots, made his own bed, and lived in a confined, four-room Moscow apartment with his wife and two daughters. At sixty-four, he rose early, did an hour of rigorous exercise, arrived at his desk by 7:30, and stayed there until around midnight.

At Reykjavik, he had startled us by saying that he was "the last of the Mohicans"—he loved reading James Fenimore Cooper—meaning that he was the last active-duty Soviet soldier who had fought in World War II. He had been in a tank unit on the eastern front.

Knowing this from the intelligence reports and from our hallway conversations in Hofdi House, I asked if he would mind telling us about his wartime experiences. He responded with a warm expression coming across his face.

Akhromeyev was only eighteen when he was stationed on a road outside of Leningrad in 1941. His unit commander had been ordered to hold the road, no matter what the German Army Group North threw at him. In riveting detail, he told how his unit did not budge, despite temperatures plummeting to twenty degrees below zero.

Meanwhile, inside Leningrad nearly a thousand soldiers and civilians were dying *each day*. More than a million and a half perished before the nine-hundred-day siege was lifted, early in 1944. The police formed special units to stop cannibalism, and arrested more than 250 people for the crime during those barbaric days.

Akhromeyev painted the horror of it all vividly, but with military precision. Just to be clear, he added in his modest manner, he had *not* been posted on that road for the entire siege. He was there a mere eighteen months. But during what he called "that relatively brief time," he never once left. He never once entered a building. He and his comrades slept in their tents, staying on that road through repeated and ruthless German panzer assaults and the brutal Russian winter.

Unlike most of his colleagues, who died or were seriously wounded, he was hit only twice. Aside from still carrying shrapnel in his body and losing hearing in one ear, he had suffered nothing more lasting.

All of us, on both sides of Shevardnadze's table, Russian and American alike, became transfixed as he related his story. Only Powell dared to speak, first asking what type of tank his unit manned. It was the T-34, a legendary weapon for its time which, according to their back-and-forths, had big guns and a sloping armor that deflected German artillery. Before long, these two old soldiers were deep into their tales of days and battles long past.

Even wonderful things must end, including this conversation after ninety minutes or so. Shultz thanked our host, and reminded us that we faced another big day tomorrow. He then thanked the marshal for sharing such rich experiences with us. With genuine sincerity, the secretary said that the young Akhromeyev's guarding the Leningrad road for those eighteen months represented what Americans most admired in the Soviet people—their personal grit and deep love of the motherland. That, he said, was inspiring to all Americans.

Akhromeyev smiled and thanked the secretary for his kind words. He then paused, looked across the table, and said, "But we all knew, Mr. Secretary, that Stalin would have had us shot if we had left the road."

I thought I heard an involuntary "Oh" emit from Secretary Shultz, sitting one person from me. Regardless, everyone then stood and bid hasty adieus. We walked into a cold, dark Geneva night in late November, with the weather seeming less frigid than when we had arrived.

THE EAST ROOM IS the largest and grandest room in the White House. It is also a room filled with American history—of presidential tributes and caskets, of children playing and the nation mourning, of private inaugurations and public ceremonies—like the signing of the intermediate missile arms treaty.

Visitors entering the large rectangular room are struck by its spaciousness and warm, golden glow. Most prominently displayed is the life-size Gilbert Stuart portrait of George Washington, his arm extended as if in welcome. Painted from life in 1796, it is the oldest object in the White House, the one heroically rescued by Dolley Madison in 1814, when the British set the Executive Mansion ablaze. A century later, a similar-size portrait of Martha Washington was commissioned and then hung on the same wall to accompany her husband.

As powerful as the feelings a first-time visitor takes from the room is the history a well-versed person brings into the room. It's where Abigail Adams famously hung the family undergarments up to dry, where Thomas Jefferson's aide and explorer, Meriwether Lewis, placed his bed and installed his office. It's where several presidents staged their inaugurations and where presidents' children played. Tad Lincoln harnessed two goats to a kitchen chair and steered them around the big room.

Union troops guarding the capital were quartered there, but had to clear out to accommodate President Lincoln's grand reception for Ulysses S. Grant upon his becoming general of the Union Army in 1864. A year later, Lincoln's body would lie in state there, as did that of John F. Kennedy nearly a century later. His casket rested on the catafalque constructed for Lincoln, which would be used again forty-one years later for another president.

Teddy Roosevelt's irrepressible daughter, Alice Roosevelt Longworth, was married in the East Room, and various other TR children roller-skated across the parquet. As did Amy Carter, who left marks from her skates in the delicate floor that weren't sanded away for thirty years.

A few minutes before 2:00 p.m. on December 8, 1987, a baritone from the U.S. Army Band—sounding like one imagines to be the voice of God—announced: "The president of the United States and the general secretary of the Communist party of the Soviet Union."

Ronald Reagan and Mikhail Gorbachev entered the East Room side by side, having strolled down the long red carpet of the Cross Hall adorned with the haunting portrait of John F. Kennedy and paintings of other Cold War presidents.

After the men entered and mounted a riser, the military band played the "Star Spangled Banner" and the "Gimn Sovetskogo Soyuza," the national anthem of the Soviet Union. Then the two men sat at a massive walnut table that had been constructed for Abraham Lincoln's cabinet. The table has a series of drawers that lock, so that Lincoln and his seven cabinet officers could safely store their papers between meetings. Reagan would have relished knowing of the table's use on January 15, 1929, when diplomats from around the world used it to sign the Kellogg-Briand Pact.

On that bright December day in 1987, some 250 guests filled the East Room. In the front row sat Secretary Shultz, wearing the only gray suit among the sea of men in black. Nancy Reagan wore a black suit top and skirt with a white ruffled blouse, while her erstwhile rival sitting by her side, Raisa Gorbachev, wore a gray ensemble highlighted by an appropriately red scarf.

On that front row was also Marshal Akhromeyev, sitting to the left of where I was sitting, two rows back. He nodded and smiled broadly when I looked over and waved a greeting to him.

The signing ceremony was rich with diplomatic tradition. The treaty had been printed on parchment paper and bound in two leather folders—one slate blue for the United States, the other burgundy red for the Soviet Union. The president and the general secretary signed each copy in eight places, their sixteen signatures scrupulously guided by a hovering diplomat, who indicated just where they should sign.

In the middle of this stilted procedure, Gorbachev turned to Reagan and, with an impish grin, asked if he might like to exchange pens. "Let's keep these pens for memory's sake," he said. Reagan considered this a fine idea and smiled as they traded pens.

Like many things after Reykjavik—including Reagan's exhortation to "tear down this Wall" and the completion of the treaty itself—this East Room ceremony nearly didn't happen. A glitch had suddenly arisen earlier that day.

Under the treaty terms, each side had to furnish a photograph of its missile, so the other could know what to identify during its monitoring. Someone noticed that the Soviets had presented us with a photo of the canister in which the missile is stored—which looks like any missile canister—and not of the missile itself, which has distinctive features. When Shultz raised the matter, Shevardnadze claimed that there was no photo of the missile anywhere, only of its canister.

Even with so much at stake—the East Room ceremony having already been prepared, the guests about to arrive—Reagan decided to hold firm. He felt that if they welshed on this peripheral provision, they would welsh later on more major matters.

We all held our breaths, waiting to see whether everything we had worked so hard to accomplish over the past fourteen months would be torpedoed at the last minute for want of a snapshot. But within the hour, the Soviets found that there *was* a photo of the missile after all. A faxed version was presented to us mid-morning—some three hours before the ceremony was to begin—with the actual photo arriving the next day. Once that crisis was resolved, the signing ceremony was good to go.

IN HIS REMARKS TO the East Room audience, President Reagan reflected how "it was over six years ago . . . that I first proposed . . . the zero option. It was a simple proposal, one might say disarmingly simple."

He took justifiable pride that one of his radical changes in U.S. foreign policy was being realized. "Unlike treaties in the past," he said, this accord "didn't simply codify the status quo or a new arms buildup. . . . For the first time in history, the language of 'arms control' was replaced by 'arms reduction'—in this case, the complete elimination of an entire class of U.S. and Soviet nuclear missiles."

Then, Reagan being Reagan, couldn't help but utter *doveryai, no proveryai*. Gorbachev, in a robust voice, interrupted by calling out, "You repeat that at every meeting!" Reagan smiled and, quick as a flash, shot back to a chuckling Gorbachev: "Well, I like it!" This was greeted with great laughter and loud applause.

Gorbachev spoke next. His remarks, like the president's, were broadcast live across the Soviet Union to an estimated 180 million of its 282 million population. In Moscow, where it was a frigid snowy night, a crowd stood for more than an hour on Kalinin Prospekt, watching on the giant screen specially constructed for the White House broadcast.

Gorbachev spoke of their mutual desire for a "nuclear-free world" and said he hoped that "December 8, 1987, becomes a date that will be inscribed in the history books, a date that will mark the watershed separating the era of a mounting risk of a nuclear war from the era of a demilitarization of human life."

. . . .

THE TREATY WAS NOT the ideal accord the two men sought when sitting around the small table in Hofdi House. It wouldn't eliminate all ballistic missiles, or all strategic weapons, or any of the other grand categories of nuclear weapons they had tossed around that table.

Nonetheless, the treaty did eliminate all intermediate nuclear missiles, thereby ending the foremost security threat that our allies faced over more than a decade. And it answered the massive Western European protests over the Euro-missile deployments, by allowing us to withdraw our missiles already deployed on their soil. Best of all, it began a steep decline in the numbers of nuclear weapons held by both superpowers—a decline that continues to this day. From this treaty, and especially from the precedent it set on verification, sprang other significant agreements concluded under subsequent presidents, including Barack Obama.

AFTER THE EAST ROOM ceremony came a private session between Reagan and Gorbachev. A few hours later, the Reagans hosted a gala state dinner at the White House for the Soviet first couple.

The next day, Shultz hosted a luncheon in the magnificent reception area on the eighth floor of the State Department building. The glitterati of Washington, New York, and Hollywood attended. In the long receiving line, Gorbachev—innately charming and superbly briefed—mustered up a quip for virtually every person he met, most for the first time.

Carol and I sat with Barbara Walters and Donald Trump and strained to get a word in edgewise at our chatty table. Gorbachev sat smiling and thumping his hand on the table near ours, while the Yale Russian Chorus sang Russian ballads and, for Shevardnadze's sake, a few from Georgia as well.

The next day, Gorbachev's last in Washington, he and Vice President George H. W. Bush held a lengthy morning discussion at the Soviet embassy. Suddenly it was noon, and they were already late for lunch with the president.

Along with Shevardnadze, they piled into the Zil limo for the brief ride up Sixteenth Street to the White House. The big boxy vehicle looked strange to pedestrians, as it barreled down Washington's busy lunchtime streets. The Zil was accompanied by the usual posse of security vans, press vehicles, and police squad cars; flanked by police motorcycles, their engines roaring loudly; and followed by a disheartening ambulance, bringing up the rear.

Even though they were already running late, Gorbachev impulsively told his driver to stop. He wanted to hop out to say hello to Americans on the street. This was a masterful move, one that the impresario of public presentation, Ronald Reagan, must have admired.

In his own version of the royals' walkabouts in England, Gorbachev clambered out of the limo and headed onto the sidewalk with his arm outstretched, greeting people exuberantly. Vice President Bush later commented, "He interacted with the people like nothing I've seen."

He happened to halt at Connecticut Avenue and L Street, the very epicenter of the law and lobbying elite. Washingtonians on their lunchtime break, or shopping at the area's boutiques, flocked to Gorbachev, leaving Bush and Shevardnadze standing by themselves, looking on.

A few seconds later, the advance cars in Gorbachev's motorcade realized that his limo was no longer behind them. Their drivers slammed on the brakes and shoved their vehicles into a breakneck reverse. The police "made furious U-turns on their motorcycles, and flatfoots beat it down the street with their hands on their holsters," reported future *New Yorker* editor David Remnick and Lois Romano in the *Washington Post*. When the American and Russian security guards finally got to Gorbachev's side, some shouted, "Keep your hands out of your pockets! Hands out of pockets!"

But hardly anyone could hear them, so loud was the commotion around Gorbachev, who was "working the crowd like a presidential candidate" with "the out-thrust hand, the ready smile, the minimalist chatter, 'Hello. Hello. How are you? Hello.'" At times, he spoke in Russian to say, "We come from two great countries," and "It was so good to come here."

One floor above, customers and waiters at Duke Zeibert's, the capital's legendary spot for power lunches, rushed onto the balcony to see what all the commotion was about. Expecting a rock star, they instead spotted a general secretary, who looked up at the expense-account crowd and waved. After a few minutes, Gorbachev climbed back into his limo to proceed to the White House, only blocks away.

Gorbachev had pressed the flesh with maybe twenty-five people, not many by U.S. campaign standards. But the impact of his gesture was profound. The American people could no longer envision the Soviet leader as a bland apparatchik, much less as a stern commissar. Henceforth, they would see him as a familiar Western-style politician, connecting with the public in a way no other Soviet chief had, or could have.

Few people ever keep the president of the United States waiting, let alone for an hour and a half. Yet the car filled with the three men was that late when it entered the circular driveway near the South Portico. But Reagan wasn't miffed. Far from it, as he walked out to greet Gorbachev with a jovial, "I thought you'd gone home!" Gorbachev explained what Reagan already knew. "I had a chat with a group of Americans."

Looking back on that episode sixteen years later, Gorbachev rightly reflected, "I think it was a wonderful encounter. . . . People of both of our countries were just tired of the strain of living under the spell of an arms race and of the Cold War for so many years."

WHILE GORBACHEV WAS WORKING the crowd on Connecticut Avenue, Akhromeyev was creating his own sensation by becoming the first Soviet official to ever visit the Pentagon.

At a welcoming ceremony on the lawn in front of the Mall entrance, he was accorded the military honors befitting a five-star marshal. He greeted each of the U.S. Joint Chiefs of Staff before moving inside to the chairman's office for a discussion. At last, Admiral Bill Crowe could talk with the man he had missed meeting at Reykjavik.

During this, their first encounter, the old troopers shared some stories and information and felt a kinship coming on. At the close of the session, Crowe invited Akhromeyev to return in 1988 to tour U.S. military bases around America.

At about the same time, across the Potomac River in the White House, Gorbachev extended Reagan an invitation to visit Moscow, likewise in 1988. Both invitations were readily accepted.

The next morning, Gorbachev, Shevardnadze, and Akhromeyev boarded their Aeroflot plane at Andrews Air Force Base to head home after what they, and virtually everyone else, hailed as a stellar summit. The three Soviet officials felt closer than ever before. They had worked together to achieve something significant, reducing nuclear arsenals as had never been done before. Unbeknownst to them was how their relationships would fray and then disintegrate, far beyond anything that had happened with the Reagan-Shultz relationship earlier that year.

TWO DAYS AFTER GORBACHEV left Washington, I left government.

By then, I had been in various federal posts for a dozen years, seven of them in the Reagan administration. The previous summer, I had told the president and Secretary Shultz that, once the missile accord was concluded—if, indeed, it could be concluded—I planned to leave. Shultz and Carlucci subsequently called me into their offices to urge me to head up USAID, the government's foreign aid agency. I considered this offer flattering yet misguided, as I knew little, actually nothing, of development economics.

As I was leaving, I recalled what Dean Acheson once said, that to leave public life is to die a little. Like him, I would miss the excitement and challenges, intellectual and, even bigger, emotional. Nonetheless, I wanted to leave office feeling that I had accomplished what I had set out to do. Nothing, I thought, could be more important than helping to conclude an arms accord, built on agreements reached at Reykjavik, which eliminated a good number of deadly nuclear weapons.

This turned out to be quite wrong. Changes in the geostrategic realm, propelled significantly by Reykjavik, would soon overshadow the nuclear cuts we had achieved.

Back as a private citizen, like everyone else in America and around the world, I would watch these events unfold with utter amazement.

CHAPTER 9

Reykjavik and the
Soviet Breakup

The Washington summit was every bit as spectacular as Ronald Reagan had hoped it would be. Wonderful events followed it—his old California friend Anthony Kennedy being confirmed as Supreme Court justice, the Washington Redskins decimating the Denver Broncos in Super Bowl XXII, and Americans piling up gold at the Calgary Winter Olympics.

Even more wonderful, though less noticed, was the U.S. Postal Service issuing a memorial stamp honoring Knute Rockne. Reagan cherished his role as quarterback George Gipp in the 1940 film *Knute Rockne—All American,* delivering the dying man's lines, which were so fitting to his character, both in the film and in his life: "Tell them to go out there with all they've got and just win one for the Gipper. I don't know where I'll be then, but I'll know about it, and I'll be happy." Reagan was happy whenever anyone called him "The Gipper"— sometimes, it seemed to me, even more than when people called him "Mr. President."

Still, nothing could match the heights of the Washington summit, with its signing of the arms pact. He and Gorbachev had gone over their other topics—SDI and the ABM Treaty, nuclear testing, strategic arms cuts—but their discussion on these was becoming perfunctory. Neither expected the other to concede and both realized that an agreement eliminating nuclear weapons was far beyond even their reach. Cutting strategic nuclear arms by half—in the manner Akhromeyev had agreed during our all-night session—*was* possible, given enough time. But there simply wasn't enough time to complete this in 1988.

While Reagan was back on track, Gorbachev was backtracking on Soviet engagement abroad. In April his spokesman announced the withdrawal of all Soviet troops from Afghanistan. That constituted a big win for the Reagan doctrine, which supported the rollback of Communist regimes anywhere, and represented a big loss for the Brezhnev doctrine, which supported the permanency of Communist regimes everywhere, if need be by the dispatch of Soviet troops.

In the spring of 1988 Reagan and Gorbachev began anticipating their third summit in three years. This too was gearing up to be some show, with the world's foremost anti-Communist entering the Communist epicenter, the man who had dubbed the Soviet Union an "evil empire" and the "center of evil in the modern world" being its welcomed guest.

THE PRESIDENT LEFT THE White House on May 25, weeks after a military dustup with Iran and days after endorsing Vice President George H. W. Bush as his successor.

The White House staff wisely scheduled three days in Helsinki for Reagan to shake off jet lag before he would arrive in Moscow for the five-day summit. Though well into his seventies, Reagan was still in stellar shape. "Since I came to the White House," he said smiling, "I got two hearing aids, a colon operation, skin cancer, a prostate operation and I was shot. The damn thing is I've never felt better in my life."

It was a warm, sunny afternoon in Moscow when Air Force One landed at Vnukovo Airport on Sunday, May 29. Among the stone-faced officials there to welcome the Reagans on their first-ever visit to Russia were three Politburo members whom the president knew fairly well.

Andrei Gromyko, the former foreign minister who had been kicked upstairs, was there to greet his fellow president. As they shook hands, Gromyko looked like he was grimacing with pain but was actually attempting to produce a smile. His rather hearty wife, Lidia, looked more genuinely pleased as she handed a bouquet of red roses to Nancy Reagan. Next in line was Eduard Shevardnadze, whom the president knew well from their hours around the Reykjavik conference table and the White House dining table. Last in the welcoming trio was Ambassador Anatoly Dobrynin.

Standing farther off on the tarmac was a group of Americans in jeans and T-shirts, with kids waving small American flags. These were the staff and family members of the U.S. embassy in Moscow, dressed like they were off to a Saturday morning Little League game. Both the president and the first lady smiled and waved when spotting this slice of Americana there in Moscow.

With the official greetings tendered and the bouquet accepted, the Reagans stood at attention as a Soviet military band and drill team marched. "Sunlight sparkled off the tubas and cymbals as the band played the national anthems of the two countries," Steven Roberts reported in the *New York Times*, "and the resounding thump of the marching units echoed in unison as they paraded past Mr. Reagan." The president had to restrain himself from saluting the smartly attired, perfectly coordinated troops of America's main enemy in the world.

Unlike at Reykjavik, the Secret Service had flown in the presidential Cadillac Fleetwood limo, assuming that any vehicle available locally would be bugged to a fare-thee-well. On the way into Moscow, the presidential motorcade was accompanied by the usual flotilla of black vans and cars filled with aides, security staff, press entourage, and medical assistants. They sped down the center of the wide highway, closed to other traffic in both directions, and flew by a tank-shaped sculpture, which marked the farthest advance of the 1941 Nazi assault, just a few miles shy of the Kremlin.

Inside the city limits, Moscow's lampposts were decorated with American and Soviet flags. Overhead, two humongous flags hung from blimps. The Moscow city fathers were clearly pulling out all stops for this visit by an American president, especially since the last one, by Richard Nixon in July 1974, had been such a downer. Besieged by Watergate even while in Moscow, he resigned weeks later.

The Reagans passed through a huge gate into the Kremlin court-yard, stopping at the Grand Palace. If anything, its name was an un-derstatement. Built in the 1830s and '40s as the tsar's local abode, it contained more than seven hundred rooms.

The first couple was led to the elaborately gilded St. George's Hall, which was nearly the length of a football field. The welcoming scene had been nicely choreographed, as the Reagans walked down a red carpet from one end of the room while the Gorbachevs approached from the other. They met in the middle—somewhere around the fifty-yard line—and warmly greeted one another.

Standing before a smattering of officials and a bank of cameras, Gorbachev told the president, "Aware of your interest in Russian prov-erbs, let me add another one to your collection: 'It is better to see once than to hear a hundred times.' Let me assure you that you can look forward to hospitality, warmth, and goodwill." That night, Reagan wrote in his diary, "There is no question in my mind but that a certain chemistry does exist between us."

Reagan's response, while equally gracious, was more substantive. He praised the missile treaty, welcomed progress on the strategic accord, and hailed the Soviet withdrawal from Afghanistan. Then he presented his own "literary saying from your past, another example of your people's succinct wisdom—*rodilsya ne toropilsya*—it was born, it wasn't rushed. Mr. General Secretary, we did not rush. We have taken our work step by step." David Remnick, then stationed in Moscow, wrote, "Although his Russian pronunciation sounds as if he is gargling pebbles, the president today once more slipped a grandmotherly Slavic proverb into his summit remarks." The proverb provoked glances around the room as many there—including Ambassador Jack Matlock, a scholar steeped in Russian history and literature—had never heard of the proverb. The president ended his remarks with words most unremarkable anywhere but there: "God bless you."

Despite the welcome's corniness, the press was eating it up. THE GIPPER VISITS THE EVIL EMPIRE ran the headline on Terrence Hunt's first summit dispatch for the Associated Press. In a classic understatement, Reagan told *Time* magazine, "I never expected to be here."

SOME FIVE THOUSAND MEMBERS of the Fourth Estate, even more than at Reykjavik, had come to cover the Soviet spectacle.

The Reagans would be staying at Spaso House, the American ambassador's stately and historic residence, some three miles from the Kremlin. Unlike at Reykjavik, the ambassador and his wife would remain in the residence while the president and first lady stayed in its guest quarters.

As the Reagans were settling in, the president's aides were registering at the Mezhdunarodnaya Hotel, which was midway between Spaso House and the Kremlin. Since Westerners are unlikely to recommend or rebook rooms at a hotel they cannot pronounce or conceivably spell, it was called "the Mezh" or, easier still, "The International Hotel."

While the American team had occupied about a dozen or twenty rooms in the Holt Hotel at Reykjavik, the White House staff now occupied 516 of the Mezh's 542 rooms. Writing about the hotel, AP's Carol Williams reported, "At night, the atrium lobby and the bars are frequented by well-dressed Soviet prostitutes, who are permitted into the premises closed to other Soviets, apparently in exchange for information about their clients." She learned that its entrances "are guarded by uniformed doormen, some of whom dissidents say are former prison camp guards."

The international press was assigned to the Rossiya Hotel. What the vast five-thousand-room hotel lacked in charm and efficiency—and it lacked almost everything in charm and efficiency—it made up in location. The Rossiya was just across Red Square from the Kremlin. On its roof, for a goodly fee, broadcasters rented space for background shots of both sites, which were even more breathtaking at night, with television floodlights on them. All four U.S. networks anchored their nightly news that week from the Rossiya roof.

It's considered bad form, and worse diplomacy, for a president to criticize his host, or host country, when abroad.

Even the conservative Republicans Richard Nixon and Henry Kissinger fawned over Mao Zedong, a man responsible for upward of 40 million deaths, when they visited Beijing in the midst of the Cultural Revolution, the very epitome of his barbarity. Likewise, FDR and Truman's meetings with Stalin; Eisenhower and Kennedy's with Khrushchev; and Nixon, Ford, and Carter's with Brezhnev—all focused on matters other than the oppression these Communist dictators inflicted upon their citizens.

In this respect, as in so many others, Ronald Reagan was the outlier president. In Moscow, he would prove troublesome to his host, not because of his deportment—Reagan could not be anything but gracious—but because of his compulsion to exalt the virtues of freedom and free enterprise.

The Moscow summit thus differed from all previous summits, including Reagan's own summits with Gorbachev. At Reykjavik, everything important happened behind closed doors in Hofdi House, but in Moscow nothing important happened behind the rose and silver doors of St. Catherine's Hall. Unlike their free-wheeling discussions in Reykjavik, the Reagan-Gorbachev discussions in Moscow constituted a diplomatic quadrille. Both men realized that, with the U.S. elections only months away, Reagan was the lamest of ducks. "The two were like actors wearily reciting a familiar script," recalled Matlock, who attended all five of their private sessions.

At Reykjavik, the leaders alternated between the negotiations realm—matters of nuclear cuts, SDI, ABM Treaty, and the like—and the grander geostrategic realm—the relative merits of Communism versus capitalism. At the Washington summit, the focus had been on the negotiation realm, completing and signing the arms accord. At Moscow, it would be exclusively on the geostrategic realm—the faults of the country hosting him and the fundamental changes needed in its system.

Along with altering the focus, Reagan also altered the process—with the primary emphasis going from private to public diplomacy. He somehow sensed that, in the new information age, with more countries becoming more open—including, in its own limited and halting ways, the U.S.S.R.—what was said boldly in local speeches, town hall meetings, and intellectual salons counted more than anything said behind the closed doors of foreign ministries, or even grand palaces. Reagan's new style of diplomacy was adopted and expanded years later, especially by Hillary Clinton as secretary of state.

HAVING SEEN THE TRANSFORMING effect of Gorbachev's foray on Connecticut Avenue, the Reagans set out on their first afternoon in Moscow for Arbat Street.

Arbat was quickly becoming the Haight-Ashbury of Moscow, where artists and entrepreneurs converged to strum their guitars and peddle their wares. The centuries-old street was getting filled with souvenir stalls, cafes, boutiques, and modish restaurants, including Moscow's own Hard Rock Café.

Although the tony Arbat was the pedestrian embodiment of *glasnost*, it still resided in a Communist land. Soon into their stroll, the president and first lady were mobbed by a friendly crowd. They were soon confronted with citizens seeking to reach out and touch them, an unaccustomed experience in Moscow. Soviet security forces may have panicked. They pushed people away and pushed the president and first lady toward their limo.

The president was shocked, writing that night in his diary: "The KGB was on hand, and I've never seen such brutal manhandling." This incident made such a deep impression that Reagan related it months later, in his Farewell Address to the Nation. "While the man on the street in the Soviet Union yearns for peace, the government is Communist, and those who run it are Communists." That's why we must still "keep up our guard" when dealing with Communists.

BUT DURING THESE DAYS of May, it was Gorbachev who had to keep up his guard. SUMMIT BEGINS WITH A CLASH: REAGAN, GORBACHEV DUEL ON HUMAN RIGHTS ran the headline of the *Chicago Tribune*'s first summit article. Steven Roberts reported in the *New York Times* that Gorbachev "was irritated, not so much at the specific points raised as by Mr. Reagan's insistence on discussing the issues at all." Reagan typically had a more equable opinion. "I introduced my favorite pitch— why he should give his people religious freedom," he wrote in his diary that night. "It was a good session & a nice way to launch the summit."

Gorbachev could have thought of a nicer way. He sent Reagan a signal via his official spokesman the next morning, "We don't like it when someone from outside is teaching us how to live." Though sent, the signal wasn't received, as that "someone from outside" ratcheted up his teaching them how to live.

Short of donning the burlap robe of an Old Testament prophet, Reagan in Moscow proclaimed the Gospel according to Friedrich

Hayek, Ayn Rand, and Billy Graham. In venues around Moscow, he said in public the type of tough talk he delivered in private at Hofdi House.

Visiting the revered Danilov Monastery—founded in the thirteenth century by Alexander Nevsky's son—the president called for "a new age of religious freedom in the Soviet Union." Most audacious was his quoting of Alexandr Solzhenitsyn—the Nobel Prize–winning author, who was still banned from public mention, let alone publication in his homeland—that "faith is as elemental to this land as the dark and fertile soil."

At the Spaso House, Reagan hosted a reception for several dozen Soviet dissidents, many of whom were picked up by U.S. embassy cars to assure their presence and safety. With reporters taking down his every word, the president urged Gorbachev "to lift all curbs on freedom of religion, stop jailing people for things they say and write, and allow citizens full freedom of emigration and travel." While *glasnost* was welcome, more was needed, especially "institutional changes to make progress permanent."

Reagan told them, needlessly by then, "I've come to Moscow with a human rights agenda."

He predicted to the assembled dissidents that "freedom will truly come to all [Russians], for what injustice can withstand your strength, and what can conquer your prayers?" Whenever he meets an atheist, he is "tempted to invite him to the greatest gourmet dinner that one could ever serve. And when we've finished eating that magnificent dinner, to ask him if he believes there's a cook."

Reagan closed with a quote from the embodiment of the Russian soul, Alexandr Pushkin: "It's time my friend, it's time. The heart begs for peace. The days fly by. It's time, it's time."

On the Soviet news that evening, Gorbachev's spokesman tried again: "What a shame he would come all this way for an important meeting and waste his time on something like this."

Undeterred, the president headed out to Moscow State University. Dwarfed beneath a massive gold hammer and sickle and a huge white plaster bust of Lenin, he spoke of the technological revolution that had helped design spacecraft and enabled the "King of Pop," Michael Jackson, to produce the sounds of a large orchestra on a single synthesizer. He told the story of college dropouts launching successful computer companies from their dads' garages. Though such a story had become hackneyed in America by then, there it took on the quality of a Russian fairy tale. The president brought it home with a lesson: "Bureaucrats are no substitute for entrepreneurs."

To conclude, Reagan spoke to the students of their future: "Your generation is living in one of the most exciting, hopeful times in Soviet history. It is a time when the first breath of freedom stirs the air, and the heart beats to the accelerated rhythm of hope, when the accumulated spiritual energies of a long silence yearn to break free."

Reagan's speech was met with thunderous applause and a standing ovation—"the most enthusiastic," Matlock noted "since the demonstration which followed his nomination at the Republican convention."

In yet another public forum, this one for Soviet artists and writers, the president championed the "permanent end to restrictions on . . . creativity . . . not just for your sake, but our own," and repeated his hope that "the works of Solzhenitsyn would be published in the land he loved so much."

Through all this, Reagan somehow didn't feel he was being confrontational. "I did not want to kick anybody in the shins," he said. "I don't think anything I said was too harsh." He had, in fact, acknowledged that *glasnost* and *perestroika* had come a long way since Reykjavik, and noted that Gorbachev had personally called the leading Soviet dissident, Nobel Peace Prize winner Andrey Sakharov and his wife Yelena Bonner, to welcome them back home to Moscow from internal exile in Gorky.

The president's most gracious remark came spontaneously the next day. After Gorbachev suggested that they take a break from their drab discussions, they strolled together through Red Square. One of the hovering reporters called out to ask Reagan whether he still regarded the Soviet Union as an evil empire. After a pause, he slowly shook his head and said "No. That was another time, another place." Gorbachev, standing beside him, flashed an appreciative grin.

The president's absolution may have been a bit premature, however. During that "spontaneous" stroll in Red Square, Gorbachev introduced him to Soviet tourists who just happened to be there then. Several of them pressed Reagan about human rights abuses in America. When White House photographer Pete Souza asked how ordinary Russians could be so bold with a visiting president of the United States, a Secret Service agent on duty told him, "Oh, these are all KGB families."

During their final evening in Moscow, the president and first lady attended a performance by the Bolshoi Ballet. Afterward, hand in hand, they strolled over to see Red Square at night, with the Kremlin and St. Basil's Cathedral's colorful onion domes brilliantly lit up. Reporters asked why they had come there, and Reagan said, "Because Nancy hasn't seen it. We've leaving tomorrow, and I didn't want her to miss it."

The president had accomplished what he set out to do at this summit, as at previous ones. The first, at Geneva, was for familiarization; the second, at Reykjavik, for negotiation; the third, in Washington, for completion of the arms accord; and this one, in Moscow, for oration of his core beliefs on the blessings of freedom.

Ronald Reagan's public preaching in Moscow—not just for basic liberties, but for their being institutionalized, and thus made irreversible—was his last real contribution as president of the United States.

The next morning, in a light Moscow drizzle, Air Force One took off from Vnukovo Airport.

. . . .

LATER THAT SAME MONTH, June 1988, Gorbachev presided over the Communist Party Conference. This was a big deal, since party congresses met every five years, but a party *conference* rarely. This, the supreme authority of the U.S.S.R., had not been called into session since Stalin's death in 1953. After considerable deliberation, the party conference created a more democratic parliament, more free-market economy, and more autonomy for the constituent republics. It thus did much of what Reagan wanted the Soviet regime to do—to extend liberty; institutionalize reforms, thereby making them permanent; and thus unknowingly sign its own death warrant.

THE NEXT MONTH, MARSHAL Akhromeyev returned to the United States for a grand tour of military installations with his counterpart, Bill Crowe.

Their six-day coast-to-coast excursion began at Camp Lejeune in North Carolina, where marines train for combat. They moved on to Virginia's Langley Air Force Base, where the marshal peered into the cockpit of a B-1 bomber, the plane designed to thwart his air defenses and deliver thermonuclear warheads on his headquarters.

They toured Fort Hood, Texas, taking a side trip to the Alamo, the site of a battle that had not turned out well for American fighting men. Then on to Ellsworth, South Dakota, where they ate in messes with American soldiers who flew and maintained strategic bombers with flight plans to Moscow. Along the way, they climbed aboard the massive aircraft carrier, U.S.S. *Theodore Roosevelt*.

Their tour was not all business. The marshal and admiral visited the wigged ones at Colonial Williamsburg and entered wigwams in South Dakota, where Akhromeyev was given yet another title by becoming Honorary Chief of the Cherokee Nation. Crowe threw his guest a down-home barbecue in his hometown in Oklahoma and took him to a local rodeo. After a speech Akhromeyev delivered in Chicago, the two stopped at a McDonald's to chow down on hamburgers and fries.

This visit between the top military officers of the two superpowers was unprecedented and, before Reykjavik, simply unimaginable. During their travels, Akhromeyev told Crowe that the two most meaningful times of his life had been when fighting for the motherland on the road to Leningrad and sitting in the East Room to witness the signing of "his" missile treaty.

The two also discussed matters of greater sensitivity and dubious probity. After their trip ended, I heard that they had set up a secret back channel. As later substantiated by Bob Woodward, they made "an alliance" for "secret, private communications" to use if either spotted anything that might lead to war. According to Woodward, they considered this necessary because "it was too easy for politicians to let a misunderstanding throw the superpowers over the brink to nuclear war."

While understandable on a human level, this was questionable on a professional level. According to the U.S. Constitution, military officers must communicate to, and follow orders from their civilian superiors. They are not to go outside the chain of command by dealing secretly with their military adversaries. While eyebrow-raising at the time, this channel was sanctified two years later by a formal U.S.-Soviet agreement for military-to-military communications. Later behavior by Akhromeyev and Crowe raised eyebrows higher.

THE SOVIET MARSHAL RETURNED home to a confused leadership and country. The mission of the 5.3 million troops he commanded had formerly been clear—to protect the motherland from America, and from subversives in brethren Communist states. But now Akhromeyev had eaten in the messes and strolled the decks with uniformed American kids, who seemed as unthreatening as their jolly boss, Bill Crowe.

The threat from within other Communist states seemed as passé. For decades, protestors taking to the streets felt fear before they were rounded up or mowed down. Now that fear had moved from the faces of the protestors onto the faces of their rulers.

During that summer of 1988, release from Communist clutches across Eastern Europe began in Poland. It was inspired by the new, and first Polish, pope, John Paul II—whose motto became "Have no fear!"—and led by an adept organizer, Lech Wałęsa. Boxed in by heavenly and earthly resistance, onetime-strongman General Wojciech Jaruzelski staged the freest elections held anywhere behind the Iron Curtain. The results were as lopsided as they had always been, but this time in the opposite direction. The anti-Communists of Solidarity won 99 of the 100 contested seats in the upper chamber, and 160 of the 161 in the Sejm, the lower chamber.

Ideas have consequences. The idea that Communist domination could be successfully challenged spread like wildfire. If it could happen in Poland, people across the region began asking each other, why couldn't it happen here?

They soon found that it could. From East Berlin to Bucharest and Budapest to Sofia and Prague, the masses began to echo the sentiments of Oliver Cromwell toward the entrenched power of the Rump Parliament he confronted in 1653: "You have sat too long here for any good. Depart, I say, and let us have done with you. In the name of God—Go."

If their dictators would not go—yet, at least—the masses would. Tens of thousands of East Germans flooded the West German embassy in Budapest. Pressed by this inflow, Hungary, long the gentlest in that brutal neighborhood, had to decide what to do with them all.

MEANWHILE, RONALD REAGAN HAD left Washington to spend August at the place he loved most, Rancho del Cielo, atop the Santa Ynez Mountain range in California. It was small—the ranch house only some nine hundred square feet when they bought it—plain, and isolated—with one winding, potholed dirt road running up to it. Nonetheless, it was the place where, truly, Reagan could be Reagan.

Every August of his presidency was spent there—clearing brush, chopping wood, erecting fences, riding horses, and sitting with Nancy, gazing out and talking quietly on the porch. The Spartan accommodations and hours spent cutting back brush weren't exactly Nancy's notion of a good time. But she was happy to see how happy he was being there, and that was enough for her.

Each morning, the president would receive his daily intelligence briefing, focused then on the stunning news from Poland. Each evening, the president and the first lady would eat simple dinners on TV trays while catching the evening news and then the Summer Olympics from Seoul.

Come the fall, the Reagans returned for their final stay in the White House. He was delighted that his hometown Los Angeles Dodgers won the World Series. Then on November 8 came the best news of all. His faithful partner, George H. W. Bush, was elected as his successor, thereby becoming the first sitting vice president to win the top post since Martin Van Buren in 1836. Bush's strong showing—tromping opponent Michael Dukakis by 53 percent to 45 percent—was the closest the American public could come to giving Reagan a third term without violating the Constitution.

"WE'VE BEEN TOGETHER EIGHT years now, and soon it'll be time for me to go," began his final address to the nation from behind the *Resolute* desk, on January 11, 1989. "But before I do, I wanted to share some thoughts."

Reagan was grateful that the people had chosen him as their president. He added—needlessly, to those who saw him in action—that he simply loved the job. He would miss gazing out his White House window each morning "at the Washington Monument, the Mall, and the Jefferson Memorial, and down the Potomac, the view Lincoln had when he saw the smoke rising from the Battle of Bull Run."

That vivid scene somehow reminded the old storyteller of a favorite story, this one "about a big ship, a refugee, and a sailor." It went like this: "In the early eighties, at the height of the boat people," an American sailor—"like most American servicemen . . . young, smart, and fiercely observant"—spotted a "leaky little boat . . . crammed [with] refugees from Indochina hoping to get to America."

When a Vietnamese refugee in that leaky little boat spotted that American sailor, he "stood up and called out to him. He yelled, 'Hello, American sailor! Hello freedom man!'"

And America, as Reagan related it, remained that "shining city upon a hill," with citizens greeted with "Hello, freedom man!" In fact, the country had become "more prosperous, more secure and happier than it was eight years ago," a stronger "magnet for all who must have freedom, for all the pilgrims from all the lost places who are hurtling through the darkness, toward home."

The pride was palpable in Reagan's voice when he said, "We meant to change a nation, and instead, we changed the world."

His concluding words from the Oval Office were quintessentially Reagan: "All in all—not bad. Not bad at all," as was his final parting: "And so, good-bye. God bless you. And God bless the United States of America."

Nine days later, Ronald Reagan left office with the highest approval rating of any president since Franklin Delano Roosevelt when he died in April 1945. Reagan's popularity was said to be even higher in Eastern Europe and the Soviet Union, where the people were clamoring to replace Communism with the liberties Reagan had extolled. They wanted to win that one, not so much for the Gipper, as for themselves—and especially for their children.

After attending George Bush's inaugural ceremonies, the Reagans strolled onto the Capitol Plaza and boarded Marine One for the short hop to Andrews, where Air Force One was waiting to carry them home to California. As the chopper slowly rose over the Capitol building, to cheers and shouts from the crowds lining the Mall below, the now-former president made a rare request to the pilot: Could he, without too much trouble, possibly circle over the White House before heading out to Andrews?

A few minutes later, looking out the window of the tilted chopper circling the White House grounds, Ronald Reagan pulled Nancy closer to him, pointed down, and said, "Look, honey! That was our little bungalow."

MR. GORBACHEV DID NOT "tear down this Wall," but it still came down in November 1989. That happened—as so much happened in the Soviet empire's final days—by a series of small patch-ups followed by a massive screw-up.

September 11 should be recalled as a day of liberation, as well as destruction. On that Monday morning in 1989, the Hungarian government announced that anyone from East Germany then taking refuge in Hungary could cross into Austria and, from there, into West Germany. That announced that the Iron Curtain was creaking open.

Euphoric East Germans honked their horns as they crossed the "green border" into Austria. Others left by rail or special buses. All were greeted at welcome stations quickly set up in Bavaria. " 'It's like Christmas,' said a young worker, as he hugged his teary-eyed girl-friend. . . . Next to them, a mother stood in silent embrace with three daughters," Serge Schmemann reported in the *New York Times*.

The East German regime was furious at its comrade brethren. It denounced Hungary's action as a "violation of treaties and international agreements" done "under cover of night and fog," even though it was being done on beautiful fall days. Hungary's foreign minister,

Gyula Horn, a true hero of that era, was sublime in understatement when acknowledging "little understanding in the Warsaw Pact for Hungary's decision."

THE NEXT MONTH, ON October 7, Mikhail Gorbachev went to Berlin to help celebrate the fortieth anniversary of that Communist regime.

Gorbachev greeted the seventy-seven-year-old East German leader, Erich Honecker—then well into his eighteenth year as Stalinist dictator—with a kiss that many considered more passionate than dictated by Communist protocol. After this ardent beginning, Gorbachev acted in a passive-aggressive manner while participating in one of history's most uncelebratory anniversaries ever.

The two Communists stood side by side to review a torchlight parade of 100,000 Communist Youth goose-stepping down the vast boulevard, Unter den Linden. Flags fluttered, torches burned high, floodlights crisscrossed the skies, à la Nuremberg 1938. Gorbachev listened as Honecker channeled Leonid Brezhnev when blaming the country's unrest on "the unbridled defamation campaign that is being internationally coordinated against East Germany."

In his own remarks, Gorbachev responded to Reagan's speech on the other side of the Wall. Someone, Gorbachev remarked, had previously said, "Let the U.S.S.R. get rid of the Berlin Wall, then we'll believe in its peaceful intentions," which was a fair summary of Reagan's main message. But Gorbachev took exception to that someone since "the postwar reality has insured peace on the continent."

While rebuking Reagan and seeming amorous toward Honecker, Gorbachev also signaled the opposite. He communicated to the grouchy old man—perhaps in words, but certainly in deeds—that he was now on his own, that he could no longer expect Soviet troops to bail him out. Gorbachev had previously ordered the half-million Soviet troops stationed in East Germany to stay put in their barracks, even while anti-regime protestors took to the streets. And Gorbachev made such unsubtle cracks as "life punishes those who come too late," which even the obtuse Honecker may have noticed.

While in East Germany, Gorbachev reviewed goose-stepping Communist Youth. But more surprising was his becoming the idol of foot-stomping anti-Communist youth. Protestors against the Communist regime within were hailing the leader of the Communist regime abroad—the very regime that had supported, even insisted upon, their oppression for the previous 40 years. Lenin's successor, the man who occupied Stalin's office in the Kremlin, was being transformed into a Gandhi-like figure of adulation. Upward of a thousand marched in Leipzig screaming "Gorby! Gorby!" when demanding greater freedoms. That demonstration would grow exponentially to 10,000 a week later, and to 100,000 the following week.

Back in Moscow by then, Gorbachev approved a speech by Eduard Shevardnadze supporting independence for all countries, including those in the Warsaw Pact. When asked on *Good Morning America* about the speech, Kremlin spokesman Gennadi Gerasimov declared "the Brezhnev Doctrine . . . dead." When probed on what might replace it, he replied cleverly, "The Sinatra doctrine," referring to "My Way," the crooner's signature song. "Every country decides on its own which road to take," Gerasimov said smiling.

Taking the cue, the East German people did it their way. They summarily ousted Honecker, who was replaced by Egon Krenz, who summarily ousted his entire cabinet. However, none of this was enough for the protestors. For the Wall was still there.

9/11 AND 11/9 WERE seminal dates in modern history. The fall of the Berlin Wall on 11/9/89 was one of the biggest events between President

Kennedy's 1963 assassination and the 2001 terrorist attacks of 9/11. Like many Americans, I can remember where I was on each of these days.

On 11/9/89, I was heading for Budapest to attend a conference on nuclear disarmament. By then, Hungary had become a new country. Its Communist Party had been disbanded, its parliamentary members had been replaced, and its constitution was being rewritten to assure civil liberties.

I took a stroll through that beautiful city on the morning of November 10, including Szabadsag Square, which was dominated by a huge monument honoring the Soviet troops that had "liberated" Hungary in 1945. Then I went for lunch with a former U.N. colleague who had become a deputy foreign minister. As I was ushered into his ornate office, he greeted me with tears.

What did I think of the news? he anxiously wanted to know.

What news? I wondered, having heard no news since taking off from Dulles the night before.

The Wall has fallen! he said with real emotion.

It took some time for me to process the information. While everyone suspected that something was about to happen, no one had suspected anything as big as the East German regime—for four decades, the staunchest and harshest of the lot—simply giving in and thereby giving up. We sat for a time in his office while I wrapped my mind around the news and he dealt with tears of joy.

Over lunch, he described his father as part of a "lost generation," his talents unused, his spirits broken, his life meaningless. And now his son, and the sons and daughters that followed, would be able to go as far as their talents would take them. I related, as best as I could recall them, the words of Thomas Paine: "We have it in our power to begin the world all over again," he wrote on the eve of America's birth. "A situation similar to the present hath not appeared since the days of Noah until now. The birth of a new world is at hand."

. . . .

BEFORE LEAVING BUDAPEST TWO days later, I took another walk around Szabadsag Square, wondering what was going to happen next and, like my Hungarian colleague, what this new world might look like.

I could not have imagined that this square would someday have another monument—across from the memorial to the Soviet troops that "liberated" Hungary in 1945—for someone who helped liberate Hungary from those troops in 1989. That there would be a seven-foot brass statue of Ronald Reagan, walking briskly and confidently—a larger-than-life figure, sculpted by local artist Istvan Mate—with words honoring him "for bringing the Cold War to a conclusion, and for the fact that Hungary regained its sovereignty in the process."

FROM BUDAPEST, I FLEW on to Moscow for another nuclear arms seminar. Reading everything I could get my hands on, I learned more about the improbable events of 11/9.

Honecker and his henchmen were replaced by a new crew, which really didn't know what they were doing. To be fair, though, no one knew what they *should* be doing—given the growing and insuppressible rebellion across East Germany.

Günter Schabowski seemed a safe choice to be the new government spokesman, having been a party propagandist and looking good on TV. On November 8 and 9, the new East German cabinet decided on new travel procedures, to take effect some unspecified time later. This news was to be embargoed, presumably until that time later. Perhaps the hapless Schabowski was not fully informed of this; perhaps he was misinformed; most likely, he was simply confused, being new in office at an awfully confusing time.

Regardless, he took to the airwaves to announce the lifting of all East German travel restrictions. Asked when this new policy would take effect, he replied, "Immediately."

Until that moment, Schabowski had been an obscure functionary of a failing regime, a gray man in a gray suit. But his few words, broadcast nationwide, moved the nation and changed the world.

They sparked an eruption, as people flocked to the Wall. East German border guards, hearing of Schabowski's announcement, started waving people through the checkpoints into West Berlin. The main thoroughfare there, the Kurfürstendamm, was soon brimming with people brimming with joy. "At Checkpoint Charlie, where Allied and Soviet tanks were locked in a tense face-off while the Berlin Wall was being erected in August 1961," reported Ferdinand Protzman of the *New York Times*, "lines of cars and people began to file across the border by late evening. Cheers, sparkling wine, flowers and applause greeted the new arrivals."

The carnival atmosphere continued with fireworks exploding above the boulevard and drinks shared along it. East German construction workers, still in their overalls and hard hats, were greeted with hugs and mugs of beer in the West. Local restaurants handed out free food. The soccer team, Hertha, based in the West but popular on both sides, gave East Berliners ten thousand free tickets for their upcoming game on Saturday. West Berlin threw three shows, all free—a rock concert featuring Joe Cocker, the Berlin Philharmonic conducted by Daniel Barenboim, and the German Opera Company performing *The Magic Flute*.

The spontaneous street festival included youngsters painting the gray concrete partitions in bright hippie colors, and climbing atop the Wall to dance, smoke grass, and generally cavort. They handed the Vopos, the formerly fearsome East German guards, bouquets. The local press was euphoric: WE'VE DONE IT. THE WALL IS OPEN! screamed the largest headlines ever across Berlin's tabloid *Bild*.

West Berlin's mayor, Walter Momper, said: "The whole city and all its citizens will never forget November 9, 1989. For twenty-eight years since the Wall was built, we have yearned for this day. We Germans are now the happiest people on earth." That had not always been the case, especially on November 9. In 1938, that was the onset of *Kristallnacht*, the shattering of glass, as Nazi thugs assaulted Jewish synagogues and stores, causing death and destruction across Germany and foreshadowing the Holocaust.

The world's media was, like everyone, taken by surprise with the fall of the Wall. Whether by good luck or sound instincts, NBC's Tom Brokaw had come to Berlin in time to report it live. With a joyous melee over his shoulder, Brokaw told his viewers that "A sinister symbol of oppression . . . has changed dramatically tonight."

Back in Washington, President George H. W. Bush had long sought to distinguish himself from the towering figure of his predecessor, to be his own man in the presidency. That day he succeeded.

Unlike Ronald Reagan, who not only welcomed change but pushed relentlessly for it, Bush valued stability above all. President Bush was "cautious," reported the lead article in the *Washington Post*, "due to apprehension . . . Bush appeared somewhat downbeat as he swiveled in his chair in the Oval Office." When reporters questioned his demeanor, Bush assured them that he was indeed "elated," but wasn't showing it since "I'm just not an emotional kind of guy."

Mstislav Rostropovich was emotional. After turning on the television, he told reporters later, "I watched these touching pictures, and I cried." The celebrated Russian cellist and conductor—whose seventieth-birthday party Reagan and Gorbachev had discussed at Reykjavik—chartered a plane and headed to Berlin. There, he rushed to the Wall and said, "*Voilà!* All I need is a chair." A chair produced, the maestro sat with his back against the Wall for more than an hour playing Bach, to express his profound feelings through the profound music of *Suites for Unaccompanied Cello*.

. . . .

OVER THE NEXT FEW days, more than 2 million East Germans did what nearly two hundred had previously given their lives to do: they crossed over to the West. Most returned home the same day, after experiencing the thrill of freedom so close but so forbidden for a generation.

While there, the easterners mobbed West German banks to pick up the one hundred marks of "welcome money," which the Bonn government had given anyone coming across since 1970. Back in East Germany, those hundred marks were worth more than one month's salary for the average proletarian in that Worker's Paradise.

The next month, the final symbol of a divided world came down. Berlin's treasured Brandenburg Gate was opened on December 22. West German Chancellor Helmut Kohl—who had been there for Reagan's speech—said that he had "often stood at the Brandenburg Gate [wondering] whether we would live to see the day when we could walk through. This is one of the happiest hours of my life." The chancellor walked through the middle arch, once reserved for kings and emperors, to shake hands with the East German prime minister.

Days later, an ailing seventy-one-year-old Leonard Bernstein, in his last year of life, came to the Wall to lead the Berlin Philharmonic in Beethoven's triumphant Ninth Symphony, supplemented with musicians from both Germanys and from Berlin's four governing powers—the United States, the U.S.S.R., the United Kingdom, and France. Bernstein decided to alter the soaring choral conclusion, "Ode to Joy," by substituting the word *Freiheit* (freedom) for *Freude* (joy).

The performance was followed by a roar from the standing audience and the ringing of church bells across Berlin. "This is the happiest Christmas of my life," Bernstein said ecstatically. While not normally religious on that day, he considered it "a historical moment sent from above."

. . . .

SOON AFTER ARRIVING IN Moscow, I heard from a Russian also attending the nuclear arms conference that Sergei Akhromeyev had become Gorbachev's top military adviser. I sent a message to the marshal asking if we might possibly be able to meet. He replied immediately that he would welcome that.

Columnist Mary McGrory had described the Kremlin offices she visited as "rather like bourgeois living rooms or even convent parlors." She must not have been in the high-rent district, because the Kremlin's third floor looked more like a five-star hotel than a convent parlor (whatever that looks like).

As I was being ushered down its red carpet, I passed stone-faced, solid-bodied guards standing against wood-paneled walls as we proceeded to Akhromeyev's office, just down the hall from Gorbachev's. Evidently, location counted as much in Kremlin power politics as in American real estate prices.

The marshal's office had a handsome wood parquet floor in a box pattern, softened by several Persian rugs. The ceiling was high, the walls covered with tan silk paper. There were no paintings or prints or photos, not even the obligatory image of Lenin. The room was dominated by an elaborate chandelier, which Akhromeyev pointed out with some pride. I gave it a cursory glance, just to be polite, since my eye had caught something more fetching. On the credenza astride his desk was a bank of phones of varying sizes and colors, including a bright red one.

Akhromeyev had changed little over the three years since Reykjavik, the two and a half years since that magical dinner in Geneva, and the two years since the East Room signing ceremony. He was fit and trim, as alert and forthright as before.

He had a military aide bring us coffee while we reminisced a bit about Reykjavik. He made the experience richer by telling me about how he had handled a few unruly, upset obstructionists among his colleagues, with Gorbachev's backing. We shared our pleasure at the arms accord, and he told me about how much he had enjoyed his grand American tour. He showed me a photo of himself in a ten-gallon hat with Bill Crowe at his side. He laughed as he told about being photographed in a full-feathered Indian headdress at an Oklahoma reservation when the chief offered it to him as a symbol of peace.

It was when our conversation moved onto the momentous news of the day—the fall of the Wall and new non-Communist governments of Hungary and Poland—that Akhromeyev turned serious. He surely felt my excitement, but sure didn't share it. Instead, some practical items were on his mind, including what to do with all the Soviet troops stationed across Eastern Europe. He had no barracks, no housing, and no work for them, once they were back in the U.S.S.R.

When a colonel came in to indicate that Akhromeyev was already late for his next meeting, I thanked him heartily for taking the time to meet me on such short notice. We shook hands and I said good-bye. The colonel escorted me back down the red carpet, past the glowering guards poised along the walls.

TWENTY YEARS AFTER THE fall of the Wall, world leaders came to Berlin to celebrate the shattering events of those times. Someone creative came up with a fine piece of conceptual art—one thousand large dominos placed along the path that the Wall once took. To Lech Wałęsa of Poland was bestowed the honor of pushing over the first domino.

Both sets of dominos—the national ones in 1989 and the plastic ones in 2009—fell rapidly in a way simply mesmerizing to watch. One week after I left Moscow, the Bulgarian tyrant Todor Zhivkov was arrested and carted off—much as he had carted off thousands of people during his thirty-five-year rule. East Germany officially stripped the Communist Party of its monopoly on power, as did Czechoslovakia, where the protests in Wenceslas Square snowballed from early November to early December. On the tenth, the grumpy old Czech Communist strongman Gustav Husak swore in a cabinet dominated by happy young anti-Communists. He was later replaced by the playwright-turned-leader of the nicely named "Velvet Revolution," Vaclav Havel. Havel later called that "a drama so thrilling and tragic and absurd that no earthling could have written it."

Of all the gripping scenes during that stampede from Communist rule, none can match the fall of the final East European domino. It came on Christmas Day 1989 in Romania, which had been ruled and ravaged since 1965 by Nicolae Ceauşescu and his scheming Lady Macbethish wife, Elena.

The wave of liberation across the region finally hit Bucharest on December 21. That afternoon, Ceauşescu strode onto a balcony of his monstrously Stalinist presidential palace to address a vast public meeting comprising, according to his security officers, of party faithful. Even without understanding a word he says, it is still gripping to watch videos of this epoch event.

Ceauşescu begins to read a typical text crammed with statistics of purported revolutionary progress. Suddenly the crowd becomes unruly and then turns rowdy. Jeers and whistles begin with loud chants of "Timişoara, Timişoara, Timişoara"—the name of the Romanian town where the anti-regime rebellion had begun the week before.

Ceauşescu stops reading his cheery, fabricated statistics and looks up. Instinctively, he raises his right arm and waves, which prompts the crowd to chant even louder. Clearly confused, the dictator loses it and begins screaming *a ostoi, a ostoi, a ostoi*" over and over again. This phrase, depending on the context, can be translated as "calm down" or "just shut up." Elena sternly steps toward the microphone and tosses in a few *a ostoi*"'s of her own.

"What's the matter with you?" the clueless Ceauşescu shouts at his people. "What's wrong with you?" Unable to stop the chanting or even to be heard above it, Ceauşescu then quits the balcony through the open door behind him.

By dawn the next day, many army units had joined the rebellion. In a scene out of a Soviet propaganda film of the 1917 Revolution, a crowd storms the presidential palace and charges up the grand red-carpeted staircase, only to find that the Ceauşescus had escaped minutes before, on a helicopter from the roof. Soon they are found, trapped, picked up, shoved into an army tank, and hauled back to Bucharest.

There they stand trial in a court every bit as kangarooish as the ones they had run for decades, but whose verdict was more just. Accused of genocide and theft upward of $1 billion, they are found guilty on all counts and sentenced to immediate death by firing squad.

After the reading of their sentence, a guard takes Ceauşescu's blood pressure. The medical procedure completed—his blood pressure deemed sufficient for his execution—several soldiers bind his wrists and Elena's and lead them into some corner of a shoddy building.

Nothing is shown of what happens next, but their dead bodies soon appear, their faces visible, and blood dripping down the dirty walkway from Elena's corpse. A newscaster then announces on Romanian television, "The anti-Christ is dead."

Thus ends Christmas Day 1989.

THERE'S AN ANCIENT CHINESE aphorism—though one wonders whether even millions of Chinese over many centuries could have concocted all the aphorisms attributed to them—that goes: "No food, one problem. Much food, many problems."

For nearly a half century, people across Eastern Europe faced one problem—home-grown tyrants installed and controlled by Moscow running every phase of their lives. With that one problem solved, many problems arose—how to go from Communism to capitalism, from tyranny to democracy, from a closed and suspicious culture to an open and trusting civil society. How to handle ex-Communist bosses—whether to put them on trial or leave them alone with their memories, whether to let them vote or even run for office, whether to set up some form of truth and reconciliation commission, like that of post-apartheid South Africa, or leave things to the history books.

Just as all unhappy families are unhappy in their own ways, each of the ex-Warsaw Pact nations made peace in its own way with its unhappy past. There were problems aplenty. But given the one problem they had faced for more than forty years, these were problems they welcomed.

MEANWHILE, MIKHAIL GORBACHEV WAS facing problems he did not welcome.

Much to his historic glory, the Soviet leader allowed the 1989 revolutions to take their course without sending in Soviet troops to squash them. But he feared that his restraint abroad would inspire, if not ignite, a similar revolution at home.

His fear was justified. Early in 1990, when the Soviet Republic of Lithuania held elections for delegates to the Supreme Soviet, the pro-Soviet candidates lost. Lithuania then declared independence, which, in a nice post-Reykjavik touch, Iceland became the first county in the world to recognize. Latvia and Estonia, the other Baltic republics, soon followed their neighbor's lead.

These mini-states—bestowed to the U.S.S.R. by Hitler in his secret 1939 pact with Stalin—mattered little in the sprawling Soviet state. But their act of secession mattered a lot. It was one thing for the legally independent Eastern Europe states to *break away* from the Soviet Union, but quite another for its constituent parts to *break up* the Soviet Union. If these tiny republics could walk out with impunity, nothing could keep the big ones—Ukraine, Belarus, Kazakhstan, even Russia itself—from doing likewise.

So Gorbachev slammed down his foot. He would not allow any secessions. He thus imposed an economic blockade against Lithuania and, in a way close to comical, ordered the mighty Soviet army to attack a Lithuanian television station.

Back in Moscow, the pace of change accelerated. A mile from the Kremlin on Pushkin Square, McDonald's opened its first restaurant in the U.S.S.R. It was mobbed, with thirty thousand Happy Meals being served on its first day. Russia's future would no longer be defined by the red bandannas of young Communists, but by the golden arches attracting young consumers.

While the Soviet economy opened a bit, Soviet politics opened a lot. The freest Russian elections ever held resulted in Boris Yeltsin, Gorbachev's nemesis, becoming Russia's first president. He publicly quit the Communist Party with a flair and accused Gorbachev of sundry sins, considering him guilty of them all until proven innocent.

IN THAT SUMMER OF 1990, Gorbachev opened the twenty-eighth Party Congress. It was to be the most wretched of those joyless affairs, and the last.

Like Davy Crockett at the Alamo, Gorbachev was then under assault from all sides. "At any time in 1990, there could have been a successful coup against him," U.S. Ambassador Jack Matlock reflected twenty years later.

Picking the most inopportune time imaginable, and without the decency to inform Gorbachev beforehand, Foreign Minister Eduard Shevardnadze announced his resignation from office. The man Gorbachev had plucked from obscurity to prominence now claimed that the country was "heading for dictatorship," when in fact it was heading for anarchy. Gorbachev was understandably irate. During what he admitted to be his "most difficult time" in office, such a move was "unforgivable." For Gorbachev, it was the most unkindest cut of all, and he never forgave Shevardnadze for it.

THE YEAR 1991 BEGAN with yet more trouble from Yeltsin, who called on Gorbachev to quit office. He led more than a half million on a march for Russian control over the people and resources then under Soviet authority.

After considerable dithering, Gorbachev finally landed on a plan, something a sports announcer might have called a Hail Mary. He offered a Union Treaty, which would grant the constituent Soviet republics self-rule while still retaining some ties to the *metropole*—a confederation, of sorts.

Gorbachev's satisfaction in having this scheme approved by a nationwide referendum lasted just under a week, before some 98 percent of Georgian voters supported outright independence, and Ukrainian voters rejected the union treaty. Other republic leaders joined them in calling for outright secession from the U.S.S.R.

By then, it seemed that the only outside leader to oppose the republics' freedom was the Leader of the Free World. On August 1, still fearful of the accelerating change and still preferring stability, President Bush delivered a major speech in Ukraine's capital warning of the dangers of "suicidal nationalism." This quickly and unkindly got dubbed Bush's "Chicken Kiev speech."

By August 1991, events in Russia and across the Soviet Union were coming to a boil. Then they boiled.

AMBASSADOR MATLOCK WAS WARNING Gorbachev about the lurking danger of conspirators.

In private, he told the general secretary that it was more than rumor that a coup was being organized against him. Gorbachev, like Caesar with the Soothsayer, "didn't take it seriously," Matlock later recalled. "As a matter of fact, he actually laughed, turned to his assistant . . . and said something about the naïve Americans."

Two days after the Ides of August, the plotters conferred and decided: It's a go.

Three days later, on August 18, Gorbachev was ensconced in his dacha on the Black Sea with Raisa, their two daughters, a son-in-law, and two granddaughters. Uninvited and most unwelcome, a delegation from Moscow, headed by the KGB chief, arrived at his door to demand a meeting.

Gorbachev ducked into a side room to call Moscow. "I was working in my office," he recalled later, "picked up one telephone, it didn't work. I lifted the second, the third, the fourth, the fifth"—there being five different phones revealing the state of Soviet technology—but "nothing. Then I tried the house phone"—a sixth!—"and realized nothing worked and I was cut off." Normally a quick study, Gorbachev had finally caught on that something serious was afoot.

He rushed to tell his family that danger loomed, perhaps even death. His household resembled that of Nicholas II in Yekaterinburg after the tsar's abdication—all huddled together and all female, save for one young male. Back then, seventy-three years earlier, the Bolsheviks came to the door, similarly uninvited and unwelcome, and proceeded to slaughter the whole family.

When Gorbachev finally received the delegation in the villa's big sunlit parlor, they demanded that he resign immediately. Instead, he fixed on each of them, flashed his iron teeth, and said coldly, "You'll never live that long."

Confronted with this unexpected rebuff, the conspirators didn't know what to do next. They hadn't planned for this—but, then again, they hadn't planned much at all. So they simply left befuddled.

For the next three days, the general secretary was held hostage by KGB and army forces legally under his command. All communications were cut off, including the special line to transmit codes from the football to the nuclear forces in case of an international crisis.

Fortunately, the guards within stayed loyal. They spread the family around the luxurious dacha for safety and, fearing poisoning, allowed them to eat only the food that had been stocked beforehand. Two of the bodyguards found old equipment in storage and rigged up a short-wave radio. This enabled Gorbachev to learn what was happening in Moscow from the stations that he had ordered to be jammed—BBC, Radio Liberty, and the Voice of America.

He heard that Tass had announced that he was ill and had to be replaced by his vice president, Gennady Yanayev. Gorbachev listened as the heavy drinker Yanayev declared a state of emergency instituted by an eight-man ruling committee, which included the powerful head of the KGB, the minister of defense, the minister of the interior, even the prime minister. He listened to reports of tanks and armored personnel carriers rumbling around Moscow.

The next day Yeltsin climbed on top of a tank outside the Russian Parliament building and urged a general strike to oppose the coup. Moscow's citizens surrounded the building and constructed barricades out of everything at hand, à la *Les Misérables*.

By nightfall it had become clear that the coup was half-baked and the conspirators half bombed, so the atmosphere lightened. Bonfires were lit around the barricades, with the young and ardent rebels joking with the young and scared soldiers. Cigarettes and vodka were passed around and tanks decorated with flowers.

President Bush, who had been power boating and power golfing at Kennebunkport, returned swiftly to the White House, where he branded the coup illegitimate and called for Gorbachev to be reinstated. That prompted Yanayev to hold his own press conference to repeat that Gorbachev was ill. With his hands clearly shaking and his words badly slurred from excess alcohol, Yanayev hardly seemed the model of physical fitness.

The U.S. president then called Yeltsin to promise his complete support. Hence Gorbachev's main enemy at home, Yeltsin, and his country's main adversary abroad, the United States, became his main supporters.

Trapped in his dacha, Gorbachev cut a videotape to show that he was in fine health and to denounce the coup. He managed to smuggle copies out and later showed the video on nationwide television, once things settled down.

By Wednesday, August 21, the air had gone out of the coup's balloon. The state-run media no longer ran anti-Gorbachev propaganda and tanks no longer roamed the streets. When communication was finally restored in the dacha, Gorbachev made his first call to Yeltsin. The words must have stuck in his craw, but he thanked Yeltsin for supporting him. He then called key Soviet leaders who had remained loyal and President Bush. That evening, the Communist Party denounced the coup staged in its name.

With that, the coup ended as it began, totally incompetently and somewhat comically. Both Yanayev and Prime Minister Valentin Pavlov had spent those days more or less soused. In a scene reminiscent of *Measure for Measure*, one Russian official told CNN that Yanayev was "so drunk he could barely be wakened" to be arrested. And Pavlov, according to his deputy, was "so drunk . . . on the night of the putsch that he could not be understood. . . . He just made no sense." A local Moscow newspaper entitled its lead article, THE COUP WAS STAGED BY DRUNKARDS.

"I don't want to make light of it," said CBS anchor Dan Rather, before doing just that, "but all they needed was a duck flying in the room to make a Marx Brothers movie out of the coup."

Others were less amused, especially Gorbachev. He publicly spoke of "seventy-two hours of total isolation and struggle," of the "terrible strain" during which "Raisa Maksimova looked as if she was close to a heart attack."

Gorbachev himself didn't look all that great when returning to Moscow at 2:00 in the morning on Thursday, August 22. According to the AP reporter at the airport then, he was "unshaven with deep lines in his face." There was no Kremlin delegation to greet him or customary KGB contingent to guard him. As a sign of the times, and especially of the times to come, he was being guarded by Russian forces under Yeltsin's command. Soon Yeltsin went back to griping about Gorbachev. "Who chose the officials?" who led the coup, Yeltsin asked rhetorically. "He did. Who confirmed them? He did."

After settling everyone back in their Moscow apartment, Gorbachev headed to the Kremlin. But it wouldn't be the same Kremlin he had left only days before.

I AROSE EARLY ON Monday, August 26, and scoured the paper for the latest on the postcoup unravelings in Moscow. The *Washington Post* ran that day's headlines in huge type: SOVIETS TO OUST MILITARY CHIEFS, with three main articles spread across the top, above the fold.

On the left was BALTICS SEE FREEDOM AT HAND telling how Lithuania, Estonia, and Latvia were heading toward independence. The middle article was about dissidents standing "in the shadow of the monumental Lenin statue" in Moscow to demand a Nuremberg-like trial of the "nation's Communist leaders for their sins of the past 74 years . . . 'This was a demonic regime,'" one protestor declared.

Getting to the right-hand article, BREAKUP OF NATION ACCELERATES by the *Post*'s Moscow correspondent Michael Dobbs, I read three paragraphs about the "sweeping purge of the military high command" as "the country hurtled further towards disintegration."

It was not until the fourth paragraph, and several sentences into it at that, when I read the most shocking news of all: "Marshal Sergei

Akhromeyev, military adviser to President Mikhail Gorbachev and former armed forces chief of staff, had committed suicide." Dobbs allocated only two of his twenty-five paragraphs to Akhromeyev, not mentioning that he had hanged himself in his Kremlin office. As I subsequently learned, the marshal had cut a piece of the drapery cord, knotted it, and tied it to his office chandelier—the same chandelier he had proudly pointed out to me—and took his life.

Almost instinctively, I telephoned Colin Powell, who had replaced Bill Crowe as chairman of the Joint Chiefs of Staff. It was not yet 7:00 a.m., but his secretary said that the chairman was in an important briefing, undoubtedly about the purge of his Soviet counterparts. So I asked that he call me back, whenever he had a chance.

She told me to hold on. Soon I heard the familiar voice: "Kenny! I thought just the same thing. It's a real shock." I hadn't said what I had called about. In fact, I hadn't said anything. But I didn't have to.

I had met and talked with Akhromeyev only a few times in my life, but he made an indelible impression on me. I thought back to the all-night session at Reykjavik, to the easygoing chats in the Hofdi House hallway, to that remarkable evening in Geneva, to our head-nodding across the East Room, and especially back to our hour together in his Kremlin office, under that chandelier.

Rumors began flying around Moscow—that Akhromeyev had been wracked with guilt over the coup, that he had been complicit in it, that he insufficiently opposed it, that he knew nothing about it, and that, as I came to believe, he had learned about it but did nothing to report or resist it. The real reason for his last act—if there ever is a real reason for such a desperate act—remains uncertain.

Nonetheless, a few things seem certain. If Akhromeyev had been clearly engaged in the coup, Gorbachev would have fired him. But he was still Gorbachev's key defense adviser when he took his own life. On the other hand, he was shunned in death by Gorbachev and his aides, which may indicate complicity in the coup. Knowledgeable people, like Georgi Arbatov, have concluded that "he was either part of" the coup attempt "or, in the best possible case, he was informed, did not protest, did not warn the president [Gorbachev] nor say anything in public." Another Gorbachev aide, who has asked to remain anonymous, told me much the same thing.

Akhromeyev left at least two and probably three suicide notes. One was for his wife Tamara, who had not spotted any sign of depression or desperation. "If we had noticed anything, anything at all," she said the following week, "we would have prevented it." His second note was made public. It could be taken to imply support for the failed coup—or not. It reads in its entirety:

> *I cannot live when my Fatherland is dying, and everything that has been the meaning of my life is crumbling. Age and the life that I have lived give me the right to step out of this life. I struggled until the end.*
>
> AKHROMEYEV 24 AUGUST 1991

Just recently, I learned that there may be a third suicide note, one written to Mikhail Gorbachev, which may be released after Gorbachev's death. If such a letter exists, it could reveal Akhromeyev's involvement with the coup and motivation for ending his life.

Regardless, it is fitting that Akhromeyev's life paralleled the life of the country he loved so well. The Soviet Union was founded within a year of his birth and perished within a half-year of his death. Likewise, the Communist Party began shortly before he joined it and ended its reign right after he died. Moreover, all three lives—those of the state, the party, and the man—ended rather pathetically.

JUST WHEN ADMIRERS LIKE Colin Powell and I could not imagine anything worse happening to Akhromeyev, it did.

After Akhromeyev's body was carried out of his office, down the red carpet away from Gorbachev's suite, his wife and daughters scheduled a quick funeral. But quicker still was how the most decorated Soviet military leader in the nation's history was airbrushed out of Soviet prominence, and soon its history.

The marshal's funeral most resembled that—not of Lenin, or of our last five-star general, Omar Bradley—but that of Willy Loman. He was buried in a public cemetery on a rainy day beneath an ordinary headstone. Due in part to the stigma of suicide, nobody attended his funeral, save for his wife, two daughters, and a few friends and relatives. There were no military brass or civilian officials there, no foreign dignitaries. There was no military honors bestowed, no music played, no salutes fired.

Even worse was to come. A week after this dreadful funeral came a dastardly act. Vandals dug up the marshal's remains, stole the uniform in which he was buried, and tossed the stripped body aside.

Thus ends the story of a man who had devoted his life to his country, a noble man serving an ignoble cause. One who lived as an ascetic and died as an outcast.

Nonetheless, Sergei Akhromeyev was critical to making Reykjavik a success and, the following year, to making the intermediate missile accord a success, as well. We shared special moments together—special for me and, I'd like to think, a bit for him as well.

THE DAY THAT AKHROMEYEV'S body was removed from his office suite, Gorbachev announced that he too was quitting the Communist Party and disbanding it altogether.

By then, more than half of the Soviet republics had jumped ship. The departure of Ukraine, the nation's breadbasket, had been the toughest for Gorbachev to take. Like with a sports team or rock band, once the key members leave, the others start looking for a way out. They don't formally abolish the group so much as simply abandon it.

Still trying to keep the few remaining republics in the U.S.S.R., Gorbachev concocted something called the Confederation of Sovereign States, which would operate as a Commonwealth lite. It wasn't much, Gorbachev readily conceded, but it was better than nothing. By then, most republic leaders preferred nothing.

Yeltsin was meanwhile grabbing control of the natural resources in Russia and all the rubles, gold, diamonds, and international reserves in the Soviet version of Fort Knox. Gorbachev called foul and warned of warfare in the region and a "catastrophe for all mankind" if the Soviet Union broke apart.

But no one was listening any longer. So no one asked if he could possibly mean that a world without a Soviet Union would be a "catastrophe for all mankind." Even in a panic, Gorbachev was too smart to believe that.

When the end came, and it came very soon, the once mighty Soviet Union ended—not as a catastrophe for all mankind, but as an afterthought of three men.

IN EARLY DECEMBER 1991, Boris Yeltsin suggested that the leaders of the three most powerful republics—Russia, Ukraine, and Belarus—meet secretly in Kiev. There, they would divvy up the national resources that were still legally owned by the Soviet Union. The Soviet leader was not invited to the meeting, nor even informed of it.

Once the three leaders reached a disposition of the Soviet resources—amicably done, since appropriating and dividing up someone else's assets is pleasant work—Yeltsin introduced a new thought. "Would you agree," he asked his colleagues casually, as if the idea had just popped in his mind, "for the Soviet Union to end its existence?"

Sure. The others *would* agree. Stanislav Shushkevich, leader of

Belarus, asked how they might announce this. Yeltsin offered to call President Bush, while Shushkevich got stuck with calling Gorbachev. Years later, Shushkevich said that "it only dawned on me afterward what . . . a momentous thing we were doing."

Gorbachev did not take the news kindly. Not at all. "Can you imagine," he thundered into the phone at Shushkevich, "what the outside world would think of this?" As Shushkevich recalled telling Gorbachev, " 'Well, actually, Yeltsin is speaking to President Bush right now.' On the other end of the phone, there was silence. And then Mr. Gorbachev hung up."

DECEMBER 25, 1991, WAS a normal workday in the Kremlin. Hence, Gorbachev went into the office as usual. But it was not to be a normal workday for him.

He sat down at his desk, straightened out a few papers, putting some in his brown briefcase, and then got ready for his final nationwide television broadcast. In marked contrast to President Reagan's bidding farewell to his countrymen, Gorbachev would bid farewell to his country.

Gorbachev had invited the CNN cameras and crew to broadcast the event live, along with the official Soviet television station. Upon hearing of this, CNN's president, Tom Johnson, knew how historic the event would be and decided to fly to Moscow for it.

Once the short event got under way, Gorbachev reached into his suit pocket to grab a pen, but found none there. Johnson, standing to the side of the desk, offered Gorbachev his pen, ironically, a Montblanc pen—the same haute bourgeois brand that Lenin liked to use. Hence, the U.S.S.R. began and ended with strokes from a German luxury writing instrument.

Johnson's CNN crew captured the moment Gorbachev signed his name at the bottom of the one-line letter: "I cease my activities as

President of the U.S.S.R." By then, the U.S.S.R. was merely the name of something that had once existed, and no longer had any activities for its president to cease.

Then Gorbachev turned over responsibility for the most powerful weapons on earth to the man he considered the most irresponsible on earth, Boris Yeltsin. Twenty years later, none of his anger had dissipated as he called Yeltsin "a scoundrel and a traitor" and beyond.

Later that day, Gorbachev telephoned President Bush to say that he would be spending "a peaceful Christmas evening" at home. Bush wished him well, and then issued a statement from the White House praising Gorbachev for working with Reagan "boldly and decisively to end the Cold War and liberate the Soviet people from Communist dictatorship." From his home in California, Ronald Reagan issued a statement saying that Gorbachev "will live forever in history" and that freedom-loving people should forever be grateful to him.

Late that afternoon, with the Moscow winter sky already dark, the red hammer and sickle flag was lowered from the pole at the top of the Kremlin. A white, blue, and red flag of the Russian Federation was raised in its place. The Cold War thus ended just as Ronald Reagan had said it would.

We won. They lost.

CHAPTER 10

Reflections and Conclusions on Reykjavik

If, as stated in the introduction, the Reykjavik summit resembles a classic mystery thriller à la Agatha Christie, then the question naturally arises, "Who done it?" In this case, we know who—Ronald Reagan and Mikhail Gorbachev. But we are less sure of the "it."

Now, long after the political theater has ended, just how—and how much—did Reykjavik matter? To many historians and the public, the answer is, "Not much."

Deciphering the summit's significance has been the key topic at four conferences over the past quarter century. While other summits have been historic—Yalta, Potsdam, Vienna, Moscow—none has inspired even one anniversary celebration, let alone four.

Reykjavik's tenth anniversary was marked by a conference on the summit's site and another at the Ronald Reagan Presidential Library. The twentieth was held at Stanford University and the twenty-fifth again at the Reagan Library.

Yet for all the discussion on it, Reykjavik remains something of a mystery, and highly contentious. Richard Nixon trashed it as the most detrimental summit since Yalta, while his close associate George

Shultz considers "Reykjavik . . . the most remarkable superpower meeting ever held," one that led to ending the Cold War.

AT REYKJAVIK, REAGAN ENVISIONED the day ten years later when he and Gorbachev would return to Iceland, bring "the last nuclear missile from each country with them," destroy those remaining missiles, and throw "a tremendous party for the whole world."

But neither man returned to Reykjavik ten years later. Reagan was already deep in the darkness of Alzheimer's disease, what Nancy called "the long good-bye." But it was a darkness that they had seen coming on.

In November 1994 Reagan's office released a handwritten letter to the American people on his stationery.* Characteristically, he was remarkably forthright, never one for burying the lead, that dark days were ahead for him. And, characteristically, he ends this, his last public communication, with gratitude, patriotism, and optimism: that bright days are ahead for America.

HAD GORBACHEV RETURNED TO Reykjavik ten years later, it would have been as a private and scorned citizen of the Russian Federation— his worst fears of losing power having, by then, been fully realized.

Though unable to make it, Gorbachev sent a letter to those of us who *did* return ten years later. Contrary to Reagan's wishes, none of us brought any nuclear missiles along (which might have caused problems getting through Icelandic customs, in any case), let alone the last ones on earth. Nor was there a "tremendous party for all the world."

---

* *A typed version of the letter appears in the notes section, as it may be hard to read on the following pages. Nonetheless, it must have been much harder to write.*

RONALD REAGAN

Nov. 5, 1994

My Fellow Americans,

I have recently been told that I am one
of the millions of Americans who will be
afflicted with Alzheimer's Disease.

Upon learning this news, Nancy & I had to decide
whether as private citizens we would keep this
a private matter or whether we would make this
news known in a public way.

In the past Nancy suffered from breast cancer
and I had my cancer surgeries. We found
through our open disclosures we were able to
raise public awareness. We were happy that as
a result many more people underwent testing.
They were treated in early stages and able to
return to normal, healthy lives.

So now, we feel it is important to share
it with you. In opening our hearts, we hope
this might promote greater awareness of this
condition. Perhaps it will encourage a clearer
understanding of the individuals and families
who are affected by it.

At the moment I feel just fine. I intend to live
the remainder of the years God gives me on this
earth doing the things I have always done. I will
continue to share life's journey with my beloved
Nancy and my family. I plan to enjoy the
great outdoors and stay in touch with my
friends and supporters.

Unfortunately, as Alzheimer's Disease progresses, the family often bears a heavy burden. I only wish there was some way I could spare Nancy from this painful experience. When the time comes I am confident that with your help she will face it with faith and courage.

In closing let me thank you, the American people for giving me the great honor of allowing me to serve as your President. When the Lord calls me home, whenever that may be, I will leave with the greatest love for this country of ours and eternal optimism for its future.

I now begin the journey that will lead me into the sunset of my life. I know that for America there will always be a a bright dawn ahead.

Thank you my friends. May God always bless you.

Sincerely,

Ronald Reagan

Yet there was an interesting seminar at Hofdi House and the Grand Hotel, hosted by the Iceland government. Nearly one hundred people attended—including two I was pleased to meet, both descendants of Bjarni Benediktsson. The American presenters included Don Regan, Maureen Reagan representing her father, Max Kampelman, and a few others of us. The Soviet delegation was led by Evgeny Velikhov, the physicist who had pushed the Soviet program on SDI and spearheaded the effort to oppose ours.

At the end of the first day, we visited Bessastadir, where Presidents Finnbogadóttir and Reagan had taken a stroll, with Reagan wearing that remarkable coat seemingly from the 1930s, and their having the most remarkable conversation about theater and politics. That evening was a dinner hosted by the current mayor of Reykjavik (with the totally unpronounceable name of Mrs. Ingibjörg Sólrún Gisladóttir) in Hofdi House. Retracing steps taken a decade earlier unleashed a flood of happiness over what we had done and sadness over what Ronald Reagan had become.

During an elegant, candlelit dinner at the table used during our all-night negotiations, I tried to listen to the speeches of the mayor, the prime minister, and the president of Iceland, but kept hearing Sergei Akhromeyev's steady voice trying to get business done around that table. Looking down the hallway, I saw the mingling of top Soviet and American officials in our first attempt at talking and laughing together, like normal people do.

Ducking into the parlor and seeing that garish mirror still there, I felt even more emotion coming on. This was where the president lounged in the corner while the U.S. paper was being redrafted on top of the bathtub, where he surprisingly returned to make sure that we were doing right by America, where we heard "They've broken!" and rushed out to learn of the summit's crash ending.

Going downstairs into the small conference room, I noticed that the portrait of Bjarni Benediktsson was still up and the weird painting of the sea crashing against the rocks still bewildering, if not depressing anyone viewing it. The guest book signed by Reagan, Gorbachev, and their aides was on display under glass in the hallway corner, where the military officers had stood clutching their briefcases.

Earlier that day, I had stopped in the U.S. embassy and asked if I might walk around by myself. Reentering the bubble brought on shivers—even though it was then filled, not with excitement and anticipation, nor with the president of the United States and the secretary of state, but with typewriters and fax paper. What Reagan had suggested would make a fine aquarium had instead become an office supply bin. "Oh, what a falling off was there," as Shakespeare put it, though in an admittedly different context.

In the middle of stacks of laser toner and copy paper, I spotted where I had squatted, leaning against those presidential knees. I paced the bubble off and found it was as small as I had remembered, some nine feet by five.

My mind filled with events a decade back, I walked around the Hofdi House parlor and hallway and into the embassy bubble as if they were sacred territory. For the first time in my life, I understood how a pilgrim must feel when approaching a holy site, and felt lucky for sensing a bit of that.

Early the next morning, I left the Holt Hotel—its lobby unchanged and its rooms as confined—and headed out to see Hofdi House as the dawn broke cold and hard over the North Atlantic. Ten years earlier, I had been too distracted and exhausted to take in the surroundings. But this morning, I was aware when leaving the historic district of the Holt Hotel, close to the U.S. embassy and ambassador's residence, that I was passing along the main shopping street, by the old city dairy and the Iceland National Archives (which Raisa Gorbachev had visited), and heading on to the Borgartun, where Hofdi House stands, on the left, by the sea.

It was as beautiful in that bright morning light as in the softer light of my memory. I waited until the sun fully rose before heading back to the Laugavegur, the main shopping street. At one of its souvenir shops, I bought a picture postcard of Hofdi House and wrote a short note— just a few sentences was all—on the back. I bought an air mail stamp and, even though I didn't know the right address, wrote the name and general location and dropped it in a Reykjavik mailbox.

PARTICIPANTS AT THIS TENTH conference, and at the three conferences that followed, differed dramatically as to the summit's significance. Reykjavik thus became a palimpsest, with different layers seen differently by different people from their different perspectives. This is not unique, especially when trying to understand great historic events. As Joel Achenbach wrote:

History isn't the thing itself, but rather a story we tell, and the story changes, new elements are added, others forgotten, myths invented, causes imagined, facts debunked. History is a process of imposing order on a chaotic process, inventing causality and finding meaning.

Eventually the story gels and one interpretation gains wide, or at least wider, acceptance.

I've already given my version of what happened over the weekend, my way of "imposing order" on what was truly "a chaotic process." What remains is to give my interpretation of Reykjavik's significance today.

This can best be done by considering four aspects of Reykjavik:

1. the *negotiations realm*, the arms control stuff on nuclear weapons, SDI, the ABM Treaty, and nuclear testing;
2. the *geostrategic realm*, related to ending the Cold War;
3. the *personal realm*, of evaluating Reagan and Gorbachev, especially as revealed over those two days; and
4. the *institutional realm*, of the government performance and particularly that of the intelligence community.

THE NEGOTIATIONS REALM

The agenda that Gorbachev proposed for Reykjavik and that Reagan readily accepted included negotiations over intermediate missiles, strategic weapons, a nuclear test ban, and the SDI–ABM Treaty package. We'll quickly evaluate all four, plus a few related topics in this realm.

Intermediate Missiles: An Undeniable Success

When Reagan assumed office in 1981, the threat of the Soviet intermediate missiles was the preeminent security issue in NATO. For five years, Western leaders and publics heatedly debated whether to proceed with deploying U.S. missiles in response to the Soviet missiles already deployed. Millions took to the streets to oppose U.S. deployments in 1983. That December, the Soviets walked out of all arms talks. "The suspensions left the super-powers for the first time in 14 years with no arms-control talks of any kind in progress," as *Time*'s 1983 "Men of the Year" cover story lamented. That suspension fueled yet more fear and yet more public protest across Europe and America.

Then, on Sunday morning in Reykjavik, Gorbachev startled one and all by agreeing to zero out his intermediate missiles in Europe and limit them to one hundred in Asia. A few months later, he dropped the one hundred in Asia, thus acquiescing to Reagan's zero option proposal of six years earlier. In December 1987 Reagan and Gorbachev signed a treaty encompassing this. And by 1991 more than fifty-five hundred Soviet nuclear warheads, which once had been aimed at key European cities, had been dismantled and destroyed.

Strategic Weapons: An Undeniable Success

Marshal Sergei Akhromeyev's 4:00 a.m. acceptance of 50 percent strategic nuclear cuts down to equal levels and Gorbachev's agreeing in principle to rigid verification provisions constituted historic breakthroughs. While no strategic treaty was concluded under Reagan, it was concluded under his successor and was, far and away, the best strategic arms accord in history.

This undeniable success did not stop with that accord, named START I and signed by President George H. W. Bush in 1991. Following that have been START II under President Bill Clinton in 1993 and START III under President George W. Bush in 2002. The latest START accord was signed by President Barack Obama in an Oval Office ceremony in February 2011.

Each agreement greatly lowered the size and dangers of the strategic nuclear arsenals. As Ronald Reagan would have put it: "Not bad. Not bad at all."

Cuts in Nuclear Weapons Overall: An Undeniable Success

Cutting nuclear weapons of all kinds—strategic, intermediate, tactical, aboard cruise missiles, aboard aircraft—was not on the agenda at Reykjavik. But it was uppermost in the minds of those at Reykjavik.

Both leaders believed strongly that there were way too many nuclear weapons of all sorts, and cared little of just what sorts they were. Reagan and Gorbachev wanted them reduced, if not eliminated. And as the owners-operators of nearly 90 percent of them, their opinions counted a good deal.

Since Reykjavik, there has been a stunning *two-thirds* decline of nuclear weapons in their countries' arsenals. The Russians now have only *one-fourth* of what they had at Reykjavik—fewer than 9,000 warheads now versus 41,000 then. We too have 9,000, in contrast to our 23,000 then. Reductions have been even steeper in deployed strategic warheads—those most threatening, poised for rapid launch and on bombers—which will be down to 1,550 on each side before long.

President Obama still feels "we have more nuclear weapons than we need"—as he stated at the Brandenburg Gate in June 2013—and seeks to shrink them down to a level last seen by either country in 1954. This dip down to 1,000 deployed strategic warheads for each might be best done, the president suggested, by "making reciprocal but nonbinding cuts."

Declines of this magnitude are rare in any realm of social science. Such a drop is even more impressive when realizing that, before Reagan, arms control entailed limiting future growth. That was how it had been done in SALT I and SALT II and how, most experts figured, it would be done for all time.

Skeptics nowadays may challenge the significance of this steep U.S.-Russian decline by pointing out that more countries now have nuclear weapons. Granted, having the world's worst weapons in the hands of the world's worst tyrants constitutes the foremost security threat of our era.

Yet this was not true at the time of Reykjavik. The main worry then was over an all-out nuclear war between the superpowers. That fear lay behind the mass marches of the disarmament movement, parents' fears of radioactive milk, fathers building basement fallout shelters, and dramas like *On the Beach* and *The Day After*. As George H. W. Bush said upon accepting the 1988 presidential nomination—eighteen months after Reykjavik—"Schoolchildren once hid under their desks in drills to prepare for a nuclear war." Indeed, we shoved our heads into Bryn Mawr Grammar School hall lockers at 10:30 on Tuesday mornings.

Clearly, there was genuine dread of a nuclear Armageddon wiping out America and life on earth, whether due to hostility, political miscalculation, or even accident. Recent research reveals hundreds of spine-chilling near misses of nuclear accidents during the Cold War. Experts believe that such dangers were real, and they are right. The Cold War was an objectively dangerous time, as well as a subjectively terrifying one.

As bad as the threats we face today are—Kim Jong-un running amok, or, God forbid, Iran deciding to obliterate Israel, or a terrorist organization with a suitcase bomb—none would constitute an existential threat to the United States or to life on earth. Kids today do not shove their heads into lockers. Fathers today do not build basement fallout shelters.

Anyone who asserts that our current predicament is more precarious than that during the Cold War either didn't live during the Cold War or wasn't alert to its dangers. Even with today's risks—especially nuclear proliferation and terrorism—it has still been *much* safer living the twenty-seven years since Reykjavik than it was living the twenty-seven years before that weekend.

Nuclear Testing: A Deniable Success
This agenda item turned out to be a success, as U.S. and Soviet/Russian

nuclear testing ended after Reykjavik—but not because of Reykjavik. Hence its scoring as a deniable success.

Here's what happened: Gorbachev sought to ban nuclear testing by getting Reagan's consent to a comprehensive test ban (CTB). Reagan agreed to include nuclear testing on the agenda, but that was about it. He would not agree to a CTB.

Hence, nothing happened at Reykjavik on nuclear testing, besides Gorbachev raising it and Reagan dodging it. But nothing *had* to happen at Reykjavik on nuclear testing.

While there has been no treaty banning nuclear testing since then, neither has there been much nuclear testing since then. The United States and the U.S.S.R. soon ended their tests, as did the other major nuclear powers. In fact, none of the five—the United States, Russia, France, Britain, or China—has tested in the twenty-first century. North Korea, the only country that has, would have done so whether a CTB existed or not.

In short, nuclear testing was an arms control issue rather than a real world issue. No arms accord treaty has stopped nuclear testing, yet nuclear testing has all but stopped anyway.

The Movement to Ban the Bomb: An Undeniable Success
Before returning to the four topics on the agenda, we should consider one other aspect of nuclear weapons, namely the movement to abolish them.

Over that weekend, each superpower leader was startled to learn how anti-nuclear the other was, and perhaps even how anti-nuclear he himself was. The high point came late on Sunday afternoon when Reagan blurted out, "It would be fine with me if we eliminated all nuclear weapons" to which Gorbachev replied without hesitation or deliberation, "We can do that."

Among Reykjavik's richest legacies has been its boost to the "ban the bomb" movement. For decades this cause was deemed too idealistic for anyone knowledgeable to join. It was a movement filled with well-meaning dreamers, folksingers, naive celebrities, outright kooks, and the occasional barmy Nobel laureate—who couldn't, or wouldn't, grasp the hard facts of the real world.

Top among those hard facts was that the knowledge to build atomic arms could not be unlearned. Once invented, once J. Robert Oppenheimer quoted the *Bhagavad Gita*—"Now I am become Death, the destroyer of worlds"—after the first bomb exploded on July 16, 1945, they could not be uninvented.

Almost overnight, Reykjavik mainstreamed the movement. It is remarkable how many Reykjavik alumni have joined Reagan in advocating abolition. George Shultz has made this a centerpiece of his post-government life, as did Max Kampelman. Jack Matlock signed on as, most unexpectedly, did Paul Nitze. At the ripe age of ninety-two, this lifelong hawk, who knew more about nuclear weapons and dealt with them longer than anyone on the Reagan team, wrote a *New York Times* op-ed piece entitled "A Threat Mostly to Ourselves." In it, Nitze said that "the simplest and most direct answer to the problem of nuclear weapons" would be "their complete elimination."

Almost as big a surprise was Bill Crowe. After telling the president that scrapping all ballistic missiles—where the Soviets enjoyed a huge advantage over us—would endanger U.S. national security, Crowe later advocated scrapping not only all ballistic missiles with nuclear weapons, but all nuclear weapons.

The drum major of this upgraded anti-nuclear pack was Shultz, who recruited Henry Kissinger, former secretary of defense Bill Perry, and former chairman of the Senate Armed Services Committee Sam Nunn to join him. The foursome's manifesto, "A World Free of Nuclear Weapons," ran in the *Wall Street Journal* on January 4, 2007, following the twentieth anniversary conference at Stanford. It said that Reagan and Gorbachev "aspired to accomplish more" than arms reductions at their meeting in Reykjavik 20 years ago—the elimination of nuclear weapons altogether. Their vision shocked experts in the doctrine of nuclear deterrence [experts like themselves] but galvanized the hopes of people around the world. The leaders of the two countries with the largest arsenals of nuclear weapons discussed the abolition of their most powerful weapons.

This new birth of respectability for the formerly flaky movement has spawned organizations like Global Zero, the Nuclear Threat Initiative, the Campaign for Nuclear Disarmament, and hundreds of others around the world.

It has fostered political activism within as well as beyond the halls of power. On Reykjavik's twentieth anniversary, the U.N. Security Council unanimously passed a resolution supporting the summit's goal of a world free from nuclear weapons. Ambassadors of the five major nuclear states each delivered a rousing address to support the resolution. It was a true Kellogg-Briand moment in Turtle Bay, one that would have delighted Ronald Reagan.

The next year, in 2007, both U.S. presidential candidates supported the anti-nuclear goal. Barack Obama claimed that this had long been his belief, while John McCain attributed his new anti-nuclear stance to his admiration for Reagan and what he proposed at Reykjavik.

On Reykjavik's twenty-fifth anniversary, Global Zero held a major conference at the Reagan Library entitled "A World Without Nuclear Weapons" featuring statements by the U.N. secretary general, the prime minister of Japan, and Mikhail Gorbachev.

The keynoter was, once again, Shultz, who began his talk by asking all those present to give a rousing three cheers for Reagan and what he had championed at Reykjavik. The assembled white-haired, pin-striped dignitaries glanced at one another and then gave a decidedly unrousing response, at best a cheer and a half. The conference participants included former U.S. senator and future U.S.

defense secretary, Chuck Hagel, and a veteran anti-nuclear leader, Helen Caldicott.

Back in the day, Reagan's daughter Patti Davis had arranged a meeting between Dr. Caldicott and her father in the White House. The Australian activist detested Reagan no less after their contentious session together. Nonetheless, at the Library bearing his name, she acknowledged that Reagan had "formed a liaison" with Gorbachev "and, over a weekend in Reykjavik, they almost agreed to eradicate nuclear weapons." She, like him twenty years before, lamented what might have been.

Their lament raises the fascinating "what if" parlor game known as counter-factual history. What if Ronald Reagan and Mikhail Gorbachev *had* signed an agreement eliminating all their nuclear weapons at Reykjavik?

In counter-factual history, we can never know. After all, it's tough enough to know things in "factual" history.

Nonetheless, I, for one, suspect that their signed agreement wouldn't have stuck. That it might have been like the 1905 summit agreement between Kaiser Wilhelm II of Germany and Tsar Nicholas II of Russia, when their accord on European security was so roundly rebuffed upon their return home that they weaseled out of the deal.

Despite heroic efforts in Iceland, the world still has nuclear weapons, and still way, way too many. Abolition remains more an aspiration than a reality or even a policy. Nonetheless, the anti-nuclear movement—so revitalized since Reykjavik and the end of the Soviet Union—has helped propel the unexpected two-thirds cuts in American and Russian nuclear arsenals without a peep of opposition from conservatives. With Reagan as the anti-nuclear poster child and Hofdi House as its emblem, they cannot really complain.

The ABM Treaty and SDI: A Deniable Success
On the ABM Treaty, Reagan agreed with Gorbachev at Reykjavik to

extend it for ten years more. That happened, and hence constituted a slight summit success. In fact, the treaty lasted fifteen years afterward, until 2002.

Over the summit weekend, Gorbachev practically claimed that the sky would fall if the treaty ever ended. It ended, and the sky is still up there. Even in Russia, the announcement of America's withdrawal was greeted with more of a collective yawn than a primal scream. Reagan's diatribe at Reykjavik—that the treaty was "uncivilized" since its underlying MAD doctrine was sheer madness—gained traction over the years. And, truth be told, few people outside the arms control community cared about the treaty in the first place.

On SDI, no single appraisal can be given. As a real Pentagon program, it has fallen far short of what Reagan and Gorbachev expected at Reykjavik.

Nonetheless, solid research and modest deployments have occurred. The United States now has ground-based, midcourse defensive systems on land in Alaska and California and at sea, and has shared that technology—not with the Russians, as Reagan foretold—but with the Japanese and Europeans. These systems could discourage or even destroy incoming missiles from North Korea or Iran, or other countries or groups that lack sophisticated decoys or other means of deception.

Even so, SDI's deployment has been disappointing. There is no robust strategic defense, as Reagan wished and Gorbachev feared would happen soon after Reykjavik. And that was twenty-seven years ago.

Still, SDI remains a good thing to do, now more than ever. A president needs an option C—some alternative to (A) accepting a nuclear blast wiping out parts of America without retaliating or (B) actively retaliating against the innocent population of an allegedly attacking country. He or (someday, maybe soon) she needs an option for strategic defense, to protect America in that most dreadful of circumstances.

A good idea in Reagan's time, it would be a great deployment in our time, for several reasons. A president may not be able to tell who, or what, launched a nuclear missile at us. A terrorist or rogue group may now—unlike in Reagan's day—be responsible, which would make an American retaliation even less likely and less moral. Second, strategic defense would succeed far better against one or a few incoming missiles than a massive launch, as from the Soviet Union.

Deploying defensive systems can prove politically beneficial, especially during a crisis, when it is most needed. Rushing Patriot missiles early in the Gulf War to the Israelis, then under nightly attack from Saddam Hussein's SCUD missiles, kept them out of that war and thus kept President George H. W. Bush's grand coalition together. Data analyzed later indicated that those Patriots were not as effective in shooting down SCUDs as reported at the time. But that was later—after Israel stayed out, after the coalition stayed together, after we won.

Likewise, deploying defensive systems in Japan, South Korea, Saudi Arabia, and other friendly nations—especially if a North Korea or Iran or some such were to brandish its nuclear power—would be reassuring. It would help preclude them from going nuclear themselves.

Last and seldom acknowledged, defensive systems actually work, and fairly well at that. Iron Dome saved lots of Israeli lives from Hamas rocket attacks in 2012. The Pentagon has run a series of successful tests of its ballistic missile defense programs. The technology has come a long way since 1986, with vastly improved detection and targeting. The possibility of someday realizing Reagan's vision for SDI prompted national security expert Thomas Henriksen to conclude: "Had Reagan bargained away the prospects" of SDI at Reykjavik, "it would have been the greatest one-sided bad bargain since Esau sold his birthright to Jacob for bread and porridge."

Despite the value of strategic defense as a military system, SDI played a far greater role in the geostrategic realm, to which we now turn.

THE GEOSTRATEGIC REALM

If Reykjavik's record in the negotiations realm is a mixed bag, its record in the geostrategic realm is a hotly contested bag.

"The Reykjavik summit was widely misunderstood, even at the time, perhaps [even] by the participants," über-participant Shultz said on its tenth anniversary. He was right, as interpretations of Reykjavik have changed as much over the decades as the weather changed over the weekend.

Deemed an abject failure when the leaders left town, Reykjavik gained esteem when the arms treaty was signed the next year. It was more valued with each strategic accord signed, and especially with the fall of the Wall in 1989 and of the Soviet Union in 1991.

"You must wait until the evening to see how splendid the day was" is an adage attributed to Sophocles. Skeptics contend that the days since Reykjavik have not been too splendid. Or that the splendor did not spring from Reykjavik, or from the Reagan years.

To be sure, Reykjavik alone did not end the Cold War. Only the uninformed or the sensationalistic could claim that it did. There is never a single cause of events in history or social science. Rather than causality, historians and social scientists uncover correlations and concurrences that may indicate, but never prove, causation.

What can be supported is that Reykjavik helped end the Cold War and in a very big way. This contention, to which I subscribe, is backed by testimony of key participants and beneficiaries, by logic, and by evidence.

First, a bit of expert testimony. Mikhail Gorbachev—as expert a witness as you could get—said explicitly that from Reykjavik sprang the "elimination of the Cold War." To him, "Reykjavik marked a watershed" that resulted in both the "elimination of the Cold War and removal of the world nuclear threat." Otherwise, "the past decade" when the Warsaw Pact, the Soviet Union, and the Cold War ended— "would have been entirely different."

The second expert witness called would be Eduard Shevardnadze, who said that Reykjavik "released the world from the Cold War confrontation." Because of Reykjavik, "the Wall was destroyed [and] a more secure and open world emerged." When he wrote this, Shevard-nadze was president of Georgia, which he called one of "many nations . . . liberated through the process begun at Reykjavik." The govern-ment of Hungary felt the same, as indicated by its statue honoring Reagan for ending the Cold War and liberating its people.

On the American side, President Reagan called Reykjavik "a major turning point" in world history, for much the same reasons, and Secre-tary Shultz seems almost unable to stop extolling its importance. Don Oberdorfer called it "the summit of the late Cold War era. All other top-level Soviet meetings pale in comparison." He and Shultz believe that Reykjavik changed the relations between the two superpower leaders and thus between the two superpowers.

Evidence indicates that personal relations count a lot in interna-tional politics, as in life. Tensions plagued the summits of the 1950s, when Nikita Khrushchev was as brutish as Dwight Eisenhower was touchy. Relations got worse when Khrushchev steamrollered the inex-perienced John F. Kennedy at Vienna. Their ill-prepared, ill-matched summit proved ill-fated. Four months later, Khrushchev built the Wall slicing through Berlin and the following year tried to sneak nuclear missiles into Cuba. As a belated demonstration of its resolve, the Ken-nedy administration augmented U.S. forces in Vietnam.

The Reagan-Gorbachev relationship had its ups and downs, the ending of Reykjavik being its most down. Nonetheless, the two liked and even admired one another. In 2001, when Gorbachev was in London for a seminar, a British academic smirked that, as everyone knew, Reagan was nothing but a lightweight. Gorbachev interrupted to take him to task. The professor, he told the audience, had it all wrong, since Reagan was "a man of real insight, sound political judgment, and courage."

Besides statements by key participants and beneficiaries, the case for Reykjavik being critical to ending the Cold War is backed by logic and evidence.

SDI never worked as Reagan wished. It worked even better.

Reagan wanted it to protect the West against the dangers of incoming Soviet ballistic missiles. But SDI ended up helping to protect the West against the dangers of Soviet militarism. A mere blink of history after Reagan stood tall at Reykjavik, the Soviet Union came down, thereby ending decades of danger. My contention is that these events were not merely coincidental.

What becomes clear when examining the record of Reykjavik is Gorbachev's quasi-apoplectic attitude toward SDI. His fear, as explained earlier, was not due to Soviet opposition to *all* defensive systems. As Reagan said frequently, they had already one deployed around Moscow. Rather Gorbachev opposed *our* defensive systems.

His inordinate fear of SDI sprang partly from the KGB's inflated estimate of its status and prospects and partly from his inflated takeaway from those inflated estimates.

Yet his fear was partly reality-based and logical. If SDI were ever deployed, it would have posed grave risks to the Soviet system. It would have negated, or at least diminished, the Soviet symbol of military power, its land-based ballistic missiles, and the aura of awesome Soviet might that accompanied them. Apart from that aura of power, the Soviet Union didn't have much going for it—surely not any economic vibrancy or political attractiveness.

Moreover, SDI hit the U.S.S.R. in its solar plexus. The Soviets lacked the technological infrastructure to compete in such a sophisticated realm. And, as Gorbachev admitted to the Politburo, the country was maxed out on defense spending.

A decade before Gorbachev came to power, I witnessed a barroom brawl between my boss, Secretary of Defense Don Rumsfeld, and then-CIA Director George H. W. Bush. They squared off over whether the Soviets were allocating 9 to 11 percent (Bush's view) or 11 to 13 percent (Rumsfeld's) of their GDP for defense. During the brief opening of some Kremlin archives, we learned that the right number was between 30 and 40 percent.

That was a staggering figure, as Gorbachev well realized. They simply could do no more. At the height of the World War II life-or-death struggle for civilization, the United States topped off at 35 percent of GNP to defense. Thus, the Soviet Union was, over several decades, allocating for the Cold War what we allocated over one or two years for the hottest of all wars.

However much Gorbachev feared SDI before Reykjavik, his fears skyrocketed there and afterward. The fact that Reagan refused to trade major nuclear cuts in exchange for confining SDI to laboratories heightened Gorbachev's suspicions. Add on how Reagan, throughout the weekend, claimed that SDI was making impressive progress, a point he emphasized in his post-Reykjavik address to the nation.

All this led to Gorbachev's assessment—stated during *his* post-Reykjavik address to his nation—that SDI endangered "the security of our country, the security of the entire world, all peoples and all continents."

Gorbachev's fear was not alleviated by Reagan's singular—and to many of us, rather silly—notion of sharing SDI with the Soviets. Gorbachev never bought it for a minute, and for good reason. Yet Reagan's notion proved wily. By lessening SDI's sting as an aggressive program, he boosted public and congressional backing for it. This in turn made SDI funding more viable and thus more terrifying to Gorbachev.

There was, however, a logical way out of all this for Gorbachev: He could make Reagan an offer he couldn't refuse. He could dangle dramatic nuclear cuts in exchange for a reasonable-sounding limitation on SDI research. This Gorbachev attempted with his linkage ploy. It failed.

Gorbachev then realized, to his shock and dismay, that there was no offer that Reagan couldn't refuse when it came to preserving SDI.

That tried and having failed, there was one other logical way out of the fix. Gorbachev could broaden and deepen his reforms, so that his country *could* compete in high-tech areas like that of SDI. That may have been what Yuri Andropov planned before his kidney gave out. It surely was what Gorbachev planned after taking that office. Years later he recalled, "We were increasingly behind the West . . . and I was ashamed for my country—perhaps the country with the richest resources on Earth, and we couldn't provide toothpaste for our people."

There were several alternative paths of reform. One was to loosen central economic control while retaining tight political control—the route taken by South Korean strongman Park Chung-hee in the 1960s and '70s and by Deng Xiaoping and Chinese leaders to this day. A second was to keep the economy largely in government hands but ease off political control, like reform-minded Gulf states are now attempting. A third was to decentralize and allow the regions to compete on their own, along the lines of Switzerland and Canada.

None of these approaches, or others conceivable, would have been easy or likely to succeed. All were tough; all were long shots. As Machiavelli put it, "There is nothing more difficult to carry out, nor more doubtful of success, nor more dangerous to handle than to initiate a new order of things." Given the realities of the Soviet Union in the late 1980s, it is doubtful that any would have worked.

But Gorbachev removed all such doubt, as the way he proceeded was *sure* not to work.

Rather than weighing alternatives, choosing the course deemed best, selling it to his colleagues and public, and then, with fingers crossed behind his back, sticking with it to give it time to work, he lurched rather mindlessly from one scheme to the next.

His economic reforms of *perestroika* ended up as a phantasmagorical construct of his own mind, one far removed from the realities of daily life back in the U.S.S.R. Its plans and accountability were kept in constant flux, its rules bollixed up, everything engulfed in a fog of uncertainty. As a program, *perestroika* was unblemished by success.

Meanwhile, *glasnost* was succeeding far too well for Gorbachev's own good. By opening the closed pages of the Soviet past, he chiseled away at whatever legitimacy the system yet retained.

As mentioned, Gorbachev designed and sold his measures as

reforms of, not replacements for, the Communist system. To be fair, he could not have done otherwise, given the political beliefs he held and political realities he faced. Yet that only added to the certainty of failure. Marx and Lenin could not be meshed with Hayek and Friedman. There could be no "Communism with a human face," as Alexander Dubček had tried to fashion in Czechoslovakia in 1968. Once the system became human, it would no longer accept Communism. Polish philosopher Leszek Kołakowski said it best: "The concept of nontotalitarian Communism seems . . . like the idea of fried snowballs." Real reform would end in regime change.

In short, Gorbachev wanted to reform the Soviet Union in the worst way possible. And that's pretty much how he did it.

Pushing his reforms to the brink of disaster, and over, was the prospect of Reagan's SDI. It functioned, not as the *cause* of Soviet reforms, but as an *accelerator* of those reforms and, even more, as a *stress accelerator* prompting major reactions in an already stressed system. Simpler said, SDI became the straw that broke the Communist camel's back.

Evidence from the historical record indicates that SDI pushed Gorbachev to become yet more determined, even frantic, to reform his system. U.S. ambassador Jack Matlock, who observed all this up close and personal from the U.S. embassy in Moscow, highlights Reykjavik's impact "to persuade Gorbachev that he had" to accelerate "reforms at home." Indeed, right after Reykjavik came that special session of the Soviet Central Committee that mandated sweeping domestic reforms.

This logical argument—that SDI accelerated a series of events that bought down the Soviet Union—is not original. In her memoirs, Margaret Thatcher does not admit many errors—no surprise there—but does fess up to one, on SDI. During her time in office, she was insistent that Reagan's SDI scheme was undermining nuclear deterrence and undercutting Western security. I was with Reagan and Thatcher several times when she—as her critics were wont to phrase it—"handbagged" his aides (but never him) on the dangers of SDI.

Yet in *The Downing Street Years*, she admits that she got this one wrong. Because Gorbachev was "so alarmed" by SDI, "it was to prove central to the West's victory in the Cold War." Lady Thatcher conceded the errors of her ways. "Looking back, it is now clear to me that Ronald Reagan's original decision on SDI was the single most important of his presidency." That's high praise indeed from someone who admired many important decisions of his presidency.

To be clear (at the risk of being repetitive), SDI in and of itself did not finish off the Soviet Union. Gorbachev and his colleagues did—partly, if not largely, in reaction to SDI. They could have shrugged it off, gone about reforms more sensibly, or even abandoned them altogether and just muddled along, Brezhnev-like. It was what SDI, along with Reagan's delegitimization campaign, did to them, and what they in turn did to their system, that finished it off.

This was evident, even at the time, at least to one perceptive person. During their last talk together, Marshal Akhromeyev told Admiral Crowe, "You didn't destroy the Communist Party. We did."

The Counterargument

This view, though not original, is not accepted widely. Its opponents would claim that none of this—not Reykjavik, not SDI, not the delegitimization campaign, not Reagan himself—had anything to do with the Soviet Union collapsing and the Cold War ending. The opponents' view has pretty much become the conventional wisdom.

It was well encapsulated by Strobe Talbott. "The Soviet system has gone into meltdown because of inadequacies and defects at its core," Talbott wrote in *Time*, "*and not because of anything the outside world has done* or not done." Jack Matlock shares this view.

It has some initial appeal. Indeed, after the stagnation of the Brezhnev era and serial deaths of Soviet leaders, the U.S.S.R. was in sad shape. Rotten to the core, their argument goes, it simply *had* to collapse.

But why did it have to? History is replete with poor countries staying poor and getting even poorer without undergoing revolution. For seventy years, North Korea has been poor and getting poorer. A state can't get much worse than to have its citizens eat bark and grass or starve, as millions there have. But there hasn't been a revolution in North Korea and none is in sight. The same has been true, though to a lesser extent, of Cuba over the past half-century.

Impoverished empires persist as well as impoverished countries. The Ottoman and Russian empires were poor and got poorer over many centuries without cratering. Edward Gibbon wrote that "the intolerable situation" of the Roman Empire's decline and fall lasted three hundred years.

Moreover, the evidence does not support the conventional wisdom. Since I began going there in the late 1960s, the Soviet Union never struck me as all that poor—especially after I lived in central Africa for a few years. It was depressing, grimy, and suffocating, for sure, but not wretchedly poor.

The data bears out this impression. The CIA *World Factbook* issued during the year of Reykjavik estimated the Soviet per capita GNP at $7,120, considerably higher than countries to which Americans flocked for their holidays—Italy ($6,096), Israel ($6,270), and Ireland ($4,440).

While not terribly poor then, the U.S.S.R. may not have been getting poorer then, either. The 1986 CIA *World Factbook* estimated Soviet economic growth at 2.5 percent for each year of the prior decade. And right after Reykjavik, the intelligence community raised that estimate upward. "The Soviet economy grew 4.2% in 1986," a front-page *Los Angeles Times* article stated, which was "twice the average growth rate for the previous decade, and considerably greater than the U.S. increase of 2.5% last year, the chief U.S. intelligence agencies reported."

Three years later, with Gorbachev's reforms accelerating, the economy started decelerating. The CIA estimates for 1988 had Soviet growth down to 1.5 percent. But it was still growth, and not fatal decline. In short, hard evidence contradicts the conventional wisdom that the Soviet system collapsed due to a precipitous economic decline from a state of dire poverty—and not because of external forces (such as the delegitimization campaign and/or the effect of SDI) or events (such as Reykjavik).

Moreover, at least some experts reject the conventional wisdom. While Talbott and Matlock are admittedly knowledgeable on Soviet affairs, they are not as knowledgeable on Soviet affairs as Gorbachev and Shevardnadze—both of whom assert categorically that Reykjavik, SDI, and Reagan had profound effects on ending the Cold War.

To assert the inevitability of the Soviet breakup—as Talbott and Matlock do—presumes that economic factors propel history to its inevitable outcome. While it may seem fitting to apply Karl Marx's methodology to Soviet history, his may not be the best tools of analysis. For this approach takes real people out of history. It substitutes grand trends and great waves for real, live decision makers, who grapple as best they can to the predicaments they confront. That approach assumes an inevitability to history's unfolding that sure doesn't feel that way to those in it at the time.

In the book *Implications of the Reykjavik Summit on Its Twentieth Anniversary*, Don Oberdorfer refutes the contention that the Soviet Union *had* to collapse due to its defects. "Nowhere was it written that the heavily armed Soviet Union would pass away peacefully. . . . It is a marvel of history." That marvel happened, Oberdorfer rightly states, "due to relationships that were forged at Reykjavik, [which] thrived in the months and years that followed. . . . With different decisions and different people, it could all have turned out very differently . . . for all humankind."

Reagan and Gorbachev never thought of themselves as corks bobbing on the Splengerian tide of history. They never thought that events were being propelled by Marxist forces toward a predetermined shore. Both men presumed that they were shaping history. And, at Reykjavik, I believe they were.

Indeed, what made that weekend so exceptional was not only its many ups and downs, turns and twists, or even its lasting and sweeping significance. It was also the leading actors of that drama—two of the most charismatic and intriguing characters of the twentieth century.

THE PERSONAL REALM

Reagan Revisited

In 2004 Henry Kissinger invited me to lunch at the Four Seasons in New York. We had known each other slightly over the years. Then, in 2001, we both joined Don Rumsfeld's Defense Policy Board, which met every couple of months.

Upon arriving, I headed toward the shrouded corners of that fabled restaurant, where the famous find privacy and discretion for their power lunches. But I was told that Dr. Kissinger preferred a table right up front, near the maître d'.

After a long talk on issues then before the Policy Board, Kissinger moved onto his favorite topic: leadership. He had fascinating facts and anecdotes about Metternich and Bismarck, Talleyrand, and Clemenceau—treating me like a one-man Harvard graduate seminar.

I interrupted his flow by asking, "What about Ronald Reagan? He clearly lacked those qualities but had accomplishments approaching theirs."

This threw Kissinger off, so much that for maybe fifteen seconds he sat silent. "Reagan is different," he said rather dolefully, "not like the others. He's sui generis. No, I cannot explain him."

If Kissinger can't, maybe no one can. Reagan is famously hard to decipher. He's baffled family members—his children, Ron and Patti, have toured the circuit speaking about the mystery of their father—as well as historians and biographers, including the best known, Edmund Morris. Having been given unprecedented access to the Reagan White

House, Morris ended up considering him a "hollow subject" without "depths to probe," even "a bone-cracking bore."

That was not only unkind, but also unfair. From the declassified notes of Reagan at Reykjavik—which were still secret when Morris published his lamentable biography, *Dutch*—we see a man with surprising depth and dexterity on the critical issues of his day.

Socrates said that "the unexamined life is not worth living." Reagan left his obviously worth-living life for others to examine. We cannot come to know Reagan by digging for his own thoughts or intentions at any given moment. He was never reflective and always reluctant to talk about himself. He refused to share whatever inner thoughts or emotions he might have had. He was, in short, the most un-Clintonian of presidents.

Yet we do know what Reagan thought and intended in grand terms. He thought Communism would end up on the ash heap of history and he intended to help put it there. He would try to make that happen by delegitimizing the evil system. This he did consistently— from his first presidential press conference, when he said that "they reserve unto themselves the right to commit any crime, to lie, to cheat" to further the Communist goal of world domination, to his Farewell Address, when he urged that we must "keep up our guard" when dealing with Communists.

Reagan intended to create a safer world by developing SDI, sharing it with the Soviets, building up America's strength, building down nuclear arsenals, and having Gorbachev "tear down this Wall." He would end his predecessors' policy of détente, considering it piecemeal at best and craven at worst.

If this be a hollow subject, it is one with considerable substance in it. Reagan got the big issues right while his smarter, more knowledge-able skeptics seemed to get so many of them wrong.

The role of lifeguard was central to Reagan's self-image and surviving the 1981 assassination attempt affected him profoundly. Saving others when he was young and being saved when he was old were two formative experiences in his life.

Reagan can best be known by his deeds. The great architect Christopher Wren is buried in his masterpiece, Saint Paul's Cathedral in London. There is no statue or headstone, only a plaque on the marble wall which reads: *Si monumentum requiris, circumspice*—if you want to see his monument, look around you.

We can look around us and see Reagan's monument—a Europe united and free, some 415 million people liberated from Communism, and nuclear stockpiles sliced and dwindling. Of course, Reagan did not build this monument by himself, any more than Wren built Saint Paul's by himself. They each designed the structure, which others helped build. Even Gorbachev recognized this, when he called Reagan "the person who had paved the way for the end of the Cold War."

We also gain insight into Reagan by realizing his narrow but deep capacity to love. His relation to Nancy, and hers to him, was something special, a real gift to them both. He and Gorbachev ignored much of the "superwife spats" between Nancy and Raisa. When asked about it later, Gorbachev said, "A lot of good things and bad things have been said about Raisa and Nancy, but I can say that both these women bore their 'first ladyships' with a lot of dignity."

We know the things Reagan did but not how he was able to do them. While frustrating, that's also true of other aspects of life. For instance, we know how well acupuncture works, and has worked over many centuries, but not so much how it works.

Likewise, we know what high achievers do but not how they do it. Mickey Mantle could never explain how he hit, fielded, or ran so superbly. When asked repeatedly by fans and biographers, he said that he didn't know either. He merely hit, fielded, and ran. He *did* know, though, that the more he thought about it, the poorer he did it. Mantle had what psychologists call muscle memory, which enables musicians and athletes to act with great skill but little thought. Dr.

Eric Kandel, winner of the Nobel Prize in Physiology or Medicine, explains it as a reflective action recalled through performance "without conscious effort or even the awareness that we are drawing on memory."

To say that Reagan had muscle memory for leadership, especially in foreign affairs, may be a great insight, or it may be trite, or even a tautology. Nonetheless, he did a lot well without a lot of deliberation. He was all Hotspur and no Hamlet.

Perhaps above all, Reagan was an actor, no longer of the Hollywood sort, but a man of action, of the Energizer Bunny sort. Hence his big "It CAN Be Done" sign on the *Resolute* desk, facing outward for all to see.

While in office, Reagan was no longer the type of actor he had been, someone trying to be someone else. After all, there was no one else he would rather be than Ronald Reagan and no role he would rather play than president of the United States.

Gorbachev Revisited

Mikhail Gorbachev is likewise sui generis. He's unique by the extent of his being reviled at home and revered abroad and by his being heralded for achieving what he sought to avoid, and even actively opposed.

Nonetheless, Gorbachev is a great man of history. When it counted most, when the Communist regimes of the Warsaw Pact faced popular revolts, he proved himself a humanist and a realist.

His record is hardly perfect. He presided over years of bloodshed in Afghanistan and weeks of bloodshed in Lithuania. In one year alone, 1990, as Soviet commander in chief, he presided over more military fatalities than those of all Americans who have died in Afghanistan and Iraq over the past dozen years. Soviet repression, with political prisoners wasting away in jail, continued long after Gorbachev got the keys to open their cells. Innocent people, good people, rotted away in the gulag.

But compared with his predecessors, Gorbachev was truly remarkable. He had no penchant for sending jackboot-wearing henchmen to round up dissidents in their apartments or to mow down protestors in the streets. He grasped the foolishness of banishing and trashing his country's most gifted citizens—the Pasternaks, Solzhenitsyns, and Sakharovs—instead of celebrating them as models for the next generation.

Gorbachev deserves high praise for allowing the Soviet Union and its empire to dissolve peacefully—especially since history furnishes few other instances of such a peaceful demise. The Ottoman and Austrian-Hungarian empires ended in the horrendous violence of the Great War, and the British and French empires ended in the aftermath of the yet-worse World War II.

On a personal level, Gorbachev also made a real impact. He was more comfortable dealing with real people than ideological constructs. He rejected Leon Trotsky's notion of a New Soviet Man, preferring authentic human beings. Aleksandr Bessmertnykh, Gorbachev's foreign minister after Shevardnadze, said during a 1993 conference at Princeton University:

> For us, of course, there were no instructions to change ourselves into human beings. But there was something that influenced us, and that was Gorbachev himself.
>
> He was an absolutely new type of top leader. He was absolutely human, accessible—a man who could love, who could curse, who could use good and unprintable language. He was an absolutely normal man, very intellectual . . . and knowledgeable.

At Reykjavik over the weekend, Gorbachev dealt honestly and respectfully. He became cranky only when Reagan ramped up another story—and certainly can be excused for that.

Unlike his predecessors, Gorbachev was right on major issues. There were way too many nuclear weapons around and they were deployed way too dangerously. There was way too much oppression at home and aggression abroad for the country's own good.

Distinct from his predecessors in these ways, Gorbachev is also distinct by being hailed abroad and hooted at home to such an extent. This began even before his country collapsed. During his 1989 trip to West Germany, ten thousand hard-hatted construction workers roared their approval when Gorbachev visited a Ruhr Valley industrial plant. He never received such tribute when visiting a Soviet industrial plant.

Gorbachev is hailed abroad for what's widely deplored at home— for ending the Soviet empire and then the Soviet Union, for presiding over what Russian leader Vladimir Putin called "the greatest geopolitical catastrophe of the century," something "for the Russian people . . . became a genuine tragedy."

Besides being widely hailed, Gorbachev has been highly awarded. In 1990 he won the greatest award of them all, the Nobel Peace Prize. The Oslo committee cited his "leading role" in the "dramatic changes [which] have taken place in the relationship between East and West. Confrontation has been replaced by negotiations. Old European nations have regained their freedom. The arms race is slowing down."

The prize went to Gorbachev alone. The committee never mentioned Ronald Reagan.

Previously, the committee had recognized joint contributions, such as Henry Kissinger and Le Duc Tho for negotiating the end of the Vietnam War (though that turned out poorly) and F. W. de Klerk and Nelson Mandela for undertaking a peaceful transition in South Africa (which turned out well). Clearly the end of the Cold War and the termination of Communist rule across Europe—both of which Reagan helped hasten—are grand, historic achievements worthy of a Nobel Prize. Freeing 415 million men, women, and children from totalitarian Communist rule will not dissipate soon, or ever.

Winning awards is wonderful, but having someone to bring those awards home to is even more wonderful. When Gorbachev won the awards trifecta—*Time* magazine's "Man of the Year" for 1987, its unprecedented "Man of the Decade" for the 1980s, and the Nobel Peace Prize in 1990—he had Raisa to share his happiness and pride.

The Gorbachevs, like the Reagans, had a special bond. Having her at his side giving political advice, which he valued highly, helped Gorbachev along his perilous path. It helped him endure the abuse heaped upon him during the Yeltsin years. It must have been tough for Gorbachev to handle the even worse abuse during the Putin years alone, after Raisa died of leukemia in 1999.

The second remarkable feature of Gorbachev was his being heralded and awarded for things he resisted, in fact, for things he detested. When taking office on March 11, 1985, he did not intend to break up the Soviet Union, to have its ideology discredited, to end its empire, to disparage its past, or to finish off the country altogether. These were not his aspirations then nor at any time that he presided over the Kremlin.

They were, however, the aspirations of the man who took the oath of office six weeks earlier, on January 20, 1985, when Reagan raised his arm to begin his second term.

Jonathan Steele, of the left-leaning *Guardian*, made the point well when he wrote: "Gorbachev won the world's biggest consolation prize . . . the Nobel peace award for losing the Cold War [and] dismantling the system his party spent 70 years creating."

In history, as in life, ironies abound.

Shultz and Shevardnadze Revisited

George Shultz has been justifiably praised for his indispensable role in the negotiations realm, bringing the intermediate missile treaty to conclusion in 1987. He was no grand geostrategic thinker on the model of Dean Acheson or Henry Kissinger, but he did not need to be. His president did enough grand thinking for the two of them. Yet Reagan could not do the nitty-gritty work on specifics that Shultz handled so deftly. They were an ideal fit.

Carefully attuned to his boss while in office, Shultz picked up his mantle after leaving office. Organizing his "gang of four" to abolish nuclear weapons, and then a larger group at the twenty-fifth anniversary of Reykjavik, has added to the meaningful life he's made for himself after government service.

Not so with his counterpart. Shevardnadze was irresponsible when breaking with Gorbachev at such a critical juncture. His post-Soviet life was no better. In 1992 a coup brought him to power as president of newly independent Georgia. His government was later accused of rampant corruption, nepotism, and electoral fraud. Citizens eventually took to the streets against his rule and tossed him out of office.

His career was thus bookended by dubious, if not deplorable actions—as the top cop in totalitarian Georgia, and the failed president of it after independence. Between them, however, were five years of success as Soviet foreign minister. Now in his late eighties and living in obscurity, Shevardnadze can look back on the late '80s with justifiable pride and joy.

THE INSTITUTIONAL REALM

In the 1980s the American political system seemed in disarray. The atmosphere in Washington was said to be poisonous, partisanship deemed worse than ever, gridlock debilitating and unbreakable. A quarter century later, the system then seems rather in array.

Despite its inevitable bumps and grinds, government delivered back then. The professional arms experts worked scores of baffling, complex problems diligently and creatively. Secretary Shultz fashioned a team out of disparate, feuding agencies to deal effectively with arms issues. It succeeded nicely in the negotiations realm, although his diplomats shied away from the geostrategic realm.

But that didn't matter, as the administration didn't need them there. Reagan served as desk officer for public diplomacy, launching the war of ideas with conviction and persuasion, and keeping it going throughout. He knew what he wanted to do in the geostrategic realm, and really needed no help in doing it.

Intelligence Reconsidered

Even as we squeezed into the bubble, we realized that the pre-summit intelligence had been wayward. Reykjavik was not going to be a photo-op, as predicted. The main fault lay with the CIA, although its assessment had been seconded by our ambassador in Moscow and theirs in Washington.

While regrettable, this is still forgivable. After all, human intelligence is tough to get right. Analysts spend loads of time trying to read the minds of people who haven't made up their minds. That's why the intelligence community is more comfortable describing what happened or what is happening than what will happen—which is what policy makers most need to know. All forecasting is dicey, as Yogi Berra put it, especially about the future.

While bad, this intelligence failure was not debilitating. Despite Don Regan's dictates, Shultz bulked up the arms team going to Reykjavik. So he had the expertise on hand to pivot when needed.

Of some consolation is how the KGB's performance was even worse than the CIA's. Its erroneous assessment of our intermediate missiles in Europe led Gorbachev to consider them "a gun pressed to [the Soviet Union's] temple" and a "serious threat to [the Soviet Union]." As told, they were nothing of the sort. But that faulty estimate prompted the Soviets to scrap their more effective, already deployed missiles to forestall our ineffective, mostly-yet-to-be-deployed ones.

Of greater consequence was the Soviet intelligence failure on SDI. This extended beyond the KGB to virtually all Soviet agencies. A Ministry of Foreign Affairs study, for instance, concluded that "the U.S. could begin testing and then the deployment of all three" strategic defense systems by 1995. Moreover the U.S. "full-scale deployment of space-based missile defense systems can be expected after 2010. We need to bear this in mind." Indeed, Gorbachev bore little else in mind all weekend long in Reykjavik.

Finally, and almost comically, the Soviet Ministry of Defense gauged SDI's effectiveness after 2010 at "approximately 99%." While this sounds impressive, it wasn't good enough, according to the ministry, since unnamed U.S. experts "think that [strategic defense] should allow, at most, 0.1% of the attacking missiles to get through." While unnamed U.S. experts might think that, nonexperts could consider stopping 99 percent of incoming missiles a whole lot better than stopping none.

More serious were intelligence failures on the broader canvas. The eminent Yale historian Lewis Gaddis wrote in 1993 that the fall of the U.S.S.R. was "of such importance that no approach to the study of international relations claiming both foresight and competence should have failed to see it coming." Yet, he noted, "None actually did so."

Despite tens of billions of dollars of yearly appropriations, the CIA—whose focus was almost exclusively on the Soviet Union then— failed to predict the Soviet collapse, one of the seminal events of modern times. According to recently declassified papers, the CIA did not entertain such a notion—and even then smothered it with caveats and footnotes—until 1989, only two years before it did happen.

The idea that the U.S.S.R. could end was unthinkable to the CIA, and to officials dealing with this portfolio, including me. Yet it was also unthinkable to the KGB, to the Supreme Soviet, the Politburo, and to the general secretary himself.

Truth be told, it was unthinkable to nearly every agency and every person on both sides of the Iron Curtain—except to Ronald Reagan. He deemed it not only thinkable but somehow inevitable.

ON SUNDAY, NOVEMBER 17, 1996, I was in the posh Hotel Bel-Air in Los Angeles for yet another Reykjavik anniversary celebration and symposium.

The conference, aptly titled "High Noon at Reykjavik," would begin the next morning at the Reagan Library. An elegant dinner was being hosted by Nancy Ruwe, the widow of the U.S. ambassador to Iceland who had been shabbily treated over the summit weekend.

I was mingling with Soviet and American veterans of Reykjavik, with whom I would be serving on panels the next day, when I spotted Nancy Reagan ambling down the hallway. She was as slight as ever, but alert and lively. As I approached her, I felt a palpable sense of sadness surrounding her, a sense that she had lost the only thing that made life worth living for her.

As she approached the reception, I greeted her by saying that I had just returned from Reykjavik. Maureen had already told her about the conference, but she still asked for my impressions of it.

Instead of answering, I began to tell her about the postcard. I described my early morning pilgrimage to Hofdi House and how that had inspired me to write a note to her husband. Since I knew neither their home address nor that of the library, I had simply addressed it to "President Ronald Reagan, Reagan Library, Simi Valley, California."

Mrs. Reagan became somewhat flustered, with a look that seemed to ask: Don't you know that my husband has Alzheimer's? That he can't read anything?

Despite her frown, she managed to ask me what I had written. I couldn't remember exactly, I told her, but it was something like this:

President Reagan—

I am in Reykjavik on the 10th anniversary, thinking back on the superb job you did that weekend. Of how well you served America, and how very proud I was to serve you, Mr. President.

MY VERY BEST TO YOU,

KEN ADELMAN

Nancy Reagan started tearing up, as did I. With people all around waiting to greet her, we seemed alone with memories we cherished— both of us about a man we considered so special and, for me, about a weekend unlike any other in my life, or in all of history.

Mourning in America

A cruel decade after Ronald Reagan wrote that he had begun "the journey that will lead me into the sunset of my life," darkness came.

He had been in a coma for days when, on Saturday, June 5, 2004, he suddenly opened his eyes. As Nancy Reagan told their daughter, Patti: "They weren't chalky or vague. They were clear and blue and full of love." He fixed those bright eyes on Nancy, and then slowly closed them. She considered it the greatest gift ever.

When the news reached Moscow, Mikhail Gorbachev hailed President Reagan for paving "the way for the end of the Cold War." In New York, Henry Kissinger said simply that "Ronald Reagan ended the Cold War." SDI, he added, had created the incentive for major Soviet concessions at the bargaining table.

Tributes flooded in from across the globe. "Icelanders will always remember the significant summit in Reykjavik," the official statement from there read, "as a turning point in world history and among the greatest moments in the nation's history." Iceland's president then, Vigdís Finnbogadóttir, recalled her conversation with Reagan about presidents, theater, and life.

In an op-ed piece for the *New York Times*, Gorbachev wrote that he could not have dealt as successfully with any other U.S. president.

Though Reagan was "a man of the right . . . he was not dogmatic; he was looking for negotiations and cooperation. And . . . the most important thing to me: he had the trust of the American people."

For Gorbachev, the relationship went beyond the professional to the personal. He "appreciate[d] Ronald Reagan's human qualities. A true leader, a man of his word and an optimist, he traveled the journey of his life with dignity and faced courageously the cruel disease that darkened his final years. He has earned a place in history and in people's hearts."

On the morning of June 7, the immediate family held a small private service at the Ronald Reagan Presidential Library, with the pastor remarking on the "outpouring of love across America." The library opened its doors to the public at noon, following the service. Over the next forty-eight hours, more than 100,000 people filed by the flag-adorned casket, which was surrounded by a five-person military honor guard. The flag on top was the one that had flown over the Capitol when Reagan was first inaugurated, on January 20, 1981.

A twenty-one-gun salute was fired on June 9 as the casket left the library to head east. It was received with full honors at the Point Magu Naval Air Station airport in Ventura. President George W. Bush had sent Air Force One to bring his predecessor back to Washington.

At Andrews Air Force Base, the coffin was placed in a hearse and then transferred to a horse-drawn caisson for a procession down Constitution Avenue to the Capitol. Silent crowds—old and young, black and white—stood five and six deep along the route to pay their respects to the fallen leader.

When the procession reached the Capitol steps, it was greeted by another twenty-one-gun salute. As the honor guard carried the coffin up the broad stone steps of the Capitol, the flag above flew at half mast, as did all flags across America that week. The Air Force band played the "Battle Hymn of the Republic" as the casket was carried into the Rotunda, by then filled with members of Congress and administration officials. It was carefully laid on the pine catafalque that had held

Abraham Lincoln's coffin there nearly a hundred and forty years earlier and John F. Kennedy's around forty-one years before.

After members of the honor guard placed wreaths at the foot of the coffin and stood at attention around the bier, Mrs. Reagan stepped forward and placed both her hands on the flag-draped coffin. Leaning over, she rested her cheek on it, said some quiet words to it, and chuckled at it. She then left on the arm of Vice President Dick Cheney, who had given a moving tribute minutes before.

The Rotunda was opened to the public for the next thirty-six hours. Some college students, who happened to be staying with us then, left our house around 10:00 that night to join the long line, stretching all the way down the National Mall and around the Reflecting Pool. They finally entered the Rotunda at 2:30 a.m. as the line of mourners walked solemnly on both sides of the catafalque draped in black velvet. More than 100,000 people paid their respects, some waiting somberly for nearly seven hours in line.

On Friday, June 11, Carol and I were honored to attend the state funeral at the Washington National Cathedral. We watched in reverent awe as four former presidents, twenty-five current world leaders, and more than two hundred foreign ministers and ambassadors assumed their places. We saw Prince Charles, Baroness Margaret Thatcher, Lech Wałęsa, Supreme Court justices, members of Congress, aged members of Reagan's so-called kitchen cabinet, and friends from movies and media, including Merv Griffin, Joan Rivers, and Barbara Walters. David Oddsson, the mayor-turned-impresario who had deftly directed Reagan and Gorbachev to open the Reykjavik drama, was there to represent Iceland.

Spaced throughout the hour-long ceremony were musical interludes, including an Irish tenor singing "Amazing Grace" and "Ave Maria," and the Marine Corps band playing a stirring rendition of the "Battle Hymn of the Republic."

Suffering from a series of harsh strokes, Margaret Thatcher could no longer speak in public. But she was not to be silenced. In a prerecorded video shown on screens around the cathedral, she told how Reagan "did not shrink from denouncing Moscow's evil empire" and gave him credit for freeing "the slaves of Communism."

Like Gorbachev in his op-ed article, Thatcher honored the man himself, talking about the effect the 1981 near-death experience had on him. "Ronnie himself certainly believed that he had been given back his life for a purpose. As he told a priest after his recovery, 'Whatever time I've got left now belongs to the big fellow upstairs.'" She concluded that, "Ronald Reagan's life was providential when we look at what he achieved."

Both Presidents Bush spoke. Sandra Day O'Connor, Reagan's first Supreme Court appointee and its first female, read Reagan's favorite passage from John Winthrop's 1630 sermon aboard the *Arabella* bound for Massachusetts: "We shall be as a city upon a hill, the eyes of all people are upon us."

After the coffin was wheeled out and placed in the waiting hearse, top dignitaries headed to the State Department for a lunch of salad, lamb, vegetables—and jelly beans.

The casket was motorcaded back to Andrews in the early afternoon for its final journey home. After two hours airborne, the pilot routed the plane—with Nancy, the family, and a few others aboard, including Thatcher—over Tampico, Illinois. Air Force One tipped a wing as it passed over a flat above the local bank where Reagan had been born, ninety-three years before. It then flew over Dixon, Illinois, where he had written in his 1928 high school yearbook, *The Dixonian,* "Life is just one grand sweet song, so start the music!"

Finally, the aircraft landed in California on a beautiful clear cool evening. More than a thousand people watched as the casket was lowered onto the hearse by an honor guard.

People lined both sides of Highway 101 to view the funeral procession. From a hillside, five forest rangers on horseback saluted. Two fire engines had extended their ladders several stories; where they touched, two firefighters stood at attention and saluted, with a huge American flag draped below them. Americans of all shades and walks of life waved small flags, saluted, or held their hands over their hearts as the Reagan caravan slowly passed by, heading toward and then up the winding road to the Ronald Reagan Presidential Library.

Behind the library, in a grove overlooking the magnificent valley with the ocean glistening in the distance, a sunset ceremony was held for some seven hundred mourners. Once again, many Hollywood friends were there—Norman Lear, Mickey Rooney, Kirk Douglas, Bo Derek, Tom Selleck, Johnny Mathis, and Wayne Newton.

Of the family members, Michael Reagan spoke first, describing how his father had always treated him like a son, never once mentioning that he had been adopted. Patti recalled her father eulogizing a dead goldfish so eloquently that she proposed killing all the other goldfish in her bowl so that they, too, could swim in that "clear blue, endless stream" her dad had portrayed as goldfish heaven. Ron Jr. began and ended, "He is home now. He is freed" and revealed his father's rather odd joy in pulling earlobes, often his own, but frequently others' as well.

With a lone bagpiper playing "Amazing Grace," the honor guard moved the casket toward a curved granite headstone engraved with the epitaph that Reagan had personally selected: "I know in my heart that man is good. That what is right will always eventually triumph. And there's purpose and worth to each and every life."

An empty space next to the president's tomb was reserved for Nancy. A huge chunk of the Berlin Wall—which had been painted in gay, psychedelic colors on November 9, 1989—was placed only yards from their gravesite.

With the sun disappearing into the horizon, Air Force fighters performed a "missing man fly-by" maneuver—four jets flying low together until one abruptly pulls up and away, leaving an empty space in the formation.

After that moving tribute, the honor guard folded the flag and its commander solemnly presented the triangle fold to Mrs. Reagan. With the casket now undecorated, she laid her cheek on its highly polished surface, kissed it, and, at last, broke down and wept. It had been a long day of coast-to-coast services, and she could hold back no longer.

Thus ended a week of mourning in America. It had been a week of emotional outpouring for the man who had been both there and not there over the previous decade; one who was remembered fondly for what he was and for what he did nearly twenty years earlier. Americans recalled his big personality, his display of exemplary character after being shot, his spontaneous humor, and his huge impact on the course of American and world history.

Obviously, most Americans had never known Reagan. But somehow they came to feel that he had known them—that he had understood their lives and cares. They loved his optimism, his conviction that America's best days still lie ahead, that it was still morning in America.

I sat for several television interviews and told tales about President Reagan, Reykjavik, and favorite moments with him. But I never felt that I did him justice.

WHILE CAROL AND I had become emotional during the funeral, what happened the day before moved me the most.

Unannounced and unexpected, Gorbachev had flown in from Moscow. He landed at what would later be named Ronald Reagan Washington National Airport and headed directly to the Capitol Rotunda. As the silent crowds continued to file slowly by the casket, Gorbachev was allowed to step inside the velvet rope alongside the honor guard. He stood there, seemingly lost in memories, for some time. He then took two paces forward, nodded pensively, and extended his right hand to rest on Reagan's casket.

"I gave him a pat," he told an interviewer hours later.

A pat and then a rub, as Gorbachev began moving his hand fondly back and forth, along the red and white stripes of the American flag covering the coffin of the fortieth president of the United States.

Acknowledgments

The happy ending of this story—a Europe united and free, a safer and more peaceful world, some 415 million people liberated from the yoke of Communism—happened because of the fortitude of many brave souls who are no longer with us, especially Alexandr Solzhenitsyn, Scoop Jackson, Vaclav Havel, Jeane Kirkpatrick, Malcolm Muggeridge, Max Kampelman, Gyula Horn, Irving Kristol, Bob Bartley, Mark Palmer, Bill Casey, Pope John Paul II, Lady Margaret Thatcher, Robert Conquest, Paul Nitze, the thousands who marched in streets and died in gulags, and virtually all postwar American presidents, but especially the two bravest and wisest—Harry S. Truman and Ronald W. Reagan—bookends of America's fortitude during the Cold War. The world is a far better place because of how it ended: we won and they lost.

Jeane Kirkpatrick and Don Rumsfeld were valuable mentors in my government posts as in my life. I will always be grateful to both.

On a more parochial level of telling the story of Reykjavik and all that flowed from it, Frank Gannon looms largest. Friend, traveling companion, and raconteur par excellence, Frank suggested the tone for the book, sketched its chapter contents, and edited it in ways that added sparkle, humor, depth, and understanding. Here's hoping that the final product comes somewhere close to what Frank envisioned when he and Carol and I embarked on this venture.

With Frank at hand, we paid a call on Jay Mandel of William Morris Endeavor, who seconded Frank's idea of focusing on Reagan at Reykjavik. After reading a few initial chapters, Jay agreed to be the book's agent, which thrilled us no end. He subsequently helped shape the material and then put it in the hands of the right publishers. He performed all this superbly.

For any author, the "first responders" are most memorable and appreciated. Tom McCloskey, Ted Bell, and Jeffrey Frank read the initial drafts and gave their suggestions, along with validation that this was, indeed, a tale worth telling. Just days after receiving early chapters, Walter Isaacson kindly called to give his hearty encouragement.

Dear friends Nord Brue and Ken Burns were as kind with their suggestions and encouragement on this project, as they have been in their friendships. Our lives wouldn't be the same without them.

Another legendary storyteller, Jay Sandrich, offered his ideas on telling this story, which, as with everything he does, were excellent. While not soul mates in politics, we are in life. Jay's mate, Linda, made a bunch of helpful suggestions, as did another dear soul of Aspen, Paul Andersen, a careful editor and close friend who has opened up grand vistas in our lives. John Fullerton, the model of an unassuming and generous man, scoured the text line by line, making corrections and real improvements. My sidekick at ACDA, Mike Guhin, went over the manuscript to make sure the arms control issues, though vastly simplified, were nonetheless accurate. As at ACDA, Mike was particularly valuable in curbing some of my natural excesses.

Doug Goodyear's enthusiasm for the material proved infectious, coming from someone with such fine judgment on both people and politics. Likewise, Mike Useem was wonderful to read the material over a weekend, and provide a "leadership moment" by urging me to keep charging. Stewart Mackinnon, the prime mover in a feature film on the Reykjavik summit—for more than six years now and running—has been a model of persistence and support.

Brother Jim, there from the start of life, has been there from the start of this project as well—guiding it along as only a bibliophile, like our mother, could do. Other family members added encouragement and guidance, daughters Jessica and Jocelyn on the text, sons Doug and Andy on the tone of the tome and the project in general.

Some of the many Icelandic gods must have steered the book toward HarperCollins and into the hands of Adam Bellow and Eric Meyers. They gave encouragement and made the book so much better, especially by letting the reader peak through the keyhole of the small conference room in Hofdi House to hear, see, and feel the most amazing discussion ever.

As for the research material, nothing was more valuable than *The Reykjavik File: Previously Secret Documents from U.S. and Soviet Archives on the 1986 Reagan-Gorbachev Summit,* edited by Dr. Svetlana Savranskaya and Thomas Blanton, and put online by the National Security Archive of George Washington University. I am most grateful for so much important material being made so accessible.

Finding photos and cartoons and securing the rights to them were handled by Nancy Rose with dedication and professionalism. One cartoon is most special, as it was created by someone most special, Mike Peters. Marian and Mike have lit up our lives over the past decade and we value them enormously. We laugh a lot together and only wish that we still had Jeff McNelly, who has a fine cartoon in the book, to laugh along with us—as does David Hume Kennerly, who generously gave two terrific photos for the book.

Many other photos came from the Ronald Reagan Presidential Library, run so well by friend Duke Blackwood, and its photo archives so competently by Steve Branch, who went the extra mile to help on this project, as did Mike Duggan when searching through mounds of correspondence in the valiant yet vain attempt to find my 1996 postcard to Reagan. Some photos and lots of other material were tracked down by a crack researcher in Reykjavik, Svanhildur Anja Astporsdottir. She described the layout of Hofdi House and of the town and related fabulous local stories, like that of Bjarni Benediktsson, which added spice to this tale of her city.

Likewise from Reykjavik came something worthy of an Icelandic saga. Out of the blue, a fellow named Eric Green e-mailed me that he had just heard about the book and prospective film and offered to help from his post as number two, deputy chief of mission, at the U.S. embassy there. He said that he had decided to join the Foreign Service back in 1983, after hearing Carol and me address him and other students at my alma mater, Grinnell College, on the joys and value of a life in international affairs. Eric's help on this project was appreciated.

Years ago, David McCullough told me that when writing history, you must like the main character, since you must live with him for years. In this, too, was I fortunate. I cherished being back with Ronald Reagan—better able, this second time around, to see his quirkiness and creativity, his personal flaws and stunning foresight, his casual and sometimes careless management but his dogged determination to change America, and then the world.

I have been lucky to be living with him again over these past few years, as I have been to be living with Carol over these past forty-two years. She made wonderful suggestions—in tone, substance, and wording for this project—as she has throughout all our projects, including that of sharing a life together.

Notes

INTRODUCTION

1 "Truly Shakespearean passions": Mikhail Gorbachev, letter to the prime minister of Iceland, the mayor of Reykjavik, and participants of the seminar on the tenth anniversary of the summit, September 10, 1996.

2 Cold War historian Don Oberdorfer: Don Oberdorfer, "At Reykjavik, Soviets Were Prepared and U.S. Improvised," *Washington Post*, February 16, 1987.

2 "wearying and grueling arguments": Ibid.

2 "no one can continue to act as he acted before": Mikhail Gorbachev, *Reykjavik: Results and Lessons* (Moscow, 1990).

3 "No summit since Yalta": Don Oberdorfer, *From the Cold War to a New Era: The United States and Soviet Union, 1983–1991* (Baltimore: Johns Hopkins University Press, 1998), 183.

4 "We were sitting around": Shultz told this story many times, including Teresa Jimenez, "Shultz Shakes Lessons of Cold War," *Los Angeles Daily News*, November 19, 1996.

1. DEPARTURES

8 the President had a few remarks: Ronald Reagan, "Remarks on Departure for Reykjavik, Iceland," October 9, 1986, Ronald Reagan Presidential Library Archives, www.reagan.utexas.edu/archives/speeches/1986/100986c.htm.

8 Days earlier: Stanley Meisler, "From Cod Liver to Hors d'Oeuvres, Iceland Seeks to Be a Good Host," *Los Angeles Times*, October 10, 1986.

9 "Get out of the way!": Michael Putzel, "Reagan Arrives in Iceland for Summit with Gorbachev," Associated Press, October 9, 1986.

9 an arm around Nancy's waist: Ibid.

10 accompanying her husband to Reykjavik: "White House Surprised by Raisa Gorbachev's Travel Plans," Associated Press, October 6, 1986.

10 settled in for the long flight: Bernard Weinraub, "The Iceland Summit: Setting the Stage; President Arrives for Iceland Talks," *New York Times*, October 10, 1986.

10 10:30 a.m. became 2:30 p.m.: Susanne M. Schafer, "Reagan Takes Over Modest Embassy Residence during Iceland Stay," Associated Press, October 10, 1986.

10 meatloaf was on the menu: Ibid.

10 The early meal service: Kenneth T. Walsh, *Air Force One: A History of the Presidents and Their Plane* (New York: Hyperion, 2003), 138.

11 presidential seal: For some odd reason, I kept this notebook on my bookshelf all these years. All references to it are from my copy.

12 Reagan deftly steered the leaders: Intermediate missiles, referred to frequently in this book, are formally called intermediate-range missiles, as they have a range between 500 and 5,500 kilometers, or 300 to 3,400 miles. The treaty banning them was usually called the INF Treaty for Intermediate Nuclear Force Treaty.

12 "an unprecedented success": Don Seller, "Summit Avoided Controversy," *Ottawa Citizen*, May 31, 1983.

12 A memo from Secretary of State George Shultz: This memo, and most of the now-unclassified material, comes from the invaluable source of *The Reykjavik File: Previously Secret Documents from U.S. and Soviet Archives on the 1986 Reagan-Gorbachev Summit* from the collections of the National Security Archive of George Washington University, Washington, DC; National Security Archive Electronic Briefing Book No. 203; Memorandum to the President from George P. Shultz, October 2, 1986, http://www.gwu.edu/~nsarchiv/NSAEBB/NSAEBB203/Document04.pdf.

13 fruit and a few jelly beans: Walsh, *Air Force One*, 138.

13 popped into the staff conference area: Ibid., 140.

13 seventy-seven notches: "1926: Lifeguarding at Lowell Park," Reagan Presidential Foundation and Library, http://www.reaganfoundation.org/life-and-times.aspx.

13 Another clear case of classification creep: Memorandum for the Honorable George P. Shultz from John M. Poindexter, October 4, 1986, *The Reykjavik File*, http://www.gwu.edu/~nsarchiv/NSAEBB/NSAEBB203/Document06.pdf.

13 According to Jack Matlock: *Implications of the Reykjavik Summit on Its Twentieth Anniversary,* edited by Sidney D. Drell and George P. Shultz (Stanford, CA: Hoover Institution Press, 2007), 109.

14 There had been top-level meetings: The meetings with Shultz and the president are reconstructed from the author's memory.

15 in its own pavilion: Frederick J. Ryan Jr., "The Airborne Ambassador: President Ronald Reagan and Air Force One," www.whitehousehistory.org/whha_publications/publications_documents/whitehousehistory_28-ryan.pdf (accessed November 26, 2012).

17 women cared little about arms control: Don Irwin, "Regan Regrets Slur on Women," *Los Angeles Times*, November 25, 1985.

17 plaque on Shultz's chair: Don Oberdorfer, "After 3½ Years at State, George Shultz Is More the Fighter and Less the Sphinx," *Washington Post*, February 3, 1986.

18 giving Shultz the longest tenure: Ray Moseley, "Shultz Leaves Global Mark," *Chicago Tribune*, December 25, 1988.

18   "I met no one in public life": Jay Nordlinger, "Around the World with Shultz—A Visit to the Former Secretary of State," *National Review*, February 11, 2008.

18   Mike Deaver recalled: Oberdorfer, "After 3½ Years at State."

19   Andrei Gromyko: Alison Smale, "Gorbachev Leaves for Reykjavik," Associated Press, October 10, 1986.

23   "elegantly attired": Ibid.

23   it went against their hosts' explicit request: Maureen Dowd, "The Iceland Summit: And a Compromise on Capitol Hill," *New York Times*, October 11, 1986.

23   the sixty-member Althing: Susanne M. Schafer, "Iceland's Officials Choose Parliament Opening over Gorbachev Arrival," Associated Press, October 10, 1986.

23   "It is unfortunate": Ibid.

23   numbered more than three hundred: Andrew Rosenthal, "Soviet Delegation to Iceland Said to Number 300 and Counting," Associated Press, October 6, 1986.

24   Quietly at first: Martin Walker, "The Man Who Warned Gorbachev," *Washington Post*, September 22, 1991.

24   They took long walks: Eduard Shevardnadze, *The Future Belongs to Freedom* (New York: Macmillan, 1991), 36–37.

25   six Soviet leaders: Robert D. McFadden, "Anatoly F. Dobrynin, 90, Is Dead," *New York Times*, April 9, 2010.

25   six American presidents: Matt Schudel, "Former Soviet Ambassador to U.S. Was Known as a Master of Diplomacy," *Washington Post*, April 9, 2010.

26   Kentucky Derby: McFadden, "Anatoly F. Dobrynin," *New York Times*, April 9, 2010.

26   outdated missiles from Turkey: Ibid.

28   "will not play a direct role in the talks": Gary Lee, "Gorbachev Aides Are Experts on U.S.," *Washington Post*, October 11, 1986.

28   "You have to understand" : Mack Reed, "The Men Who Broke the Ice in Iceland," *Los Angeles Times*, November 19, 1996.

28   That would only become clear: *The Reykjavik File*, http://www.gwu.edu/~nsarchiv/NSAEBB/NSAEBB203/Document06.pdf.

31   he was young: Jim Gallagher, "Gorbachev's Rapid Rise to Power," *Chicago Tribune*, August 19, 1991.

32   Soviet specialist: Serge Schmemann, "The Emergence of Gorbachev," *New York Times Magazine*, March 3, 1985.

32   "What a chic lady is Mrs. Gorbachev!": Ibid.

32   "a refreshing change": Gallagher, "Gorbachev's Rapid Rise."

32   319 committee members: Howard A. Tyner, "Gorbachev Chosen," *Chicago Tribune*, March 12, 1985.

33   youngest Soviet leader: Gallagher, "Gorbachev's Rapid Rise."

33   A now-declassified CIA report: "Gorbachev's Economic Agenda: Promises, Potentials, and Pitfalls," written in September 1985 and contained in *Ronald Reagan: Intelligence and the End of the Cold War* (Washington, DC: Center for the Study of Intelligence, 2011), 51.

34 "a working session in a working atmosphere": Rolf Soderlind, "A Strange Place for a Summit," United Press International, October 4, 1986.

34 twenty-five hundred journalists: Marcus Eliason, "Iceland Opens Its Media Center," Associated Press, October 8, 1986.

34 3,117 foreign journalists: Susanne M. Schafer, "A Summit's a Summit, but Reykjavik Is not Geneva," Associated Press, October 11, 1986.

35 "a remarkable achievement": Eliason, "Iceland Opens Its Media Center."

36 ABC News alone sent a team of fifty: John Carmody, "The TV Column," *Washington Post*, October 8, 1986.

36 CNN brazenly publicized: Ibid.

36 Intelsat scrambled: Bill McCloskey, "Media Communications Set Up Rapidly in Iceland," Associated Press, October 11, 1986.

36 half the city's hotel rooms: Soderlind, "A Strange Place."

36 a third of all its rental cars: Ray Moseley, "Iceland to Trot Out Its Keystone Kops," *Chicago Tribune*, October 9, 1986.

36 "emergency powers": Larry Thorson, "Iceland Swamped by Influx of Officials and Journalists," Associated Press, October 4, 1986.

37 The whole house: Susanne M. Schafer, "Reagan Takes Over Modest Embassy Residence during Iceland Stay," Associated Press, October 10, 1986.

37 Nonetheless, reporters Daniel Schorr: Jane Leavy, "Friday, the Rabbi Was in Reykavik [*sic*]," *Washington Post*, October 10, 1986.

38 Gorbachev's letter in response: Letter to the President from M. Gorbachev, September 15, 1986, *The Reykjavik File*, http://www.gwu.edu/~nsarchiv/NSAEBB/NSAEBB203/Document01.pdf.

40 Hermansson later related: Edmund Morris, "Push and Shove in a Cold Climate," *Forbes FYI*, November 1986, 120.

2. ARRIVALS

41 Shevardnadze quipped: "Why Reykjavik? It's Quiet—and Has a U.S. Air Base," *Los Angeles Times*, September 30, 1986.

41 While protests elsewhere: Curt Suplee, "The Intro to Iceland," *Washington Post*, October 10, 1986.

41 "one of the strangest places on Earth": Soderlind, "A Strange Place."

42 only elected female president: Michael Putzel, "Reagan Arrives in Iceland for Summit with Gorbachev," Associated Press, October 9, 1986.

42 black on Thursdays: Rolf Soderlind, "Iceland Readies for Superpower Summit," United Press International, October 10, 1986.

42 armor-plated limousine: Ibid.

43 holding candles: Putzel, "Reagan Arrives."

43 assortment of antlers: Schafer, "Reagan Takes Over."

45 Reagan liked that notion: Interview in the Reykjavik newspaper *Morgunbladid* in June 2004, as reported and translated by researcher Svanhildur Anja Astporsdottir.

45   "affecting him already in 1986": Dagur B. Eggertsson, *Forsoetisraoherrann Steingrímur Hermannsson* (Reykjavik: Aevisaga, III, 2000), summarized by Astporsdottir.

46   a bulletproof Zil limo: Andrew Rosenthal, "Gorbachev Takes Up Residence in Reykjavik Harbor," Associated Press, October 10, 1986.

47   *Top Gun*: Soderlind, "Iceland Readies."

47   *Georg Ots*: Rosenthal, "Gorbachev Takes Up Residence."

47   "wonderful, very romantic": Bryan Brumley, "Life on Ship Romantic for Raisa Gorbachev," Associated Press, October 11, 1986.

48   "payoff match the pomp": Howard Rosenberg, "Media in Action at Reykjavik," *Los Angeles Times*, October 13, 1986.

48   hired Gray & Co.: Joan Mower, "Iceland Turns to Washington Publicists to Help Handle Media Horde," Associated Press, October 7, 1986.

49   steam . . . was mistaken . . . for smoke: Soderlind, "A Strange Place."

49   Roger Rosenblatt wrote: "On the Field of Ancient Peacemaking," *Time*, October 20, 1986, 25.

49   Along the steepest: Meghan O'Rourke, "Iceland," *New York Times Magazine,* October 6, 2013, 104.

49   "wouldn't spill a drink": John Barbour, "The Site of the Summit Is Literate, Proud, and Independent," Associated Press, October 9, 1986.

49   international press center: Marcus Eliason, "Iceland Opens Its Media Center," Associated Press, October 8, 1986.

50   In Iceland: O'Rourke, "Iceland," *New York Times Magazine*, October 6, 2013.

50   Visiting in 1872: Byron Farwell, *Burton: A Biography of Sir Richard Francis Burton* (New York: Penguin, 1990), 303.

50   "We are the descendants": Curt Suplee, "The Intro to Iceland," *Washington Post*, October 10, 1986.

51   intoned ABC's Peter Jennings: *World News Tonight*, ABC News, October 9, 1986.

52   Hofdi's history: *Hofdi: The City of Reykjavik's House for Official Receptions*, published by the city of Reykjavik.

52   Einer Benediktsson: Matthew C. Quinn, "Historic 'Haunted' House Hosts Summit," United Press International, October 10, 1986.

53   "bumps in the night": Ibid.

54   So if any resided: Notes of Astporsdottir based on local articles during the summit.

3. MINDS AND MOODS GOING INTO HOFDI HOUSE

58   "end of the discussion": Robert McNamara, "The Long Road to Reykjavik," *Time*, October 20, 1986, 34.

58   In 1963 President Kennedy: John F. Kennedy, Address to the American People, July 26, 1963, http://www.ratical.org/co-globalize/JFK072663.html.

61   When the Soviet intermediate missile: This is the SS-20 missile, which had three warheads. The U.S. intermediate missile, or medium-range missile, was the Pershing II, which had a single warhead on each missile.

61   Soviets precluded it: This was the Carter administration's 1978 "dual decision"—for the United States to begin deploying in 1983, in designated NATO countries, its Pershing II ballistic missiles and its cruise missiles to counterbalance the previously deployed Soviet SS-20 missiles targeting Europe, up to equal numbers of warheads—unless an arms control agreement precluded the need for such U.S./NATO deployments. This last provision was added because NATO foreign ministers needed an arms control aspect to the missile deployments and not because many of them thought this was likely, or even possible.

62   outside of Colorado Springs: Story recounted by Martin Anderson, in *Revolution: The Reagan Legacy* (Stanford, CA: Hoover Institution Press, 1988), 81–84.

63   In a letter to a friend: *Letters from the Desk of Ronald Reagan,* edited by Ralph E. Weber (Random House Digital, 2010), 279.

64   Union of Concerned Scientists: David C. Morrison, " 'Star Wars': A Thriving Cottage Industry," *National Journal*, May 23, 1987.

64   Arms Control Association: Eliot Brenner, "Objections to 'Star Wars,' " United Press International, October 19, 1986.

65   "Why are you doing this?": Thomas C. Reed, *At the Abyss: An Insider's History of the Cold War* (New York: Presidio Press, 2004), 234–35.

67   The editorial quoted: One can also question the conventional claim of the *New York Times* being the most influential publication in America. Ten days after the *Times* so vigorously endorsed Mondale, the nation vigorously endorsed Reagan. He swept the nation, winning forty-nine states. Mondale won one, his home state of Minnesota, and that by only a whisker (49.72 percent to 49.54 percent).

71   "We started with the wrong move": Shown on the "Greatest American" series of the Discovery Channel.

71   On a staff memo: Jack F. Matlock, *Reagan and Gorbachev: How the Cold War Ended* (New York: Random House, 2005), 214.

72   "Nancy Reagan's great rival": "Gorbachev's Wife Charms Parisians," United Press International in *Chicago Tribune*, October 4, 1985.

72   watched videotapes of Mrs. Gorbachev: Helen Thomas, "Spouse Meetings Closely Watched," United Press International, November 11, 1985.

72   "left her sense of style at home": Paula Butturini, "First Ladies Call a Truce in 'Style Wars,' " United Press International, November 21, 1985.

73   "there was no contest": Donnie Radcliffe, "First Ladies, Firsthand," *Washington Post*, November 21, 1985.

73   Julius Bengtsson: Stanley Meisler, "Two Leaders Fence with Press—And Hair Style Is Critiqued by Mr. Julius," *Los Angeles Times*, November 21, 1985.

73   the release of Anatoly Chernyaev's notes: Anatoly Chernyaev Notes from the Politburo Session, September 22, 1986, *The Reykjavik File: Previously Secret Documents from U.S. and Soviet Archives on the 1986 Reagan-Gorbachev Summit* from the collections of the National Security Archive of George Washington University, Washington, DC, http://www.gwu.edu/~nsarchiv/NSAEBB/NSAEBB203/Document02.pdf.

74   Five days before taking off: Anatoly Chernyaev's Notes, Gorbachev's Instructions to the Reykjavik Preparation Group, October 4, 1986, *The Reykjavik File*, http://www. gwu.edu/~nsarchiv/NSAEBB/NSAEBB203/Document05.pdf.

74   They were nothing of the sort: Nor did the peace movement realize how the U.S. Pershing II missile, prized for its mobility like its counterpart the Soviet SS-20, would have become immobile when needed—if not by the West German government then surely by the peace movement itself.

75   "limit of our capabilities": Chernyaev's Notes of October 4, 1986, *The Reykjavik File*, http://www2.gwu.edu/~nsarchiv/NSAEBB/NSAEBB203/Document05.pdf.

76   "we will lose!": contained in various memos on the *The Reykjavik File* website, http://www.gwu.edu/~nsarchiv/NSAEBB/NSAEBB203/index.htm.

76   "It will be difficult": David Holloway, "The Soviet Preparation for Reykjavik: Four Documents" contained in *Implications of the Reykjavik Summit*, 80.

77   Reagan's delegitimizing campaign: Chernyaev Notes from the Politburo Session, October 8, 1986, *The Reykjavik File*, http://www.gwu.edu/~nsarchiv/NSAEBB/NSAEBB203/Document08.pdf.

78   belongs to someone else: Discovery Channel series on great Americans, dealing with Reagan.

4. SATURDAY IN REYKJAVIK

82   According to legend: The legend and history are summarized by Astporsdottir from Icelandic sources.

83   wine-colored blotch: Eleanor Hoover, "Whatever Mikhail Gorbachev's Other Worries, the Birthmark on His Head Isn't One of Them," *People*, November 18, 1985; "Photographs Show Mark on Gorbachev's Head," Associated Press, March 12, 1985.

83   high concentrations of blood vessels: Frederic Golden, "Health Horizons; Medicine; Shedding New Light on the Skin," *Los Angeles Times*, October 6, 1991.

84   to do business together: The conversations in the four Reagan-Gorbachev Hofdi House sessions are reconstructed mainly from the American notes, but at times from the Russian notes, or occasionally from a combination of the two sets of notes. The key words in quotes are all taken from the notes, except for a change in tense, from past to present, and in pronouns, from third-person (natural to a notetaker) to second-person (natural to a conversation). For instance, if the notes read: "The President said what he proposed differed in three respects from Gorbachev," the conversation here would read: "Reagan told Gorbachev, 'What I'm proposing differs in three respects from what you're proposing.'" The parts quoted are only a small fraction of the leaders' ten and a half hours of dialogue, so quite a bit was left out when selecting the most significant and relevant to understanding the men and the issues. Moreover, inferences were made from the two sets of notes as to their tone, voices, and moods during the conversations. Since I was not in the room with them, and those who were in the room could not precisely reconstruct those elements decades later, I based such inferences on the recorded words—much like an actor and director base their emotions on the written words of playwrights or scriptwriters. These notes, which

were classified for many years after Reykjavik, have been assembled in *The Reykjavik File: Previously Secret Documents from U.S. and Soviet Archives on the 1986 Reagan-Gorbachev Summit* from the collections of the National Security Archive of George Washington University, Washington, DC, and put online: the American notes are at http://www.gwu.edu/~nsarchiv/NSAEBB/NSAEBB203/Document09.pdf and the Russian notes are at http://www.gwu.edu/~nsarchiv/NSAEBB/NSAEBB203/Document10.pdf.

86 not acknowledging one another: I was disappointed, but not surprised, that of all the White House photos of the Reykjavik summit not one included the two football-carrying military officers—even in the background. But, as mentioned, this remains the most vivid image in my mind from the weekend.

87 Bjarni Benediktsson: Considerable research on Benediktsson was conducted by Astporsdottir, including material from his biography and many other Icelandic sources.

89 another way to make his point: Oddly, this is in the Russian notes and not the American notes. But Reagan no doubt said it since no notetaker, Russian or otherwise, could have made it up. Plus, it was something Reagan was to say many more times.

90 She was not even identified: Maureen Dowd, "The Iceland Summit: Charm and Cough Drops," *New York Times*, October 12, 1986.

91 changing outfits several times: William J. Eaton, "The Reykjavik Summit: Changes Clothes 4 Times," *Los Angeles Times*, October 12, 1986.

92 "Good morning" and "It is beautiful": Bryan Brumley, "Life on Ship Romantic for Raisa Gorbachev," Associated Press, October 11, 1986.

92 Halldor Laxness: Dowd, "Iceland Summit," *New York Times*, October 12, 1986.

92 "Nancy is well!": Eaton, "The Reykjavik Summit," *Los Angeles Times*, October 12, 1986.

92 "there were no bureaucracies": I obtained a videotape of parts of that conference from Dr. Robert Meyers, the chairman of Global Zero, which organized the session. Shultz's remarks, as those of others, are on the Meyers homemade videotape.

92 Even someone: quoted in Charles Moore, *Margaret Thatcher: The Authorized Biography* (New York, Alfred A. Knopf, 2013), 565.

94 Immediately after: Again, I was disappointed, but not surprised, that there was no photo of the bubble in Reykjavik. The White House photographer, who usually snaps the president every few minutes, took relatively few photos indoors that weekend. And no other photographer was allowed inside the embassy, residence, or Hofdi House—at least that I saw or know about—during the weekend.

98 "On Saturday": John Carmody, "The TV Column," *Washington Post*, October 8, 1986.

98 At 3:30 p.m.: National Security Archive, *The Reykjavik File*, www2.gwu.edu/~nsarchiv/NSAEBB/NSAEBB203.

100 Reagan then accused Gorbachev: The Soviet radar at Krasnoyarsk, missed for many years by U.S. intelligence agencies despite regular U.S. satellite coverage of that area, was deemed a clear violation because it faced outward, in a way most likely used for detection and response to incoming missiles and was thus explicitly banned by the ABM Treaty. As mentioned, neither Gorbachev nor Shevardnadze ever denied it was a violation.

107 "improper for me to go": Eaton, "The Reykjavik Summit."

108 Maintaining the ABM Treaty: Hoffman, "The Soviet Preparation" in *Implications of the Reykjavik Summit on Its Twentieth Anniversary*, edited by Sidney D. Drell and George P. Shultz (Stanford, CA: Hoover Institution Press, 2007), 61.

109 "The most politically volatile issue": Kenneth Adelman, "Beyond MAD-ness," *Policy Review* 17 (Summer 1981): 77–85.

109 Granted, when his memoirs: Ronald Reagan, *An American Life* (New York, Simon & Schuster, 1990), 608.

110 Another pre-Reykjavik memo: Hoffman, "The Soviet Preparation," 58.

112 "the dawdling is worse": Byron Farwell, *Burton: A Biography of Sir Richard Francis Burton* (New York: Penguin, 1990), 303.

113 Joan Baez: Steve Goldstein, "The Doings at Superpower Weekend," *Philadelphia Inquirer*, October 12, 1986.

114 Indeed, the *New York Times*: Bernard Weinraub, "Reagan-Gorbachev Meeting Opens with Plans to Pursue Arms Pact and Rights Issues," *New York Times*, October 12, 1986.

114 Less understandable: Bernard Weinraub, "Summit Aftermath: Outlook for Bargaining on Arms," *New York Times*, October 14, 1986.

116 He had previously accused: Cliford J. Levy, "Georgi A. Arbatov, a Bridge between Divided Superpowers, Is Dead at 87," *New York Times*, October 3, 2010.

116 Earlier that day: "Soviet Spin Control," *Time*, October 20, 1986, 28.

117 University of Minnesota experiment: David Remnick, "The Evolution of Max Kampelman," *Washington Post*, January 23, 1985.

118 Albert Wohlstetter: James Gerstenzang, "Perle Wages Behind-the-Scenes Crusade against Kremlin," *Los Angeles Times*, November 11, 1985.

119 Wohlstetter steered him: Sidney Blumenthal, "Richard Perle's Nuclear Legacy," *Washington Post*, November 24, 1987.

120 "Prince of Darkness": Gerstenzang, "Perle Wages Behind-the-Scenes Crusade."

126 Arbatov mustered flattering words: Paula Chin, "Death of a Soldier," *People*, September 16, 1991.

5. SUNDAY MORNING IN REYKJAVIK

131 What he would later call: Ronald Reagan, *An American Life* (New York, Simon & Schuster, 1990), 675.

131 Shultz later recalled: George P. Shultz, *Turmoil and Triumph* (New York, Charles Scribner's Sons, 1993), 765.

133 Gorbachev began: "Previously Secret Documents from U.S. and Soviet Archives on the 1986 Reagan-Gorbachev Summit, National Security Archive of George Washington University, Washington, DC, *The Reykjavik File*, http://www.gwu.edu/~nsarchiv/NSAEBB/NSAEBB203.pdf.

136 Most matter of factly: Saying that there would be one hundred Soviet missiles in Asia was shorthand for there being one hundred *warheads* on Soviet missiles in Asia. As mentioned, the Soviet SS-20 missile contained three warheads, while the U.S.

Pershing II contained one. Consequently, there would *actually* be only thirty-three Soviet missiles in Asia, but one hundred warheads on such Soviet missiles in Asia. In this book, as in the negotiations themselves, I use that shorthand to make things simpler.

137 "I would agree": Don Oberdorfer, "When Reagan and Gorbachev Reached for the Stars," in *Implications of the Reykjavik Summit on Its Twentieth Anniversary*, edited by Sidney D. Drell and George P. Shultz (Stanford, CA: Hoover Institution Press, 2007), 117.

146 she led her cavalcade: "Gorbachev's Wife to Meet Children Who Wrote to Soviet Leader," Associated Press, October 9, 1986.

147 "I am an atheist": "Gorbachev's Wife Visits a Church, but Cuts Short Itinerary," Associated Press, October 12, 1986.

148 too imperative to be tied up: Anatoly Chernyaev's Notes, Gorbachev's Instructions to the Reykjavik Preparation Group, *The Reykjavik File*, October 4, 1986, http://www.gwu.edu/~nsarchiv/NSAEBB/NSAEBB203/Document05.pdf.

6. SUNDAY AFTERNOON AND EVENING IN REYKJAVIK

157 This Margaret Thatcher: Thatcher, *The Downing Street Years* (New York, Harper-Collins, 1993), 472.

158 diplomatic two-step with Eduard Shevardnadze: The exact wording of these two attempts is presented in Shultz's memoirs, *Turmoil and Triumph* (New York, Charles Scribner's Sons, 1993), 769.

160 "Ten years from now": Although Reagan was twenty years older, the story has Gorbachev the quasi-demented one, unable to recognize his pal, Reagan, ten years hence. Being the one who tells the story clearly has its advantages.

162 *Tom and Jerry* cartoons: George de Lama and Terry Atlas, "A Look behind The Summit Curtain," *Chicago Tribune*, October 16, 1986.

162 share both facilities: Matthew C. Quinn, "Historic 'Haunted' House Hosts Summit," United Press International, October 10, 1986.

164 Mrs. Reagan come to Reykjavik: Jack F. Matlock, *Reagan and Gorbachev: How the Cold War Ended* (New York: Random House, 2005), 232.

165 Some among us: Ibid., 238.

165 "I'd done exactly right": Ronald Reagan, *The Reagan Diaries*, edited by Douglas Brinkley (New York, HarperCollins, 2007), 444.

166 "excited speculation": Tom Shales, "The Valleys and Peaks of Summit TV," *Washington Post*, October 13, 1986.

172 "debates that became very pointed": Gorbachev's letter to the prime minister of Iceland, the mayor of Reykjavik, and participants at the tenth anniversary, September 10, 1996.

173 Meanwhile, upstairs: Shultz, *Turmoil and Triumph*, 774–75.

173 "You could have said 'yes!' ": de Lama and Atlas, "A Look Behind."

173 "I was mad": *Reagan Diaries,* 444.

173 It certainly showed: The full interview is at http://millercenter.org/president/reagan/oralhistory/james-kuhn.

174 Kuhn recalled: Ibid.

175 "won't shoot down any missile": Eliot Brenner, "Objections to 'Star Wars,'" United Press International, October 19, 1986.

176 "Weary, glassy-eyed": "Sunk by Star Wars," *Time*, October 20, 1986, 20.

178 The president opened his remarks: "The Iceland Summit: How Leaders See It; Remarks by Reagan and Gorbachev after Reykjavik Talks: Mr. Reagan," *New York Times*, October 13, 1986.

181 an hour and forty minutes: Lou Cannon, "Reagan-Gorbachev Summit Talks Collapse as Deadlock on SDI Wipes Out Other Gains," *Washington Post*, October 13, 1986.

181 And he delivered the answer: Ibid.

7. DEPARTURES AND IMMEDIATE FALLOUT

186 "the president stayed for overtime": Jack Nelson, "Summit Ends in Failure after Deadlock on 'Star Wars' Issue," *Los Angeles Times*, October 13, 1986.

187 no-holds-barred campaign: Eleanor Clift, "Administration Eager to Tell Its Side of Summit," *Los Angeles Times*, October 15, 1986.

187 "quite easy to reach an understanding": Anatoly Chernyaev's Notes of October 12, 1986, *The Reykjavik File: Previously Secret Documents from U.S. and Soviet Archives on the 1986 Reagan-Gorbachev Summit* from the collections of the National Security Archive of George Washington University, Washington, DC, http://www.gwu.edu/~nsarchiv/NSAEBB/NSAEBB203/Document19.pdf.

190 "Tune in tomorrow night": Nelson, "Summit Ends in Failure."

190 Andrei Gromyko: Serge Schmemann, "Summit Aftermath: Russians Seem to Sense Victory," *New York Times*, October 14, 1986.

191 Soviet state television: Thom Shanker, "Soviets Assail U.S. but Hold out Hope," *Chicago Tribune*, October 14, 1986.

194 All around town: All descriptions of Reykjavik returning to normal taken from Marcus Eliason, "The Summit Circus Leaves Town, Leaving Reykjavik Unfazed," Associated Press, October 13, 1986.

201 "a sad day": "Lugar: Reagan Did not 'Blink' at Summit," United Press International, October 12, 1986.

201 SDI would lose its support: Christopher Connell, "Lawmakers Divided on Arms Talks Impasse in Iceland," Associated Press, October 12, 1986.

202 "immediately pull": Sara Fritz, "Nunn Asks Reagan to Drop Zero-Missile Offer," *Los Angeles Times*, October 17, 1986.

202 "A grand and historic opportunity": Owen Ullmann, "Summit Offered Hope, Reagan Says Missile Defense 'Key' to Banning All Nuclear Arms," *Miami Herald*, October 14, 1986.

202 "make anyone suspicious": Nicholas M. Horrock, "Regrets Mask Sign of Success," *Chicago Tribune*, October 14, 1986.

202 Les Aspin, called: Russell Watson, "Can a Deal Still Be Cut?" *Newsweek*, October 27, 1986.

202 "the best deal": Connell, "Lawmakers Divided."

202 "the most significant discussions": Helen Dewar and Edward Walsh, "Defense Budget Ceiling of $290 Billion Negotiated," *Washington Post*, October 15, 1986.

202 Adding to the cacophony: All quotes taken from *Time*, October 27, 1986, 37–41.

204 Reagan loved talking: Jackie Calmes, "Live from the Oval Office," *New York Times*, July 10, 2013, 1.

204 behind the desk at 9:00 p.m.: The president's address in full is presented at "Address on the Meetings with Soviet Premier Gorbachev," University of Virginia, Miller Center, October 13, 1986, http://millercenter.org/president/speeches/detail/5865.

207 The general secretary opened: The speech is contained in Mikhail Gorbachev, *Reykjavik: Results and Lessons* (Moscow, 1990). All italics in the text are mine, not his.

209 The top administration troika: The figures on U.S. and Soviet press briefings all come from "Forward Spin," *Time*, October 27, 1986, 24 and 25.

211 Fifteen Soviet spokesmen: Ibid.

215 "if the President's purpose": "Derailment at Reykjavik" (editorial), *New York Times*, October 13, 1986.

215 "the widespread impression": "In the Reagan World, with No Missiles" (editorial), *New York Times*, October 19, 1986.

215 "Reykjavik produced a roller coaster": "Burned in Iceland" (editorial), *New York Times*, October 28, 1986.

216 Despite such trashing: Yanelovich Clancy Shulman poll, *Time*, October 27, 1986, 27.

217 "Our efforts with the press": "Arms Control Follow-Up to Reykjavik," Summary of the Secret National Security Planning Group Meeting, October 27, 1986, provided by the Ronald Reagan Presidential Library.

219 "Mr. President": A muffled version of what the chairman said is contained in the bowdlerized notes of the Situation Room session, but a vivid version remains in my memory since it was such a dramatic statement.

221 After returning from his Brussels briefing: George P. Shultz, *Turmoil and Triumph* (New York, Charles Scribner's Sons, 1993), 775.

8. FROM THE WORST TO THE BEST OF TIMES

224 In a *Time* interview: "The Nation," *Time*, November 26, 1986.

226 Shultz had made such a threat: In late 1985 when the president approved a CIA plan requiring ten thousand government employees to submit to random lie detector tests, Shultz threatened to resign and Reagan then dropped the notion. Sara Fritz and Norman Kempster, "Shultz Offered to Quit 3 Times in Last 4 Years," *Los Angeles Times*, July 24, 1987.

228 "We will [in that case]": Anatoly Chernyaev's Notes, Gorbachev's Instructions to the Reykjavik Preparation Group, October 4, 1986, *The Reykjavik File: Previously Secret Documents from U.S. and Soviet Archives on the 1986 Reagan-Gorbachev Summit* from the collections of the National Security Archive of George Washington University, Washington, DC, http://www.gwu.edu/~nsarchiv/NSAEBB/NSAEBB203/Document05.pdf.

228 Gorbachev had to push: Though Matlock had scant regard for SDI, he believed that

Reykjavik propelled Gorbachev to reform at home (Jack F. Matlock, *Reagan and Gorbachev: How the Cold War Ended* [New York: Random House, 2005], 249). What at Reykjavik, besides SDI, could have propelled that? Reagan and Gorbachev had agreed in principle on cutting, if not eliminating, offensive nuclear weapons. Yet, Matlock did not, and does not, believe that SDI played a role in ending the Cold War.

229 A CIA report: "Gorbachev's Economic Agenda" in *Ronald Reagan: Intelligence and the End of the Cold War* (Washington, DC: Center for the Study of Intelligence, 2011), 52.

231 Two weeks later: Paul Nitze, *From Hiroshima to Glasnost: At the Center of Decision-Making—A Memoir* (New York: Grove Weidenfeld, 1989), 443.

232 With their allotted time: Antony R. Dolan, "Four Little Words," *Wall Street Journal*, November 8, 2009.

233 "With a fervor and relentlessness": Ibid.

233 Twenty years later: Romesh Ratnesar, "20 Years after 'Tear Down This Wall,'" *Time*, June 11, 2007.

233 "It's the right thing to do": Ibid.

235 Chancellor Helmut Kohl: Jason Keyser, "Reagan Remembered Worldwide for His Role in Ending Cold War Division," *USA Today*, June 7, 2004.

235 Nor does Jack Matlock: It's interesting to note that Matlock's book, which purports to be a definitive work on—as his subtitle has it—*How the Cold War Ended*, not only lacks any mention of Reagan's speech, but expends only a dozen words on the fall of the Wall.

246 The East Room is the largest and grandest: George de Lama and Terry Atlas, "U.S.-Soviet Arms Treaty Signed Gorbachev, Reagan Hail a New Era," *Chicago Tribune*, December 9, 1987.

247 Abraham Lincoln's cabinet: Ibid.

247 250 guests: David K. Shipler, "The Summit; Reagan and Gorbachev Sign Missile Treaty and Vow to Work for Greater Reductions," *New York Times*, December 9, 1987.

248 two leather folders: Lou Cannon and Don Oberdorfer, "Reagan, Gorbachev Sign Nuclear Missile Treaty," *Washington Post*, December 9, 1987.

248 "Let's keep these pens": Janet Cawley and George de Lama, "U.S., Soviets Sign Arms Pact; Leaders Open Summit Talks," *Chicago Tribune*, December 9, 1987.

249 "*doveryai, no proveryai*": Ibid.

249 estimated 180 million: Alison Smale, "Gorbachev Co-Stars with Reagan on Big Screen in Moscow," Associated Press, December 8, 1987.

249 Kalinin Prospekt: Celestine Bohlen, "Signing Televised in Moscow," *Washington Post*, December 9, 1987.

251 "like nothing I've seen": Donald M. Rothberg, "Gorbachev Joins Bush for Campaign-Style Sidewalk Tour," Associated Press, December 10, 1987.

251 The police "made furious U-turns": David Remnick and Lois Romano, "Soviet Leader Stops in the Name of Glasnost," *Washington Post*, December 11, 1987.

252 "like a presidential candidate": Rothberg, "Gorbachev Joins Bush."

252   "two great countries": Remnick and Romano, "Soviet Leader Stops."

252   Gorbachev had pressed the flesh: Diane Duston, "Gorbachev Mixes with Crowd; Gets Rave Reviews," Associated Press, December 10, 1987.

252   "I thought you'd gone home": Remnick and Romano, "Soviet Leader Stops."

252   Looking back: Thom Shanker, "Gorbachev Honors His Enemy and Friend," *New York Times*, June 11, 2004.

9. REYKJAVIK AND THE SOVIET BREAKUP

256   three days in Helsinki: "Reagan to Rest in Finland, the Way Station to Russia," Associated Press, May 25, 1988.

256   "The damn thing": Joyce Purnick, "Washington Talk; Roasting Reagan: Guess Who Laughed Last," *New York Times*, March 30, 1987.

257   Andrei Gromyko: Susanne M. Schafer, "Gorbachev and Reagan Open Summit," Associated Press, May 29, 1988.

257   "Sunlight sparkled": Roberts, "The Moscow Summit: The Serious Side, Reagan and Gorbachev Begin Summit Parley in the Kremlin; 'Strike Sparks' on Rights Issue," *New York Times*, May 30, 1988.

258   Inside the city limits: Michael Putzel, "Gorbachev and Reagan Open Fourth Summit; Clash on Human Rights," Associated Press, May 29, 1988.

258   "There is no question": Ronald Reagan, *The Reagan Diaries* (New York, Harper-Collins, 2007), 613.

258   "it wasn't rushed": "Moscow Summit: The Serious Side; Transcripts of Reagan and Gorbachev Remarks," *New York Times*, May 30, 1988.

259   David Remnick: "Reagan to Gorbachev: '*Rodilsya, Ne Toropilsya*,'" *Washington Post*, May 30, 1988.

259   the Associated Press: Terence Hunt, "Reagan's Summit: The Gipper Visits the Evil Empire," Associated Press, May 28, 1988.

259   Some five thousand members: Carol J. Williams, "Summit Takes Over Soviet Capital's Busiest Buildings," Associated Press, May 28, 1988.

259   Mezhdunarodnaya Hotel: Ibid.

261   "The two were like actors": Jack F. Matlock, *Reagan and Gorbachev: How the Cold War Ended* (New York: Random House, 2005), 298.

262   writing that night: Reagan, *The Reagan Diaries*, 613.

262   SUMMIT BEGINS WITH A CLASH: George de Lama and Ray Moseley, "Summit Begins with a Clash: Gorbachev, Reagan Duel on Human Rights," *Chicago Tribune*, May 30, 1988.

262   Gorbachev "was irritated": Roberts, "Moscow Summit," *New York Times*, May 30, 1988.

262   "I introduced my favorite pitch": Reagan, *The Diaries*, 613.

263   "a new age of religious freedom": "Moscow Summit: Preaching to the Unconverted; Excerpts from Reagan Talks to Dissidents and at Monastery," *New York Times*, May 31, 1988.

263   picked up by U.S. embassy cars: Alison Smale, "Reagan to Meet Moscow Refuseniks,

Dissidents," Associated Press, May 30, 1988.

263 "to lift all curbs": Thom Shanker and Ray Moseley, "Reagan Keeps Focus on Rights," *Chicago Tribune*, May 31, 1988.

263 "institutional changes": "Moscow Summit: Preaching to the Unconverted."

264 Moscow State University: Lawrence Martin and Jeff Sallot, "Reagan Continues to Pitch U.S. Life at Moscow Summit," *Globe and Mail* (Canada), May 1, 1988.

264 Reagan spoke to the students: Nicholas M. Horrock, "Reagan Summit Trip Calmed U.S. Anxiety," *Chicago Tribune*, June 5, 1988.

264 Reagan's speech was met: Matlock, *Reagan and Gorbachev*, 302.

264 "permanent end": Martin and Sallot, "Reagan Continues to Pitch."

265 "Oh, these are all KGB families": "A Front-Row View of Obama's White House," NPR, January 15, 2009, http://m.npr.org/story/99353598.

265 Bolshoi Ballet: "Reagans Say Goodbye to Moonlit Moscow," *Chicago Tribune*, June 2, 1988.

267 During their travels: Richard Pearson and Martin Weil, "Soviet Marshal Akhrome-yev Found Dead," *Washington Post*, August 26, 1991.

267 As later substantiated: Bob Woodward, *The Commanders* (New York, Simon & Schuster, 2007), 40.

267 Later behavior by: Akhromeyev's questionable behavior will be discussed later.
Bill Crowe, whom I personally liked a lot, was a bit too political for my taste. After serving as chairman of the Joint Chiefs under President George H. W. Bush, Crowe retired and shortly thereafter publicly endorsed Bush's opponent, Bill Clinton, in the 1992 presidential election. Candidate Clinton, then under attack for draft dodging and being anti-military, mentioned Crowe's endorsement constantly and used it effectively in the campaign. Of course, he won and soon thereafter appointed Crowe to the preeminent diplomatic post, U.S. ambassador to the Court of St. James's. To me, it was bad enough for the highest ranking U.S. military officer to enter the political fray immediately after retiring. But then to turn against the president under whom he served in the highest post of his profession was worse. The London appointment for Crowe gave it a further stench.

268 won 99 of the 100 contested seats: Ronald E. Powaski, *The Cold War* (New York: Oxford University Press, 1998), 266.

271 "It's like Christmas": Serge Schmemann, "Hungary Allows 7,000 East Germans to Emigrate West," *New York Times*, September 11, 1989.

271 "under cover of night and fog": Ferdinand Protzman, "Clamor in The East; East Berliners Explore Land Long Forbidden," *New York Times*, November 10, 1989.

277 "A sinister symbol": Tom Shales, "The Day the Wall Cracked," *Washington Post*, November 10, 1989.

277 President Bush was "cautious": David Hoffman and Ann Devroy, "Bush Hails 'Dramatic' Decision," *Washington Post*, November 10, 1989.

278 substituting *Freiheit* for *Freude*: Ed Siegel, "Bernstein Captures the Joy of Freedom," *Boston Globe*, December 26, 1989.

278 "happiest Christmas": Stephanie Griffith, "Bernstein Brings 'Ode to Freedom' to Berlin," *Los Angeles Times*, December 25, 1989.

279 Columnist Mary McGrory: "From Moscow, the Party Line," *Washington Post*, November 17, 1985.

281 Gustav Husak swore in: "Upheaval in the East: Czechoslovakia's Seven Weeks of Drama," *New York Times*, December 30, 1989.

281 Havel later called that: He said this on public television in February 1990 when asked how he felt as a dramatist about the theatrics of 1989.

281 Even without understanding: https://www.youtube.com/watch?v=Pm53beoUZ4Q and https://www.youtube.com/watch?v=wWIbCtz_Xwk and https://www.youtube.com/watch?v=HjbYhVDwd6k, among other websites.

282 Accused of genocide: "Romania's 11-Day Revolution," *Associated Press*, December 25, 1989.

283 Lithuania then declared independence: "Main Events of Six Years of Perestroika," Associated Press, August 19, 1991.

284 "At any time in 1990": Bridget Kendall, "New Light Shed on 1991 Anti-Gorbachev Coup," *BBC News*, August 17, 2011.

284 Picking the most inopportune time: Michael Dobbs, "Shevardnadze Quits as Foreign Minister," *Washington Post*, December 21, 1990.

285 98 percent of Georgian voters supported: "Day by Day, Historic Year Unfolds," Associated Press, December 20, 1991.

285 Ukrainian voters rejected: "Chronology of Breakup of Soviet Union," Associated Press, December 10, 1991.

286 "As a matter of fact": Kendall, "New Light Shed."

286 "I was working in my office": Michael Parks, "Soviet President Feared for His Life," *Los Angeles Times*, August 23, 1991.

288 "so drunk": "Aide Says Key Coup Plotter Was Drunk When Arrested," Associated Press, August 30, 1991.

288 And Pavlov: Gerald Nadler, "Pavlov, Yanayev Were Inebriated at Key Coup Meeting," United Press International, August 30, 1991.

288 THE COUP WAS STAGED BY DRUNKARDS: Ibid.

289 "seventy-two hours": " 'Everything Was Done to Break the President Psychologically,' " *Washington Post*, August 23, 1991.

289 "close to a heart attack": Francis X. Clines, "After the Coup; Gorbachev Recounts Telling Plotters: 'To Hell with You,' " *New York Times*, August 23, 1991.

289 According to the AP reporter: Mark J. Porubcansky, "Gorbachev Denounces Coup Plotters," Associated Press, August 22, 1991.

290 took his life: Wendy Sloane, "Gorbachev Adviser's Suicide Puzzles Soviet Officials," Associated Press, August 26, 1991.

290 Knowledgeable people: Paula Chin, "Death of a Soldier," *People*, September 16, 1991.

291 Akhromeyev left at least two: Ibid.

291 Just recently: While I was doing research in the summer of 2013, in response to my repeated inquiries, an aide close to Gorbachev informed me of the third suicide note and the possibility of its being made public after Gorbachev's death. He asked that I not use his name.

294 Gorbachev would bid farewell: Alan Cooperman, "Gorbachev Resigns, Says Has 'Confidence' in Commonwealth's Leaders," Associated Press, December 25, 1991.

294 Montblanc pen: Interestingly, like Lenin, Mao Zedong used the luxury pen in his lifelong campaign against opulent capitalists as well. See http://kolkataonwheelsmag-azine.com/kolkata-life-style/culture-tradition/no-longer-mightier/.

295 "a peaceful Christmas evening": Don Oberdorfer, "Gorbachev Resignation Ends Soviet Era," *Washington Post*, December 26, 1991.

10. REFLECTIONS AND CONCLUSIONS ON REYKJAVIK

297 George Shultz: Shultz, *Turmoil and Triumph* (New York: Charles Scribner's Sons, 1993), 776.

298 he was remarkably forthright: The letter reads:

My Fellow Americans,

I have recently been told that I am one of the millions of Americans who will be afflicted with Alzheimer's Disease.

Upon learning this news, Nancy & I had to decide whether as private citizens we would keep this a private matter or whether we would make this known in a public way.

In the past Nancy suffered from breast cancer and I had my cancer surgeries. We found through our open disclosures we were able to raise public awareness. We were happy that as a result many more people underwent testing. They were treated in early stages and able to return to normal, healthy lives.

So now, we feel it is important to share it with you. In opening our hearts, we hope this might promote greater awareness of this condition. Perhaps it will encourage a clearer understanding of the individuals and families who are affected by it.

At the moment I feel just fine. I intend to live the remainder of the years God gives me on this earth doing the things I have always done. I will continue to share life's journey with my beloved Nancy and my family. I plan to enjoy the great outdoors and stay in touch with my friends and supporters.

Unfortunately, as Alzheimer's Disease progresses, the family often bears a heavy burden. I only wish there was some way I could spare Nancy from this painful experience. When the time comes I am confident that with your help she will face it with faith and courage.

In closing let me thank you, the American people for giving me the great honor of allowing me to serve as your President. When the Lord calls me home, [words scratched out] whenever that may be, I will leave with the greatest love for this country of ours and eternal optimism for its future.

I now begin the journey that will lead me into the sunset of my life. I know that for America there will always be a bright dawn ahead.

Thank you my friends. May God always bless you.

Sincerely,

Ronald Reagan

302 This is not unique: Joel Achenbach, "Gettysburg," *Washington Post*, April 28, 2013.

305 Reductions have been even steeper: Hans Kristensen and Stan Norris, *Bulletin of the Atomic Scientists* (May 2012 and May 2013); Natural Resources Defense Council's Archive of Nuclear Data, Arms Control Association, and the U.S. Department of State, http://www.state.gov/t/avc/rls/207020.htm.

305 President Obama still feels: Jackie Calmes, "Obama Asks Russia to Join in Reducing Nuclear Arms," *New York Times*, June 20, 2013.

305 This dip down to 1,000: In an article published in 1984 while still in office, I advocated this approach as far more practical and productive. "Arms Control With and Without Agreements," *Foreign Affairs* 63(2) (Winter 1984/85): 240–63.

306 Recent research: Eric Schlosser, *Command and Control* (New York: Penguin, 2013).

308 this lifelong hawk: Nitze, "A Threat Mostly to Ourselves," *New York Times*, October 28, 1999.

309 The assembled white-haired, pin-striped dignitaries: Material about the Global Zero conference, and a short, homemade video were provided by the Global Zero chairman, Dr. Robert Meyers.

310 That it might have been like the 1905 summit: Formally called the Treaty of Björkö or the Treaty of Koivisto, it was a secret mutual defense pact signed aboard ship on July 24, 1905. It never went into effect.

311 The United States now has ground-based: There are currently thirty ground-based interceptors, twenty-six at Fort Greely, Alaska, and four at Vandenberg Air Force Base. "Missile Defense Interceptor Misses Target in Test," *New York Times*, July 6, 2013.

312 The possibility of someday: Thomas Henriksen, "The Legacy of Reykjavik," *Implications of the Reykjavik Summit on Its Twentieth Anniversary,* edited by Sidney D. Drell and George P. Shultz (Stanford, CA: Hoover Institution Press, 2007), 36.

313 Gorbachev—as expert a witness: Letter of September 10, 1996, to the prime minister of Iceland, the mayor of Reykjavik, and participants at the tenth anniversary.

313 The second expert witness called: Shevardnadze's letter to the prime minister of Iceland, May 22, 1996.

314 In 2001, when Gorbachev: Jack F. Matlock, *Reagan and Gorbachev: How the Cold War Ended* (New York: Random House, 2005), 326.

316 Years later he recalled: Robert G. Kaiser, "Gorbachev: We All Lost Cold War," *Washington Post*, June 11, 2004.

318 U.S. ambassador Jack Matlock: Matlock, *Reagan and Gorbachev*, 249.

319 Yet in *The Downing Street Years*: Margaret Thatcher, *The Downing Street Years* (New York: HarperCollins, 1993), 463.

319 During their last talk together: Paula Chin, "Death of a Soldier," *People*, September 16, 1991.

319 "The Soviet system": Strobe Talbott, "Rethinking the Soviet Menace," *Time*, January 1, 1990. Italics added.

320 The CIA *World Factbook*: 1986 CIA *World Factbook*, http://archive.org/stream/world-factbook86natiilli#page/120/mode/2up. These CIA estimates on the Soviet economy were fraught with problems of ruble-dollar convertibility and a host of even more

arcane technical difficulties, on top of the CIA's difficulty in knowing just how the Soviet economy functioned. The estimates were often wrong.

320 the Soviet economy: Robert C. Toth, "Soviet Economy Shows Rapid Growth in 1986," *Los Angeles Times*, March 27, 1987.

321 "Nowhere was it written": Don Oberdorfer, "When Reagan and Gorbachev Reached for the Stars," *Implications of the Reykjavik Summit*, 117–18.

322 the best known, Edmund Morris: Edmund Morris, *This Living Hand and Other Essays* (New York: Random House, 2012).

323 his lamentable biography: *Dutch: A Memoir of Ronald Reagan* (New York: Random House, 1999).

324 We can look around: The 415 million number was attained by simply adding the 1990 populations of Warsaw Pact nations that were no longer Communist.

324 Even Gorbachev recognized this: *The Early Show*, CBS, June 11, 2004.

324 When asked about it: Thom Shanker, "Gorbachev Honors His Enemy and Friend," *New York Times*, June 11, 2004.

324 Dr. Eric Kandel: Jane Leavy, *The Last Boy: Mickey Mantle and the End of America's Childhood* (New York: HarperCollins, 2010), 158.

326 Aleksandr Bessmertnykh: Oberdorfer, "When Reagan and Gorbachev," 117.

327 Gorbachev is hailed: April 24, 2005, Annual State of the Union Address.

328 Jonathan Steele: *Guardian*, October 16, 1991.

330 A Ministry of Foreign Affairs study: David Holloway, "The Soviet Preparation for Reykjavik: Four Documents," *Implications of the Reykjavik Summit*, 57, 58.

331 Finally, and almost comically: Ibid., 60.

331 Yet, he noted: Jacqueline Stevens, "Political Scientists Are Lousy Forecasters," *New York Times*, June 23, 2012.

331 According to recently declassified papers: Bruce D. Berkowitz, "U.S. Intelligence Estimates of the Soviet Collapse: Reality and Perception," in *Ronald Reagan: Intelligence and the End of the Cold War* (Washington, DC: Center for the Study of Intelligence, 2011), 21–28.

332 Despite her frown: The Ronald Reagan Presidential Library made a valiant attempt to find the postcard, but without success. If it made it to the library, the postcard may not have been cataloged since it was well past the presidential years and Reagan himself was by then unable to read it. Besides, the Reagan Library dispenses with all public correspondence more than five years old. While I do not remember the exact words, I well remember the sentiment, as it is expressed here.

EPILOGUE: MOURNING IN AMERICA

335 As Nancy Reagan told: Ann Gerhart, "A Widow's Heartfelt Farewell," *Washington Post*, June 11, 2004.

335 "the end of the Cold War": *The Early Show*, CBS, June 11, 2004.

335 In New York: Kissinger had said the same thing eight years earlier. Jere Hester, Michelle Caruso, and David Eisenstate, "Words of Hope," *New York Daily News*, August 13, 1996.

335 Iceland's president: Taken from Reykjavik newspapers in June 2004, as reported and translated by Astporsdottir.

335 In an op-ed piece for the *New York Times*: Mikhail Gorbachev, "A President Who Listened," *New York Times*, June 7, 2004.

337 nearly a hundred and forty years earlier: Rudolph Bush, "A Time to Remember," *Chicago Tribune*, June 11, 2004.

337 Mrs. Reagan stepped forward: Ken Fireman, "Ronald Reagan 1911–2004: Our Final Hail to the Chief," *Newsday*, June 12, 2004.

337 the state funeral: I was startled to read later that Mikhail Gorbachev was there at the funeral, since neither Carol nor I saw him that morning. Otherwise, I would have gone over and greeted him.

337 musical interludes: Ann McFeatters, "A Nation Bids Farewell," *Pittsburgh Post-Gazette*, June 12, 2004.

337 Margaret Thatcher: Ibid.

338 Reagan "did not shrink": Margaret Thatcher, Eulogy for President Reagan, Margaret Thatcher Foundation, June 11, 2004, http://www.margaretthatcher.org/document/110360.

338 Sandra Day O'Connor: David Von Drehle, "Reagan Hailed as Leader for 'The Ages,'" *Washington Post*, June 12, 2004.

338 top dignitaries: Sonya Ross, "Thatcher, Gorbachev Lead Foreign Leaders Paying Respects to Reagan," *Associated Press*, June 12, 2004.

338 including Thatcher: McFeatters, "A Nation Bids Farewell."

338 tipped a wing: Jeff Zeleny, "Reagan Laid to Rest," *Chicago Tribune*, June 12, 2004.

338 *The Dixonian*: The yearbook is displayed in the Ronald Reagan Presidential Library.

338 More than a thousand people: Steve Chawkins, "Farewell to a President: Lasting Memories Gleaned Along the Final Leg," *Los Angeles Times*, June 12, 2004.

339 "I know in my heart": Ryan Pearson, "Reagan Entombed in Underground Crypt at Hilltop Presidential Library," *Associated Press*, June 12, 2004.

340 "I gave him a pat": Robert G. Kaiser, "Gorbachev: 'We All Lost Cold War,'" *Washington Post*, June 11, 2004.

Index

About the Author

Ken Adelman was President Ronald Reagan's arms control director. He was at Reykjavik during the 1986 superpower summit with Mikhail Gorbachev, and accompanied President Reagan at three superpower summits in all. He has also served as a U.S. ambassador to the United Nations and as assistant to the secretary of defense. After leaving government, he taught Shakespeare at Georgetown University and George Washington University, and national security studies at Johns Hopkins and Georgetown universities. He is the author or coauthor of five previous books, including *Shakespeare in Charge* and *The Defense Revolution*.